Achieving

Primary
ICT

Knowledge, Understanding
and Practice

Achieving QTS

Primary
ICT
Knowledge, Understanding and Practice

Third edition

Jonathan Allen
John Potter
Jane Sharp
Keith Turvey

LearningMatters

First published in 2000 by Learning Matters Ltd
Reprinted in 2001.
Second edition published in 2002.
Reprinted in 2002.
Reprinted in 2003.
Reprinted in 2004 (twice).
Reprinted in 2005.
Third edition published in 2007.

© Jonathan Allen, John Potter, Jane Sharp, Keith Turvey
British Library Cataloguing in Publication Data
A CIP record for this book is available from the British Library.

ISBN 978 1 84445 094 7

Cover design by Topics – The Creative Partnership
Text design by Code 5 Design Associates Ltd
Project management by Deer Park Productions, Tavistock, Devon
Typeset by PDQ Typesetting Ltd, Newcastle-under-Lyme
Printed and bound in Great Britain by Cromwell Press Ltd, Trowbridge, Wiltshire

Learning Matters Ltd
33 Southernhay East
Exeter EX1 1NX
Tel: 01392 215560
info@learningmatters.co.uk
www.learningmatters.co.uk

Contents

v

Introduction

CLASSROOM STORY

In the corner of a classroom, Albert (85) is searching the Commonwealth War Graves database (**www.cwgc.org**/) with a group of Year 6 children. They are searching for information about local people from the village who lost their lives in the Second World War; people Albert grew up with and went to school with. The children are fascinated by the information Albert shares with them about these people who until now were merely names engraved on the War Memorial in the centre of the village. However, Albert is equally fascinated as the children demonstrate how they can access information about how, when and where these people fell, and where their graves are. Albert wants to know more and so do the children. These children go on to create a multimedia presentation with images, text and audio from interviews with Albert about the plight of local people during the Second World War.

Encapsulated within this brief extract is the power of technology to act as a catalyst for rich educational experiences for all generations. This snapshot offers a glimpse of the important role technology has to play in lifelong learning; both the children and the 85-year-old were united in their quest for information. Technology can have relevance for all, in whatever phase of life they may be, which raises important and challenging issues for people undertaking primary teacher training and embarking on their careers as newly qualified teachers, thus:

• **What does it mean to be a teacher and lifelong learner in the information society?**

Such a question prompts us to examine our values and beliefs about the purposes of education, the contexts in which people learn and the roles that teachers might play in facilitating such rich educational opportunities described in this classroom story. Digital literacy will no doubt be a vital factor in enabling both teachers and children to exploit the creative potential of new technologies throughout their learning lives, and this is complicated by the fact that technologies are in a constant state of change and pervade all areas of our lives from work to leisure. Despite there remaining a significant digital divide between those with access to technology in the home and those without, many children in our society enjoy rich digital lives outside of school, downloading and sharing music, interacting in online multi-user games environments, and engaging in various forms of communication from e-mail to instant messaging. So what can we as teachers learn from these informal uses of technology outside of school and what effect might the constantly changing technological landscape have upon our uses of technology within school? Teachers need an understanding of the ways in which they can use information and communications technology (ICT) to support and enhance their teaching across the curriculum. They also need an understanding of how children develop an ICT capability, which enables them to deal with information critically in a rapidly changing world. These are pedagogical issues and indeed the development of new technologies often necessitates a shift in pedagogical approach in order to exploit fully the educational potential of the technology.

This book in the *Learning Matters QTS Series* has been written to support primary teacher trainees and newly qualified teachers to develop their understanding of these pedagogical issues as they investigate the ways in which ICT supports teaching which enables children to develop confidence, capability and competence as lifelong learners in the information society. The requirements of teachers in England are clearly identified in the National Curriculum and the Standards required for Qualified Teacher Status. This book identifies clear links with these requirements, but also addresses the wider context in which ICT has an impact on learning and teaching.

This introduction will briefly discuss some of the recent national policies and initiatives regarding the development of ICT in schools in order to set the background. The notion of ICT capability as expressed in the pupils' National Curriculum will be explored with reference to the QCA schemes of work for ICT. There will then be a discussion of ICT capability and the features of ICT, which make a distinctive contribution to learning and teaching. Finally, consideration will be given to the Professional Standards for QTS, which form part of an ongoing continuum of professional development for pre-service and in-service teachers. The Standards require all teachers in all subjects and phases to use ICT appropriately and effectively in their work. This is a much broader brief than the focus on ICT capability expressed in the pupils' National Curriculum, but it is important to consider the wider application of ICT in some detail in order to develop an understanding of the conceptual framework which needs to underpin a teacher's professional capability with ICT.

Some of the story so far

There has been significant government expenditure on ICT infrastructure in the recent past, which is indicative of the important role many believe technology can play within our schools. Although no longer in existence, the National Grid for Learning (NGfL) was established in 1998, managed and funded through the government's agency for ICT, the British Educational Communications and Technology Agency (Becta). This was essentially an online portal to web-based resources for teachers and children. Similarly other linked services emerged such as the Virtual Teacher's Centre (VTC), also no longer in existence. The main thrust of government policy at this time was to connect every primary school to the Internet and ensure that all teachers had a basic level of ICT competencies. In-service training was offered to schools by a variety of providers funded through the National Lottery's New Opportunities Fund (NOF). However, the potential of these initiatives was limited by the lack of access to broadband connectivity in schools. This prompted a second wave of investment from the government which has been directed again mainly at infrastructure and hardware, with broadband connectivity and interactive whiteboards introduced into many schools. The status of ICT was also raised within the National Curriculum. The use of ICT across the curriculum and within a range of teaching and learning styles is seen to be vital to the success of the government's Primary National Strategy (PNS), which seeks to provide children with an exciting and creative curriculum.

ICT capability and the National Curriculum

When asked what should be in the National Curriculum for ICT, many people will suggest 'keyboard skills...copy and paste...using Internet Explorer'. In other words, their response tends to focus upon specific skills within particular pieces of software, skills and software that often reflect current practices within work and leisure environments. However, this notion of a purely skills-based ICT curriculum is flawed for a number of reasons. The work and leisure spaces that today's children will inhabit throughout their lives will be technologically very different from the present and subject to change; consider how networks have transformed many people's work and leisure practices in the last decade. Furthermore, a purely skills-based ICT curriculum is not fit for the stated aims of a twenty-first-century education as expressed in the introduction to *Excellence and Enjoyment* which states that when there is enjoyment in learning, *children learn to love learning* (DfES, 2003). So how do teachers facilitate in children such a disposition to learning with and about ICT, and how do we ensure that rather than merely equipping children with a set of increasingly anachronistic skills and techniques in a fast changing world, we enable them to develop autonomy in their learning with and about ICT? Children need a much deeper knowledge and understanding of the role that technologies might play in their lives, a critical understanding.

In order to begin to address this issue it is useful to ask ourselves some key questions:

- **What are the deeper, fundamental concepts at the heart of ICT as a subject, which are less susceptible to change than the outward physical components such as hardware and software?**
- **Why do we use ICT?**

In asking these questions we begin to uncover the underlying principles of the National Curriculum for ICT. Rather than a distinct or extensive set of skills and techniques within given applications, what we find is a clear identification of the purposes for which ICT is used, thus:

- **finding things out;**
- **developing ideas and making things happen;**
- **exchanging and sharing information;**
- **reviewing, modifying and evaluating work as it progresses.**

These four strands within the programmes of study for ICT encompass a range of skills and higher-order knowledge and understanding. On one level, in order to use ICT to 'find things out' through using the Internet, children will need to know how to use the tools on a navigation bar – whether it be Internet Explorer, Safari or Firefox. However, they will also need to be able to identify what information they need, search effectively and efficiently for it and interpret that information accurately taking into account the validity and reliability of the source. This level of higher-order thinking is dependent upon a deep understanding of the ways in which information is managed, structured and developed on the Internet in comparison with other sources of information. Similarly, if children are going to be able to use technology throughout their lives to 'share and exchange information' they will need to develop a deep understanding of the ways in which information can be created and manipulated to communicate effectively with different audiences. When young children first begin to combine image and text in their presentations and work, they are often but not always quite easily satisfied with their outcomes. However, as their ICT capability develops they begin to exercise more critical judgement about the way they combine elements such as text, still and moving image, and audio within their work, developing a greater awareness of audience and a higher level of critical judgement about these elements of their creative outcomes with ICT.

The four strands of the programmes of study for ICT begin to unravel for teachers this complex relationship between skills, knowledge and understanding in ICT. A further strand – breadth of study – indicates the expectation that children will develop their skills, knowledge and understanding through working with a range of information; exploring a variety of ICT tools; working collaboratively; and comparing the different uses of ICT inside and outside school. It can be useful to think of these strands as both distinctive and inter-related. Think back to the opening classroom story and it is possible to identify different aspects of the programmes of study coming into the foreground at different points within the children's activities. It is worth considering the programmes of study for ICT in detail as they describe a basic framework for developing ICT capability for both children and teachers (see table). As you study the table think carefully about and try to visualise the types of activities children might undertake. Focus on a particular strand and ask yourself what characterises increasing ICT capability within this strand.

Knowledge, skills and understanding	Key Stage 1 Pupils should be taught:	Key Stage 2 Pupils should be taught:
Finding things out	• How to gather information from a variety of sources • How to enter and store information in a variety of forms • How to retrieve information that has been stored	• To talk about what information they need and how they can find and use it • How to prepare information for development using ICT, including selecting suitable sources, finding information, classifying it and checking it for accuracy
Developing ideas and making things happen	• To use text, tables, images and sound to develop their ideas • How to select from and add to information they have retrieved for particular purposes • To try things out and explore what happens in real and imaginary situations	• How to develop and refine ideas by bringing together, organising and reorganising text, tables, images and sound as appropriate. • How to create, test, improve and refine sequences of instructions to make things happen and to monitor events and respond to them • To use simulations and explore models in order to answer 'What would happen if...?' questions, to investigate and evaluate the effect of changing values and to identify patterns and relationships
Exchanging and sharing information	• How to share their ideas by presenting information in a variety of forms • To present their completed work effectively	• How to share and exchange information in a variety of forms, including e-mail • To be sensitive to the needs of the audience and think carefully about the content and quality when communicating information
Reviewing, modifying and evaluating work as it progresses	• To review what they have done to help them develop their ideas • To describe the effects of their actions • To talk about what they might change in future work	• To review what they and others have done to help them develop their ideas • To describe and talk about the effectiveness of their work with ICT, comparing it with other methods and considering the effect it has on others • To talk about how they could improve further work
Breadth of study	• Working with a range of information to investigate the different ways it can be presented • Exploring a variety of ICT tools • Talking about the uses of ICT inside and outside school	• Working with a range of information to consider its characteristics and purposes • Working with others to explore a variety of information sources and ICT tools • Investigating and comparing the uses of ICT inside and outside school

Programme of study: ICT National Curriculum

The QCA scheme of work for Key Stages 1 and 2

In order to facilitate the implementation of the National Curriculum for ICT and develop children's ICT capability through challenging and relevant experiences, the ICT Scheme of Work has been published by the Department for Education and Skills (DfES) and the Qualifications and Curriculum Authority (QCA). However, it should be noted that this is not statutory and although a useful exemplar of a practical planning framework, many schools develop their own schemes of work in the spirit of excellence and enjoyment. Teaching for creativity and creative teaching with ICT requires teachers to think imaginatively about where purposeful links might be made between ICT and other curriculum areas. For this reason a flexible approach to any given scheme is often essential. The optional scheme exemplifies a whole-school approach to:

- **develop ICT capability in an organised, systematic and rigorous way which encourages progression;**
- **develop ICT processes, skills and techniques;**
- **develop ability to apply ICT capability to support language, communication and learning in other areas;**
- **explore perceptions, attitudes and values in relation to ICT in the wider society;**
- **build on children's previous and wider experiences of ICT;**
- **identify learning intentions and approaches to assessment within planned activities.**

The QCA scheme of work provides a sequence of units, or activities, which can be used though Key Stages 1 and 2, providing a degree of flexibility and coherent progression linked to the programmes of study and the attainment levels. The units can be incorporated into the school's whole curriculum framework and the activities related closely to work in other subject areas and planned activities in the school. It offers an exemplar for medium- to long-term planning as it is addressed within a whole school and as such, it also provides a useful framework for short-term lesson or activity plans. A summary of the units, which indicates the progression in activities and expectations, is presented in the following table:

Key Stage 1	
Year 1 Units	**Year 2 Units**
1A An Introduction to modelling 1B Using a word bank 1C The information around us 1D Labelling and classifying 1E Representing information graphically: pictograms 1F Understanding instructions and making things happen	2A Writing stories: communicating information using text 2B Creating pictures 2C Finding information 2D Routes: controlling a floor turtle 2E Questions and answers
Key Stage 2	
Year 3 Units	**Year 4 Units**
3A Combining text and graphics 3B Manipulating sound 3C Introduction to databases 3D Exploring simulations 3E Email	4A Writing for different purposes 4B Developing images using repeated patterns 4C Branching databases 4D Collecting and presenting information: questionnaires and pie charts 4E Modelling effects on screen
Year 5 Units	**Year 6 Units**
5A Graphical modelling 5B Analysing data and asking questions: using complex searches 5C Evaluating information, checking accuracy and questioning plausibility 5D Introduction to spreadsheets 5E Controlling devices 5F Monitoring environmental conditions changes	6A Multimedia presentation 6B Spreadsheet modelling 6C Control and modelling – what happens when? 6D Using the internet to search large databases and to interpret information

ICT scheme of work: DfES and QCA

From ICT to e-learning; from subject to learning and teaching strategy

Many teachers, teacher-educators and policy-makers have grappled with the question of what contribution new technologies bring to learning and teaching. The plethora of technological tools now available from web-based virtual learning environments (VLEs) to mobile hand-held devices such as PDAs, electronic voting systems and digital video cameras has led many to look for new ways of describing and classifying the role of information and communications technologies in learning and teaching. The term 'e-learning' encompasses learning and teaching strategies, which draw upon this range of technologies. Furthermore, for the first time e-learning as a specific strategy is identified in the standards for Qualified Teacher Status (QTS), thus providing a clear expectation that newly qualified teachers will demonstrate critical judgement, confidence and expertise in applying e-learning strategies throughout their work to improve the quality and standard of children's education. From this perspective, teachers need to have knowledge, skills and understanding of the ways in which information and communications technologies can support their professional practice. That is, teachers need to be able to make informed decisions about when, when not and how to use e-learning strategies effectively in their teaching and children's learning. In order to unpick this issue it is useful for teachers to consider the features of ICT, which can make a distinctive contribution to practice. What are the characteristics that can be exploited in order to make a contribution as a resource, as a tool and as a catalyst for new ways of working in the curriculum?

Interactivity can engage users at a number of levels, from the playing of a computer game in a child's bedroom to investigating the geographical features of the Himalayas via Google Earth. Both of these activities have in common the ways in which ICT can give immediate and dynamic feedback to decisions and actions made by the user. Whether undertaking a search of the world wide web, investigating a graph of the changes detected by a temperature sensor over a period of time or editing a multimedia presentation, these activities enable children to make decisions, see the consequences and act upon feedback accordingly. However, the degree to which children engage and interact will very much depend upon the way in which the teacher has framed these activities. Furthermore, the role of the teacher in encouraging the children to explore, to learn from dead ends and frustrations and to develop perseverance in trying out ideas and learning from feedback is vital in maximising the educational value of the experience for the children.

The **provisionality** of ICT enables users to make changes, try out alternatives and keep a trace of their developmental ideas. The advantages of this can be recognised immediately in the writing of text with a word processor, which can facilitate continual editing and development of ideas. However, recent advances in the speed and storage capacity of computers have extended this feature to the digital manipulation of still images, moving images and sound. Such advances puts within children's and teachers' grasp a range of new modes of expression and enable them to become creators of rich multimedia. However, as with interactivity, teachers have a vital role to play in promoting positive attitudes to working with and exploiting the provisionality of ICT. They can model, discuss and make explicit the processes of evaluation, changing ideas and reviewing work whether this is with text, still images, moving images, sound or a combination of these.

Another key characteristic of ICT is the **capacity and range** of ways in which children and teachers can access vast amounts of digital information in the form of text, visual images and sound. The modes by which information is communicated with technology continue to diversify as file capacity and processor speed increases across the range of technologies from mobile phones to desktop computers. However, with this increasing multi-modality comes the need for children to be able to make sense of this information and critically evaluate its authority and authenticity. Whilst teachers continue to play a vital role in enabling children to make sense of text from an early age, reading images (still, moving, animated) and considering the impact of sound in a multi-modal text will also be key to children's capacity to make sense of an increasingly rich multimodal world.

The **speed and automatic function** of ICT allows tasks of storing, changing and displaying information to be carried out by technology, enabling users to read, observe, interrogate, interpret, analyse and synthesise information at higher levels. Many routine activities such as capturing and organising data, monitoring change, carrying out calculations, drawing graphs and presenting findings can be done using ICT, leaving the children time to ask questions and think about the meaning of the information with which they are presented.

These distinctive characteristics of ICT offer a useful framework for teachers in thinking about the contribution of ICT to learning and teaching throughout the curriculum as well as their wider professional role. However, it is important to understand that these features do not lie solely within the technology. It takes a thinking teacher to realise and exploit the full potential for interactivity, provisionality, capacity and range or speed and automatic function offered by an interactive whiteboard or any piece of hardware or software.

Qualifying to teach: Professional Standards for QTS

There has been a significant shift in the new standards in that they are now designed to provide a continuum of professional development for both pre-service and in-service teachers well beyond their qualification and induction period. ICT is referred to both explicitly and implicitly within the new Professional Standards for QTS, as can be seen from studying the table below, which outlines the expectations for trainee teachers and newly qualified teachers with regard to ICT.

Recommended for QTS	Induction period
Professional knowledge and understanding	
<ul><li>Pass the professional skills test in ICT</li><li>Know how to use ICT to support their teaching and wider professional activities</li><li>Know the assessment requirements and arrangements for ICT</li><li>Have a secure knowledge and understanding of ICT to enable them to teach effectively across the age and ability range for which they are trained to teach</li><li>Know and understand the relevant statutory and non-statutory curricula, frameworks, including those provided through the National Strategies, for their subject/curriculum areas and other relevant initiatives</li></ul>	<ul><li>Know how to use ICT to support their teaching and wider professional activities</li><li>Know the assessment requirements and arrangements for ICT</li><li>Have a secure knowledge and understanding of the subjects/curriculum areas they teach including: the contribution that their subjects/curriculum areas can make to cross-curricular learning, recent relevant developments and related pedagogy</li></ul>
Professional skills	
<ul><li>Use a range of teaching strategies and resources, including e-learning, taking practical account of diversity and promoting equality and inclusion</li><li>Provide opportunities for learners to develop their ICT skills</li></ul>	<ul><li>Use a range of teaching and learning strategies and resources, including e-learning, adapted to meet learners' needs</li><li>Identify and provide opportunities for learners to develop ICT and thinking and learning skills appropriate within their phase and context</li></ul>

In examining these standards it is possible to identify three key areas for trainee teachers and newly qualified teachers to focus upon when considering their professional development with ICT. These are represented in Figure 1 and have been presented in this way to emphasise their interdependency and interconnectedness. As well as considering the ways in which the features of ICT support children's learning, teachers can also use ICT to improve their own professional efficiency in administrative tasks, maintaining links with their professional networks and resources for their subject. Thus, teachers who use ICT purposefully in a wide range of their work are likely to be more confident and competent in developing the use of ICT in teaching and learning across the curriculum with children. However, to be truly effective they will also need a deep knowledge and understanding ICT as a subject.

Together with the explicit reference made to ICT in the new Standards for QTS, there are also many areas of the Standards where ICT may have a significant role to play. For example, trainee teachers and newly qualified teachers are also expected to

- **have a creative and constructively critical approach towards innovation;**
- **know how to personalise learning and provide opportunities for all learners to achieve their potential.**

Figure 1 Key areas for professional development

It is well established that ICT has the potential to empower children with a wide range of learning needs through its adaptability and interactivity. Indeed, it could be argued that ICT has made most impact in schooling in the area of special educational needs where software, hardware and peripherals can be designed to bypass a number of physical and cognitive learning difficulties. Thus technology has a significant role to play with regards to inclusion and the *Every Child Matters* (DfES, 2004) agenda facilitating accessibility in education. Consequently, it is the responsibility again of thinking teachers to use their professional skills, knowledge, understanding and judgement as to how ICT may or may not be appropriate within these contexts.

Moving on

As you read this book it will become clear that it is grounded in a view of ICT as a powerful teaching and learning tool throughout the school curriculum and beyond, into many areas of children's learning lives. The emphasis is placed upon children becoming discerning and creative users of technology as opposed to passive recipients of information through technology. In order for children to develop such critical, confident and expansive dispositions towards technology they need opportunities to develop their ICT capability over time, through using and applying their skills, knowledge and understanding across a range of purposeful and meaningful contexts. ICT capability will not be developed through simply being invited to drag and drop a few objects around an interactive whiteboard every now and then in a whole class lesson although this is not to deny the educational potential of the interactive whiteboard. The challenge for teachers is to develop children's knowledge and understanding through planning and providing meaningful opportunities for sustained engagement with technology; opportunities in which children themselves are required to explore, reflect, review, ask questions and share ideas openly. Trainees and new teachers need also to take responsibility for the development of their own capability, through personal study, working with others, planning classroom experiences and developing networks of professional support, providing strong role models for the children as they themselves become confident, informed and critical users of technology.

REFERENCES AND FURTHER READING REFERENCES AND FURTHER READING

Becta, **www.becta.org.uk/** Accessed 30 January 2007

Commonwealth War Graves Commission (CWGC) **www.cwgc.org/** Accessed 30 January 2007

DfES, *Primary National Strategy* **www.standards.dfes.gov.uk/primary/** Accessed 30 January 2007

DfES (2003) *Excellence and Enjoyment* **www.standards.dfes.gov.uk/primary/publications/literacy/ 63553/** Accessed January 30 2007

DfES (2004) *Every Child Matters: Change for children in schools* **www.everychildmatters.gov.uk/ publications/** Accessed 30 January 2007

QCA, *National Curriculum in Action* **www.ncaction.org.uk/** Accessed 30 January 2007

TDA (2007) *Draft revised QTS Standards* **www.tda.gov.uk/teachers/professionalstandards.aspx** Accessed 30 January 2007

Section A
Teaching and learning with primary ICT

Introduction to issues in planning, assessing and recording in primary ICT

Section objectives and chapter content

This section is concerned with all issues related to planning, assessing and recording with ICT throughout the whole of the primary age phase. The curriculum for the Foundation Stage will also be addressed in a separate section on ICT in the Early Years setting.

Given that good planning depends on a thorough analysis of the situation before you even start working, the opening chapters provide a consideration of the background knowledge you need to acquire in order to deliver real learning opportunities for the children you teach.

In 'ICT in your classroom' we will consider the literal, physical management of a range of technologies in learning areas. The different levels of resourcing will be characterised so that you can begin to assess the situation in your placement school more quickly. We will consider what the various strategies are for dealing with high-, medium- and low-resource situations. For example, we will consider the very different management strategies to be employed when working with children in a primary school with a network room full of computers or when working with one stand-alone machine in the corner. We will also look at the implications of recent initiatives in primary schools and see how some of these initiatives are taking ICT in UK schools forward at a very rapid rate. There will also be reference to wider agendas which are having an influence on primary schools, such as 'Excellence and Enjoyment' and 'Every Child Matters'.

As far as possible throughout the parts of chapters which are concerned with resources we have attempted to be completely generic, that is to say, we have not specified a particular platform (PC, Mac, etc.). Some example titles of software or other specific resources may be given, but only where absolutely necessary to explain a concept further. There is so much software available for schools at all levels for all of the computer platforms that it would be impossible to create a list that would be applicable or viable in all settings. Local authorities (LAs) and schools themselves will have such lists and justifications for the choices they have made in terms of ease of use, applicability to the age phases they are being used with, and so on. They may use their own sites to explain connections between specific titles and curriculum content, thereby aiding in the planning process.

In the chapters 'Planning primary ICT' and 'Planning primary ICT in subject teaching' we will consider the context of the National Curriculum and its impact on the teaching and learning of the subject as well as looking at the way in which this works with the various strategies and schemes and schemes of work for teaching and learning. We will look at how to map the schemes of work back onto the new curriculum and negotiate the different emphases in the documentation. We will also address the ways in which some LAs and schools have planned for ICT, using the QCA schemes of work as a template, but also adjusting it to suit local needs and priorities. ICT exists in all subjects of the National Curriculum, so this section will also look at how to plan within the core curriculum (English, maths and science) and its associated strategies (now brought together as the *Primary National Strategy*) as well as within the Foundation subjects in order to maximise the potential of ICT for all learners. This will specifically address the Standards for qualification as a teacher on courses of Initial Teacher Training set out by the Training and Development Agency (see below for a fuller explanation).

'Planning ICT in the Early Years' will look specifically at ICT in the context of the Early Learning Goals as defined for children who are in the Foundation Stage (see *Curriculum Guidance for the Foundation Stage*, QCA, 2000).

'Assessment and Recording in Primary ICT' will look at how to go about evaluating children's development with ICT in order to inform planning. It will consider a range of strategies designed to provide a quick overview of a class as well as a more detailed and individually targeted assessment of the needs of a given learner.

'Researching primary ICT' will be of particular interest to those training in the primary phase as ICT specialists or who are undertaking an assignment during their training, perhaps as part of M level work or as a research project validated within their degree or PGCE. It will include an activity looking at recent classroom-based case studies.

Links to the requirements for initial teacher training

Where directly applicable there will be references throughout this section to the relevant parts of the Standards for Qualified Teacher Status.

As you will be aware from documentation for your course of study, the Professional Standards for Qualified Teacher Status (henceforth 'the QTS Standards') set out the requirements against which you will audit yourself and/or be assessed by your training provider or awarding body. They are presented in the form of 33 statements grouped under the following three headings:

1. Professional attributes (which includes items under 'Relationships with children and young people', 'Frameworks', 'Communicating and working with others' and 'Personal professional development').
2. Professional knowledge and understanding (which includes items under 'Teaching and learning', 'Assessment and monitoring', 'Subjects and curriculum', 'Literacy, numeracy and ICT', 'Achievement and diversity' and 'Health and well-being').
3. Professional skills (which includes items under 'Planning', 'Teaching', 'Assessing monitoring and giving feedback', 'Reviewing teaching and learning', 'Learning environment' and 'Team working and collaboration').

You will see that there is explicit mention of ICT in 'Professional knowledge and under-standing' and you will be able to identify elements in many of the general headings above which lend themselves to the professional use of ICT and which will enable you to meet the Standards. Throughout the text there will be references to the Standards associated with the reflective tasks which will enable you to use the book to help you accumulate evidence towards the award of QTS.

1
ICT in your classroom

Chapter objectives

This chapter is intended to focus thoughts on the organisational issues around teaching with computers in primary schools. We will consider the practical, physical aspects of locating equipment and look at how this impacts on planning. We will look at strategies for organising in the different resource settings in schools. We will also consider the pressure on the timetable and how best to meet the needs of the pupils and enable them to benefit from and enjoy using ICT in their learning.

The national background

First, to look back at the recent past, new entrants to the teaching profession are fortunate to be joining it at a time of continuing, well-funded change in ICT in schools. Since the late 1990s in England there has been enormous spending on ICT infrastructure, hardware and software in schools. However, change on such a huge scale is not without its logistical difficulties and much still depends on how the additional spending on ICT in schools has been managed at school level and at Local Authority (LA) level.

The evidence, from inspections by OFSTED and others, has suggested year on year that the use of computers and other ICT resources in schools, such as interactive whiteboards, is, in some cases, becoming more prevalent and better integrated into subject teaching. However there is concern at the widening gap between schools that are at the cutting edge and using ICT widely and pervasively and those that have not yet begun to integrate it into their teaching and learning. Even in areas where there is rich provision of equipment, and/or Internet connections, it is possible to find evidence that the computer is not always fully or usefully integrated into the curriculum. For a fuller discussion of these reports and the relevant research into ICT in education, please see Chapter 6.

Part of the issue lies with the variation in the quality of the development plans at local and at school level as well as with the wide variation in advisory support to schools. In turn, some of the variation can be put down to the 'bid culture' in which the innovation has taken place. In some initiatives, LAs make bids for funding to central government on the basis of a costed development plan. Schools sometimes have to bid to LAs for a share, and so on. No two neighbouring LAs have managed this in exactly the same way, so you will notice variations when you move between your placement schools.

Allied to the expansion in hardware provision has been the connection of every school to the Internet and to subsequent opportunities for collaboration communication, as well as home–school links. This used to be referred to as connecting schools to the National Grid for Learning and you may still see references to this now-defunct term in school documentation. To this end, LAs in many parts of the country aligned themselves with the emergent 'Regional Broadband Consortia' (RBCs) which are public–private partnerships providing fast, relatively low-tariff Internet access for schools and, in many cases, a virtual learning environment (VLE) of one kind or another through which the learning community interacts. They also – usually – assist schools in protecting children from unsuitable content through the deployment of firewalls and servers which screen sites and searches.

A further major element of spending early on was an acknowledgement of the need to train teachers in schools. The New Opportunities Fund (NOF) was set up with Heritage (Lottery) money. Again, although NOF funding and training have now ceased, you may well encounter references to it in staffroom documentation or in conversation.

A further intention of government policy in recent years has been to provide subsidised laptops for teachers. Significant pilot projects, such as the Becta multimedia Portables for Teachers pilots (see **www.becta.org.uk** for further information), had found that giving teachers laptops greatly increased their use of ICT in the curriculum for teaching and administration. In order to benefit from the scheme teachers had to be part of a school which was registered with the above-mentioned NOF training scheme. Some of the teachers with whom you will be working may well have benefited from this scheme. The present form of subsidy for equipment is at the local level and is usually in the hands of the management of a school.

Other major initiatives have had differing levels of emphasis in different local authorities in schools. In some LAs, personal ownership of computers has been pursued in the form of projects which focus on the use of handheld equipment such as PDAs (personal digital assistants). In other LAs the use of laptops has been seen as something to be encouraged through bulk purchase schemes alongside trolleys for storage and charging of the equipment. The aim here has been to diversify ICT provision away from the static fixed computer lab and put the technology in the hands of the learners.

You may well also encounter local projects and initiatives based in the realm of digital media, recording and presenting video and audio resources, digital movie-making, podcasting and so on. There is a fuller discussion of this in future sections.

Finally, it is almost certain that at some stage you will encounter a classroom with an interactive whiteboard; and, to a greater or lesser extent, these larger interactive displays are having an influence on pedagogy in schools. At some stage you will need to negotiate your own response and the sections on planning which follow will point you in the direction of resources and research which will assist you in making the sometimes complex decisions involved.

The local background

When you visit schools for your placements you will find that teachers are at many different points in the processes and initiatives described above. They may:

- **have completed substantial amounts of training;**
- **be in the process of completing it during your training year;**
- **be about to bid for the training or equipment for the following academic year.**

It is important to know about the training which the teachers have had or are about to undergo because it will impact on the background atmosphere and levels of enthusiasm for ICT in subject teaching in the school. Practising what you know alongside serving teachers who are engaged in their own training may be of benefit to all involved in the process. Indeed, many schools may welcome your input if they feel you can contribute skills gleaned in college training.

In more general terms there has been a perceived lack of confidence on the part of some teachers. Occasionally, this is characterised as 'reluctance'. It is certainly true that some teachers find it enormously threatening to be delivering a subject which employs skills which they do not feel themselves have, but which the children may (and it is worth stressing that word 'may') possess. If this is indeed the case, it requires teachers to be in a different power relationship with the children they are teaching.

There may also be no support structure for teachers in their school situation. At school level, there may be no ICT co-ordinator. Good ICT co-ordinators who attend training and pass it on to colleagues, give generously of their time and knowledge are not always readily available. At LA level, it may be that there is no active advisory team encouraging good practice and recommending hardware and software. In both these cases there has been a failure of management to see the necessity of putting money into human resources. Too much time and money can sometimes be spent on hardware and software and not enough on the human resources needed to develop and promote excellence in ICT in the classroom. You may well see evidence of this in your placement school.

One other issue to note is the perceived 'skills gap' between teachers and children at home. Year on year, home ownership of computers is increasing. It would be wrong to assume that it was all going into the study bedrooms of middle class students. It is possible to find levels of computer ownership in deprived areas of Inner London, for example, where six-year-old children are experienced users of the latest software. Many of these children are, when they get to school, used as surrogate ICT co-ordinators, showing both teachers and children alike how to sort out printing problems, load useful pages from the Internet and how to close down the computer properly so that it comes back to life the next day.

As alluded to above, it would be wrong for teachers to allow the feeling to grow that children know more than they do. They may sometimes know more about the mechanics of the Internet, software and hardware at a basic level (though most training more than adequately allows teachers to catch up with this). What children do not know, and the reason why they need the teacher to be using it with them, is how to apply it in their developing subject knowledge. They require the teacher to be a guide or facilitator. In return, where there are skills gaps opening up between teachers and pupils, some form of mutual exchange of information and ideas helps both parties interact constructively around computers.

Resource levels in schools: a rough guide

This section attempts to categorise schools according to the resource settings at different levels. Three types of resource setting are described on a continuum from high resource to medium resource to low resource. It is useful to characterise resource settings in this way because you will be able to make a judgement about particular organisational strategies if you can learn to observe and sum up the situation in a placement school quickly.

The school in which you are placed will be somewhere along the line of development and will not necessarily have all elements of the different resource settings represented. Furthermore, schools develop and change year on year. A school previously described as being low resource may move on quite rapidly in a year in, for example, the case of a school just receiving its allocation of government funding.

A further issue – which is partly included below – is the human resource setting in the school. A school with very low numbers of computers may still be doing well in ICT due to excellence in organisation and involvement of all staff. Similarly a school which looks good with a network room full of computers may in fact be keeping the door locked and doing nothing with them. The situation is complex.

Table of Resource level definitions

High resource setting

Portable computers such as laptops or PDAs are used to distribute ICT around the school
There is a network room used by groups and the wider community (sometimes) as a hub for ICT development activities
Printing – in colour when necessary – is available at every station.
The Internet connection is a fast affordable broadband connection supplied and moderated by an LA
There is a technician who regularly attends to maintain equipment in good working order
Digital cameras and digital video cameras are available for use by teachers and pupils
There are interactive whiteboards available to use in many teaching spaces and their use is informed by good pedagogical decisions, not always teacher-led; pupils often have control of the resource
Appropriate software is available for every age phase
There are also stations connected to the network available in the classroom to carry on with work begun in the network room. These may be in the form of rechargeable laptops or handheld PDAs
Programmable toys are available for teaching and learning across the curriculum
The school is implementing a cohesive strategy, including an ongoing development plan with high levels of LA support
There is a policy for acceptable Internet use
There is a fully implemented scheme of work
Teachers, pupils and the wider community make use of the local authority VLE where the school has a vibrant and well-used web presence

Suitability for placement as a trainee:

This is an excellent setting for learning how to integrate ICT fully into the curriculum and develop ICT capability at the same time.

Medium resource setting

A working computer and printer in every classroom
A network room with computers removed from classrooms and placed there to capitalise on resources
Some programmable toys are available
A digital camera is available to borrow and some short video clips are sometimes used
Repairs are dealt with fairly promptly, though it may take up to half a term
Interactive whiteboards are present in some classrooms and sometimes used but rarely by pupils and often in a didactic and limited way to reinforce teacher-directed pedagogy
A scheme of work is being implemented

The school has the first stages of a development plan in operation and there is a sense that ICT is valued and that within the next two or three years the school will move forward and become a high resource setting

A policy on safe and acceptable Internet use is being developed and there are plans to launch a school website soon

Suitability for placement as a trainee:

Although not at the very cutting edge, this is a good situation in which to develop skills of organising for ICT and a trainee may still learn and even contribute something to the partnership school.

Low Resource setting:

An older, frequently broken computer in the classroom or one between two

One or two interactive whiteboards which have never been switched on because the teachers are still waiting to be trained

Overhead projectors are used on the whiteboard surface

Low staff morale, low spending on ICT, no ICT co-ordinator, no technician

Frequent sightings of batik and plant pots placed over computers

No scheme of work in place

No ink cartridges or ribbons in the printers

Poor software titles with children from Year 1 to Year 6 doing the same thing on the computer (copy typing, doodling in a Paint package, playing a number or spelling game, probably the same one each time)

A school website is some way off although the school phone number is available through OFSTED or the LA.

In OFSTED terms, the school is not providing the entitlement to ICT resources for its children and staff are not receiving their entitlement to professional development.

Suitability for placement as a trainee:

This is a very difficult placement in which to gain the required standard in ICT in Subject Teaching and you will be heavily dependent upon your college for support.

PRACTICAL TASK PRACTICAL TASK PRACTICAL TASK PRACTICAL TASK

Observing the ICT setting 1: The computers and other hardware

The government has spent unprecedented amounts of money on ICT in Education in recent years and much of it has been spent on various hardware and equipment in schools. Schools have a degree of choice over how they organise their resources for ICT and this early observation task is designed to raise awareness about organisation and use of ICT in teaching and learning. The sections which follow will take up issues around school organisation and discuss how they may have come to certain pedagogical decisions.

Although in itself a Foundation subject, ICT is in every subject area across the curriculum and you will see it being used in a range of settings, including in areas of learning in the Foundation Stage. Make notes on what is being used and on where it is being used. Remember that ICT includes computers and more. Use these questions as prompts for your note-taking. Have a look at all the places in the school where computers may be in operation.

- **What do you see?**
- **Is there a computer in the classroom?**
- **Or are all the computers grouped in an ICT suite?**

- Is there a mixed economy of some in the classroom and some in an ICT suite?
- Are there any portable computers available, either laptops or PDAs?
- Is there an interactive whiteboard in the classroom or Foundation Stage setting?
- How is it being used?
- Who is using it?
- Are there scanners or digital cameras or digital video cameras?
- Can children and teachers access the Internet easily?
- Is it available in the classroom or ICT suite or both?
- Does this appear to be a quick connection?
- Is it filtered in any way to protect the children?
- Does it go straight onto the Internet or onto a special local authority network?
- Does the school use a local virtual learning environment (in London, for example, this may be provided by the London Grid for Learning, elsewhere by other Regional Broadband Consortia)?
- Does there appear to be interesting primary school software around in the school?
- How does it appear to be organised?
- Has the school subscribed to appropriate web-based software for learning?

Find out what is available and, if you can, list six to eight titles with their subject area and age range.

The notes which you make should be brief and comprise up to two sides of A4. They should be written with enough detail to give you a snapshot of ICT in use across the curriculum in your school.

Read them again in the context of the opening sections of this chapter. What do your observations and reflections tell you about the kind of ICT setting in which you will be operating?

Observing the ICT setting 2: Human Resources

Observe how the class teachers organise the ICT for their children. Remember that unless they have supportive ICT co-ordinators or senior managers, a programme of staff development and working equipment, they may well be struggling with ICT. They will welcome your support but you must never make them feel threatened by your access to more recent knowledge and ideas possibly gained in work experience. Remember that the teachers are there to help you learn. Whatever you can give back to the school as a trainee who is learning about ICT in subject teaching, has to be offered but tactfully and with due regard for the teachers' professionalism.

Observe the children themselves as they work with ICT in the school. They are the best source of information about what is going on with computers in the classroom. They know about the equipment. If it is old, they know which keys stick. They tend to know how to get round the deficiencies of the equipment, such as the printer which jams regularly.

The games-playing children, those who have computer games consoles at home of one kind or another, often have a robust attitude towards computers of all sorts. They are aware of 'cheating' to get to different levels. Sometimes they will indulge in various key presses which may cause havoc with onscreen displays; sometimes they may discover for the class, newer, more efficient ways of doing things. Whatever the situation, it is always worth listening to what children say about computers and considering and valuing their contributions to the whole class body of knowledge about ICT.

Observe the classroom and learning support assistants wherever possible. Where available, they are a valuable source of knowledge and support about computers in the classroom. Some authorities are already in the business of providing training for classroom assistants in ICT. Listen to what they say and involve them in your planning. Mutual respect and good communication are the keys to working well with classroom assistants in all areas of the curriculum.

How do the children and adults use the interactive whiteboard? Is the teacher always in control? Which curriculum areas predominate? Do they use the software that comes with the board or do they sometime show web pages, images, DVDs through the projector?

Find out about the parents and governors and ICT. Parents, like children, have a wide range of ability and experience and an even wider range of concerns with ICT. They may be thinking about a purchase for their child and will often ask about a particular piece of hardware or software. They will assume, rightly or wrongly that you are an individual, fully trained to deal with such enquiries.

Some parental concerns will be around the use of the Internet in your school, how it is organised and so on. They may be hinting at whether or not the school has an acceptable use policy and adequate protection for their children from unsuitable material on the world wide web.

Governors may raise many of the same issues with you and the school will be held responsible for the materials which the children may, in all innocence, be accessing if the school is not providing access through an education provider or through a filter which it is maintaining itself.

RESEARCH SUMMARY RESEARCH SUMMARY RESEARCH SUMMARY

Bridget Somekh (Somekh and Davis, 1997) characterises three ways in which teachers approach the use of ICT. In the first two of these, teachers either use ICT as a tutorial tool, delivering content to pupils or as a tool for carrying out tasks in 'content-free' software that does not necessarily depend on fully exploiting the features of ICT (she calls the computer a neutral tool in this mode). Finally, the third way of using the computer is as a cognitive tool to support active learning on the part of the children concerned (see Somekh and Davis, 1997). These provide a useful framework for examining practice, either your own or practice observed in school.

Organisational strategies for working in different resource settings with children

ICT is an entitlement no matter which situation you are working in. In all settings there are organisational issues which need to be addressed. This section looks at bringing ICT into the world of the classroom in the low resource setting and the high resource setting.

Organising ICT in high resource settings

In a high resource setting, it is quite likely that you will be able to share the experience of the lesson with the children by means of a large display. This will be in the form of a large monitor, projector and screen or an interactive whiteboard (sometimes you will see this written in abbreviation as 'IWB'). It could be by being able to take control of the screens at the individual stations and replacing them with the teaching screen via some network software. In schools where there is no such display facility you will have to gather the children together in a space in front of one of the monitors. Teaching in network rooms without a large display is very difficult and you will need to learn strategies for overcoming this from observing the other teachers and/or classroom assistants.

There are additional levels of complexity in computer labs (sometimes called network rooms) and you must be on the alert for children who are still thinking in terms of stand-alone use. In the first place, make use of the large display or screen-grabbing facility to demonstrate the procedure for logging on. Remind the children that they do not have to sit at the same machine each week. Remind them about the importance of their password. Here are some different models of practice:

- **Whole-class logon with the same username and password into a general area on the network for that class.**
- **Children with a unique username and password.**
- **Children with group logon names and passwords.**

Before teaching the children on a network, make sure that you understand the process of logging on yourself. Ask the ICT co-ordinator (or technician) before starting (remember to ask for your own username and password as a guest on placement at the school). Children are often given their own area on the network in which to save their work. It is important that you follow the same protocols as they are used to. Every school network is slightly differently organised and you will need to take time to learn this for yourself so as not to make potentially serious mistakes (children are no more forgiving than adults of those whom they suspect had a hand in losing work on which they have spent a considerable amount of time).

As a rule, unless the children are very young, they should be taught how to log on and log off by themselves. This is part of learning about network literacy, a concept that has newly arrived in primary schools in recent years, a situation in which, previously, children and teachers worked with one stand-alone computer in the corner of the classroom. One strategy is to have all the passwords and usernames on index cards, used at the beginning of the session and collected at the end.

Whole-class demonstrations can, and should, still take place. But they need to be a sensible length, enabling the children to make the best use of what may be their only time in the week when they are on the machines. After all, lesson management ought to be easier with no activities going on other than use of the systems. The teacher can provide more direct input for the children.

In a school where there is access to distributed technology, such as laptops or PDAs, many of these issues do not arise at all. In their place, other factors need to be taken into account, such as battery life, ownership, sharing, storing and so on. At any rate, it is important that you follow the protocols of the school in this area as in others. Many teachers remark on how much simpler it is to integrate the use of technology when mass access to portable or handheld computers comes to their classroom, rather than having to take everyone down to a computer lab. It becomes as much a part of the provision as the use of traditional items in the classroom.

The planning chapter and sections will look in detail at how to manage ICT resources to approach knowledge and skills across the curriculum. It is important to remember that children can contribute to the whole-class understanding and skills development in ICT and that there should be an opportunity for them to do so at times during, or at the close of, the session. The plenary, for example, can really come alive in a networked environment if the children are encouraged to use software for presentation of their projects for all to see. Schools in high resource settings which are capable of publishing on the Internet or their own Intranet will be able to further enrich the motivational opportunities for children writing or creating multimedia for a wider audience.

Organising ICT in low resource settings

Lower resource settings are far less common (see section on monitoring ICT). However, they still exist and can also be foisted in a school when a network room or set of laptops is out of use (or block-booked by another teacher). In a setting in which a single computer is shared by a class of 30 children, first bring the computer to the carpet area where it can be seen by everybody. This immediately brings the computer out of its corner and into the world of the classroom. There may, of course, be physical reasons why you cannot do this. If there are, do what you can to overcome them or borrow areas big enough to do it somewhere else in the school. Just getting started with a piece of software should involve the whole class. This does not need to be of the same order of time as for the initiatives in literacy and numeracy; although at the beginning with software they have not encountered before, when screens look very unfamiliar to the class, it would be worth spending longer on them.

The aim is still to allow the computer to be a part of the general resource provision of the classroom more fully. A question-and-answer style lends itself to this situation. Allow the children to contribute, even to provide tips for other users. Discuss with them the difficulties that they have overcome in familiarising themselves with the onscreen layout of the particular piece of software. Whole-class sessions can be enhanced by the following examples and principles:

- **Ask the children to discover during the session, and then report back on, different ways of doing the same thing. In a writing program for example, how to make text appear in a different font size or colour.**
- **Stress regular, practical instructions. One such regularly repeated instruction should be 'Save before you print', droned to children day-in day-out in order to persuade them that they should indeed save before they print in order to avoid the inevitable heartache which arises when a document gets lost in a malfunctioning printer.**
- **As is the case with all good primary practice, question children who don't always jump up and down with the answer (don't favour the loud over the quiet).**
- **Invite children to contribute to the discussion strictly girl –boy – girl – boy.**
- **Do not allow one gender or group of children to dominate.**
- **Stress the team-building aspects of sharing strategies so that they/we can all use the computer efficiently and safely.**
- **Involve children in a discussion about safety – monitor position, length of time, seating and so on.**
- **Let everyone become an expert... don't always ask the same child who is managing their own Internet business from their bedroom at home.**
- **Value what they say even when it is patently wrong. Help them to discover a better way constructively (e.g. 'That's a good suggestion but...').**

The suggestions in the list above are part of good practice for any teaching situation. There is no reason why the use of technology should result in adopting different values around communication and sharing, etc. Technology sometimes challenges assumptions that we have around teaching and learning, indeed it often stimulates debate about the first principles of education, but it should never be an end in itself. There has to be a sound pedagogical reason for using it in a given situation and we will return to this theme in the section on planning below.

Regular whole-class input increases the shared level of knowledge in the classroom about the use of the computer. It will also repay you in terms of stress reduction to have a regular period of whole-class instruction in the basics of a particular piece of software. You will reduce the number of times that you have to say the same thing over and over again to groups of two to three children.

Becoming independent and increasingly competent in basic ICT skills will engender in the children a sense of responsibility for their work. It may be something that many of the children know from home but there will be others for whom you are providing the only access to newer technology. From an early age, as children progress through the school, they are expected to take on more responsibility for knowing where their equipment is, where their possessions are, where they're going next and so on. It should be the same for ICT. Children can be shown the importance of looking after electronic forms of their work, just as they learn the importance of looking after their draft books. They will need to be shown how to save and retrieve their work and the importance of backing up work.

All of these activities allow you and the children to start to think of the computer as a part of the world of the classroom. More than that, they foster a belief amongst all users in the classroom that they can become competent and confident manipulators of ICT.

The alternative model of instruction, a version of the cascade model, whereby one or two children learn it and teach others over a period of time discreetly while other children get on with the real work, allows the more negative messages about ICT to be disseminated. Amongst these more negative messages are:

1. There are ICT experts who know everything and must always be consulted before you do anything.
2. ICT is something that happens in a corner of the room away from the mainstream and is never discussed and nothing to do with the rest of the school day.

Show children that you are also a learner. ICT will be less threatening to you as a teacher if you enter into the situation as a learner alongside them. It is wrong to give children the impression that you or anyone else knows all they need to know about computers. Frustrating as it may be, the truth of the matter is that we are all always learning about ICT. Once one thing is learned you can be sure another parameter will enter the equation. It is OK to make mistakes. If the basic care of the equipment is known and respected, there is not much harm that can be done by trying different solutions to problems.

At the same time it is important in the low resource setting to establish and maintain a rota. Rotas ensure that there is equality of access and of opportunity in the classroom. However, they should not be fixed once and for all at the start of an academic year. The acquisition of ICT skills is a dynamic process, always changing. After whole-class input, in the beginning of working with a new piece of software or hardware, children need time to practise. Longer rota periods can be gradually shortened as children gain more skills and independence.

Organising ICT for special educational needs

Children who have special educational needs have the right to access to the whole curriculum including ICT. The nature of the needs dictates your response to it as a teacher. Often ICT has been identified as being of particular benefit to a given learner in a given situation.

Sometimes, if the child is on the SEN register, the child will have ICT hardware and software use identified as part of her or his Individual Education Plan (IEP) and you will need to incorporate this in your planning and organisation. Some examples might include:

- software which addresses the needs of a dyslexic child;
- hardware which allows access to the computer for a child with motor impairment;
- browser windows which open up in larger fonts for visually impaired children;
- portables or laptops with specialist software loaded for very particular needs (this might include one specialist device or laptop assigned to one child in particular);
- specialist hardware for those who are using wheelchairs, e.g. specialist keyboard mounts or switching devices.

Some companies are dedicated to finding solutions for access for children with SEN and they will welcome enquires about their software and suggestions for future development. They are usually smaller companies who depend on a close relationship with the schools and children with whom they work. The annual British Educational Technology and Training exhibition (known as the BETT show and held in January in London each year) includes a Special Needs Village for you to examine at first hand such solutions.

For children with SEN in your class it is important to discover if they require any additional access to the computer in the form of hardware that makes it easier to point and click at menu items or enter text. Some examples include:

- A Concept Keyboard – a device which allows touch-sensitive areas to be created on a flat A4 or A3 board which can be set up to input particular items of text or commands. Teachers can tailor the Concept Keyboard to the particular needs of an individual child using authoring software provided. The software also includes printing facilities.
- A Touch Window – a device which attaches to the front of a monitor allowing the user to touch areas of the screen as a replacement mouse click to gain access to the menus in given software.
- Big Keys – a larger-format keyboard for children with fine motor control difficulties.
- Switches – on/off rack-mounted switches for wheelchair users and others which equate to left and right mouse clicks.
- Trackballs – large inverted mouse systems where the user is able to move a larger ball over a bigger area to point and click.
- Small mice – smaller point-and-click devices for smaller hands with motor control difficulties.

In terms of software for special educational needs, there is a very wide range indeed. Most of it can be used to access the curriculum including the units of work in the ICT scheme of work by means of levelled menus and different screen setups.

There is also a case for appropriate tutorial software for some children with dyslexia or language delay because it will address very specifically the multi-sensory approach needed to allow such children to acquire strategies to catch up with language development.

REFLECTIVE TASK

Organising ICT for children who have special educational needs
- Find out about children in your class with SEN.

- Does their IEP require that they use ICT?

- Is there, in fact, dedicated equipment for use by one child?

- Would this be hardware, software or both?

- Does the child have a special needs assistant who will work with them on their ICT?

- How does their need for specialist ICT Input impact on your organisation of the class?

- Is there a programme of review for determining success levels of the ICT equipment with their special educational need?

- Is there someone you can discuss the situation with?

- What are the feelings of the parent on the use of ICT by their child during the week? Do they have materials or equipment at home which they are using support her or him? Does it complement what you are doing or do you need to make adjustments to it?

RESEARCH SUMMARY RESEARCH SUMMARY RESEARCH SUMMARY

ICT and SEN

Research by Lie, O'Hare and Denwood (2000) in Scottish schools shows that although word processing is believed to have a positive effect on the compositional process for children with specific writing difficulties there are further significant background factors around motivation, cognition, medical factors and the whole learning environment.

The argument throughout this book and this chapter in particular is about seeing the possibilities for ICT use within the context of the whole class, or, in this case, the individual learner with special educational needs. ICT is a tool for the enhancement of the learner's education within the context of the whole child and not simply an intrinsically 'good thing'.

Organising ICT for children with English as an additional language

ICT offers many benefits to young learners in the primary classroom who are learning and using English as an additional language (EAL). The Internet brings many audio and video resources across the curriculum within reach. Children who are learning English at the earliest stages can access parts of the curriculum by means of such media.

As a child begins to acquire more English, the computer, if properly managed, allows her or him to experiment with forms of written and spoken English in an unthreatening and motivating environment. Some additional tutorial software may be appropriate but talking word processors can be just as effective, with immediate feedback provided on composition. The biggest benefit is in areas where the child can experiment with open-ended software alongside peers.

Community languages with their own alphabets and letter systems are available through font add-ons in Office software. Amongst other uses, these can be employed to produce signs and instructions in the appropriate language. In turn, this goes some way to demonstrating that the language of that child is valued in the context of the school and is an excellent way, again, of bringing the ICT into the world of the classroom.

For younger children in this context, sensitive adult intervention and peer support are crucial. There should be plenty of opportunity to try to move conceptual development along by talk in the home language alongside support for learning English.

The choice of software or web-based resource should include elements which allow for the child to choose menu items by pointing and clicking, to have sections of text spoken, to allow access to pictures, music and video. Multimedia authoring packages including some digital video activities (see the relevant section below) can be useful in this context. There is enormous potential for producing home-grown resources in dual language format. This would be an exciting project for Year 6 for the Multimedia Authoring Unit. Resources could be created for any age in the school by the older children asking parents, siblings, and other adults to help to record in the home language.

Organising ICT for children with English as an additional language carries the same responsibilities and requirements as for organising any area of the curriculum for them, namely:

- **Never assume the level of language-learning – find out.**
- **Differentiate for levels of English appropriately; do not assume that all EAL learners are the same or have the same learning style.**
- **Make sure that EAL children understand all of the processes involved in switching on and off, logging on and off and saving work.**
- **Check and re-check understanding with sensitive questioning.**

A SUMMARY OF **KEY POINTS**

This chapter has considered the background to the use of ICT in your classroom, providing important contexts for your understanding of planning issues.

> **We have seen that there are different management strategies for different resource levels for ICT.**

> **We have considered the needs of learners with special educational needs in the various contexts.**

> **We have considered the needs of children for whom English is an additional language.**

Moving on

Consider the wide range of resources you have seen and the ways in which they have been organised. On teaching practices you will have some freedom to change them but not so much as when you move into your induction year. What kind of organisation of resources have you seen that has been most successful? What will you try to replicate in your own classroom? Where do you see the future of classroom design taking the use of ICT in teaching and learning? It may well be that you will have some input into the design of a learning space at some stage during the years of classroom rebuilding that lie ahead. Hopefully you will be able to take some ideas about the design of learning spaces into your future career and relate them back to the sorts of choices you make about the technologies you use.

FURTHER READING FURTHER READING **FURTHER READING** FURTHER READING

Ager, R. (2003) *ICT in primary schools.* London: Routledge

Duffty, J. (2006) *Primary ICT: Extending knowledge in practice*. Exeter: Learning Matters

Freedman, T. (1999) *Managing ICT.* London: Hodder & Stoughton

Lie, K., O'Hare, A. and Denwood, S. (2000) Multidisciplinary support and the management of children with specific writing difficulties, *British Journal of Special Education,* 27 (2) June

McFarlane, A. (ed.) (1997) *Information technology and authentic learning*. London: Routledge

QCA (2000) *Curriculum guidance for the Foundation Stage*. London: QCA

Somekh, B. and Davis, N. (eds) (1997) *Using IT effectively in Teaching and Learning: Studies in pre-service and in-service teacher education*. London: Routledge

2
Planning primary ICT

Chapter objectives

The requirements of the QTS Standards suggest that trainees focus on subject-related opportunities to work with ICT that make a significant contribution to the learning of the pupils. At the same time as acquiring these skills of planning within subject teaching, however, trainees will need to be mindful of the developing ICT capability of their children. The capability and the application in subject teaching are very closely bound up together. Planning which addresses one without at least considering the other will not work. Good planning depends on a thorough analysis and negotiation of factors around the children, including their capabilities and needs.

ICT Planning and the Professional Standards for QTS

While learning how to plan for ICT in subject teaching, trainees will be cognisant of the need to know about their children's ICT capability in order to pursue opportunities to exploit and extend it. It will be part of a set of factors which makes up good lesson planning, in the same way that planning a useful daily mathematics lesson in shape and space, for example, takes into account the children's wider experiences, mathematical capabilities and opportunities to enhance and develop them. They do not exist in a separate world; they are inextricably linked. Trainees must look at the context of the features of ICT which make it a learning tool – one amongst many – and decide on whether it is appropriate to the learning outcome for which they are currently planning. At the same time, unless other factors are taken into account (and, as previously stated this means, as a minimum, knowing about the children's existing ICT capability and the resources available in the school), planning will be, at best, ineffective and, at worst, potentially counterproductive.

The Standards themselves are clear on a number of issues which relate to planning and all of which, to a greater or lesser extent, suggest an integrated vision of skills, contexts and uses of ICT in teaching and learning. Here are some of the key principles from within the Standards on which to draw when thinking about planning in the light of new technology, together with some instances of their relevance:

> Those recommended for the award of QTS should:
> Have high expectations of children and young people including a commitment to ensuring that they can achieve their full educational potential... (from Q1 in Professional Attributes)

High expectations must extend to the use of technology in schools in an era of continual change and adaptation and in an era in which young learners may (stress the word 'may') have access to all sorts of ICT at home and elsewhere away from the classroom. Having high expectations means knowing where the children are in the first place. It presupposes for ICT that some kind of conversation has taken place which locates the children's ICT knowledge and experience. In this way ICT is no different from any other territory of learning. It needs to be mapped accurately by reference to the learners and what they bring to the setting. It will not do, for example, to teach how to underline fonts to someone who is designing their own web space at home. It will have to be a different set of expectations for these learners.

> *Those recommended for the award of QTS should:*
> *Have a secure knowledge and understanding of their subjects/curriculum areas and related pedagogy...*
>> (from Q14 in Professional Knowledge and Understanding)

For ICT this means being aware of where to go for support in knowledge and understanding and not simply in the way of finding appropriate 'content' for subject teaching by when and how to use that content and with what sort of pedagogy in mind. There are very many resources produced by LAs, software publishers and the government (as well as informally through the networks which teachers establish for themselves) which lend themselves to particular visions of pedagogy

> *Those recommended for the award of QTS should:*
> *Know and understand the relevant statutory and non-statutory curricula and frameworks, including those provided through the National Strategies, for their subjects/curriculum areas...*
>> (from Q15 in Professional Knowledge and Understanding)

In order to take ICT in subject teaching forward there needs to be some knowledge of, and negotiation with, the emergent strategies and frameworks. This means, at a basic level, monitoring the requirements and documentation through a series of websites and mailings, mainly centred on the DfES standards website. It also means being open to ideas disseminated to the school and your training provider which relate the themes of ICT to subject teaching.

> *Those recommended for the award of QTS should:*
> *Know how to use skills in... ICT to support their teaching...*
>> (from Q17 in Professional Knowledge and Understanding)

This standard is virtually self-explanatory. It implies a degree of adaptation of personal existing ICT skills into the teaching situation. It is not enough to know a great deal about how ICT works yourself if you cannot translate this usefully into teaching and learning. Some of the issues around the overlap of skills and personal knowledge will be discussed in sections which follow.

> *Those recommended for the award of QTS should:*
> *Design opportunities for learners to develop their... ICT skills*
>> (from Q23 in Professional Skills)

This is also relatively simple to interpret in the light of planning for teaching with ICT. It means being able to see opportunities in whatever sessions you are designing for the convergence of skills of ICT and purposeful learning with the technology in a given subject. As a concrete example, publishing small books in the classroom will give a sense of writing for a purpose, for a target audience and perhaps focusing on particular aspects of literacy teaching. At the same time, the mix of text and graphics, the negotiation with scanners, printers, cameras and other peripherals help to develop ICT skills within a real context.

> *Those recommended for the award of QTS should:*
> *Use a range of teaching strategies and resources including e-learning...*
>
> (from Q25 in Professional Skills)

E-learning is defined here in its broadest sense and links with overall governmental targets for the use of both online and offline resources. It also clearly aligns e-learning as both a resource and a subset of skills in its own right. It means seeing opportunities for using web-based learning platforms, online software, and resources in the classroom (including IWBs).

> *Those recommended for the award of QTS should:*
> *Establish a purposeful and safe working environment*
>
> (from Q30 in Professional Skills)

The word 'safe' above means being physically well organised in the space whether you are in a network room or bringing a portable resource to the classroom. It is about being aware of everything that can contribute to a safe working environment around technology. A fuller discussion appears elsewhere in the book but, at this juncture, it's worth demarcating the range of thinking in health and safety as starting from who plugs and unplugs the equipment to dealing with trailing cables, to safe, possibly height-adjustable seating, and monitoring levels of screen-time.

The word 'purposeful' above relates to having some clear idea of what is happening and where it is taking the learners in terms of their knowledge and experience. More than that, as in other subjects, it means being able to communicate this. In planning terms this means being very clear about the learning objective. We will see, below, how we might identify these learning objectives and opportunities in subject teaching in all subjects. For the purposes of the award of QTS this means each trainee knowing about ICT objectives and opportunities in the core curriculum (English, maths and science) and, where relevant, in their chosen specialist subject. The sections which follow will analyse the situation further in a range of contexts and will then go into each individual subject area (including the strategies for the teaching of literacy and numeracy) in search of such opportunities.

> *Those recommended for the award of QTS should:*
> *Ensure that colleagues working with them are appropriately involved in supporting learning and understand the roles they are expected to fulfil...*
>
> (from Q33 in Professional Skills)

This has been included because there are many occasions in classrooms now where you will be responsible for the work of other adults in the setting. With ICT this means being sensitive to the needs or otherwise of those teachers and helpers. Again, this means being fully apprised of the situation regarding skill levels and expectations of everyone in the setting.

Effective planning – analysing the situation

Effective teaching depends heavily on effective planning. ICT in subject teaching and ICT as a subject in its own right are no exception to this rule. In turn, effective planning depends on a thorough analysis of the situation at the outset. Many writers have identified this link and some have produced books for teachers in training which summarise and synthesise the best of the available research. Chris Kyriacou provides an overview of studies which have looked at lesson effectiveness in his book, *Effective Teaching in Schools* (Kyriacou, 1997). One of the studies reported, that of Cooper and McIntyre (1996), looked at the teaching and learning in a series of lessons in terns of what both the teachers and the pupils felt. Analysis produced the following list of key items which contributed to lesson effectiveness:

- *Clear learning goals for pupil learning*
- *Helping pupils to contextualise the content in terms of their own experience and knowledge*
- *Providing a supportive social context for learning*
- *Enabling pupils to engage in the learning process in a number of different ways*
- *Willingness of the teacher to modify learning tasks in the light of pupil circumstances*

(Kyriacou, 1997)

All of these factors are of immediate direct relevance to teachers planning for any subject in the curriculum. When it comes to the use of ICT in subject teaching or ICT in its own right, there is an added layer of complexity because of the impact of the resource setting of the school (see previous chapter). Some questions need to be raised to take account of this and added to the generic areas above. At the outset, as a minimum, teachers preparing to use ICT in their teaching need to be asking at least these few questions:

- **What do we know about the children's existing knowledge, skills and understanding in the subject?**
- **What has been their previous experience with ICT?**
- **What does the National Curriculum set out for the children in this class?**
- **What does the relevant strategy, scheme or framework suggest at this level?**
- **What am I therefore expecting the children to achieve?**
- **How will I differentiate the activity to reflect the different needs and abilities in the class?**
- **What relevant pieces of theoretical writing and/or case studies are there to support my planning?**
- **What will be the demands on me in terms of my own knowledge, skills and understanding of ICT?**
- **What is the resource setting for the school and how does this impact on what I can plan for the class?**
- **What are the additional time costs and constraints on me when planning to use ICT?**
- **What kind of grouping or organisation am I planning for?**
- **How do I go about the physical management of the activity?**
- **Are there any further cross-curricular links?**
- **How will I go about including the whole class in the activity?**

Finally (and we will consider this in far more detail in the relevant chapter below):

- **What are the assessment and record keeping opportunities in the activity?**

Planning is, of course, cyclical in nature. No sooner have you reached the last question than you realise it must be used to answer the first question in the next batch of planning. Good planning should create assessment opportunities because good assessment informs good planning.

Towards a lesson planning pro-forma for ICT

It makes sense to try to collect these questions into headings which you can use to ensure that you cover all of the necessary elements, each time you plan. As part of your training year, you will develop, or be given assistance in developing, lesson planning pro-formas of various kinds. Some will provide very detailed outlines of what is going on in a session whereas others will be shorter. As you gain experience through the year, what seems like a very detailed and time-consuming activity initially, will become part of your professional life and second nature to you as a practising and reflective teacher.

Without attempting to prescribe a model which works in all settings, on all courses, in all classrooms, here is a possible set of headings for a detailed, longer format, plan. Most of the headings are in common use for curriculum planning in all subjects and are relatively easily adapted to ICT in subject teaching and ICT as a subject in its own right.

LESSON OVERVIEW
Describe the lesson in brief before going on to outline the detail of how it will operate and the rationale under the remaining headings.

SCHOOL/CLASS CONTEXT
Describe under this heading the context of the children, their school, and their class within the school.

LEARNING NEEDS OF THE CHILDREN
Use this part of the plan to map out the learning needs of the class in both general and specific terms.

GROUPING/TIMING
Is this lesson plan for the whole class, a group, a pair or an individual? Is it an activity which you would like a group to work on all week, or different groups of children to work on through the week? How long will the activity last?

RESOURCES
Outline here how the resources for ICT are set out in the school. What, in particular, is available to you to use during the session you are planning? Make a list of everything you need to hand to make the lesson work.

THEORETICAL CONTEXT
Are there any readings which underpin the thinking behind the plan for this lesson, either for you or for the children? An example for you might be one where you have identified, through your use of ICT, a different way of approaching a particular lesson. You find that, for example, 'IT can support the process of professional development as well as providing a stimulus to rethinking the teaching process', (Somekh and Davis, 1997).

NATIONAL CURRICULUM/FOUNDATION STAGE CURRICULUM CONTEXT
What aspects of the programmes of study from *Curriculum 2000* are you teaching? Consider the ICT and any links to other subjects. List the main cross-curricular focus. If you are working in an Early Years setting, what elements of the Curriculum for the Foundation Stage are you hoping to work with during the activity?

SCHEME OF WORK CONTEXT

From the school scheme of work, or the QCA scheme of work, outline the unit, or aspect of the unit, that you are covering with the children. Show how it progresses from the previous one studied.

YOUR OWN LEARNING NEEDS

Take some time to note down any concepts you need to revise and review before teaching the children. Are there any aspects of any hardware, software or websites you are using which you need to consider before starting the activity?

ORGANISATIONAL MEMORY JOGGERS

Do you know all you need to know about passwords, location of keys to the computer suite, computer cupboard, etc.? Have you checked on availability of all of the items you need to run the lesson?

OTHER ADULTS

Do you know how many, if any, other adults are available to support the teaching of the lesson? Have you copied the plan for them and indicated what you would like them to do?

LEARNING OBJECTIVES

List the main objectives of the activities using the scheme of work as a map for learning.

DIFFERENTIATION

What do you expect different members of the class to achieve in terms of their different ability levels? How will you help children who are experiencing difficulties with ICT? How will you develop further the skills, knowledge and understanding of the most able in the class? What do you expect the majority to have achieved by the end of the lesson? There is some good guidance given in the QCA scheme of work which can be used as a starting point for differentiation. See the next chapter.

LEARNING NEEDS – EAL

How will you support children in your class who have English as an additional language?

LEARNING NEEDS – SEN

How will you support any children in the class with special educational needs? Are there particular physical needs, for example, which could be met by means of alternative access devices?

ASSESSMENT OPPORTUNITIES

What are the assessment opportunities in this particular lesson? Will you focus on the whole class, or an individual? How will you use other adults who may be around to assist in the process? (See the assessment chapter for a fuller discussion of the issues around assessing ICT.)

KEY QUESTIONS

What are the key questions which you will ask the children during the lesson which draw out the teaching and learning objectives? How will you maintain the dialogue with children who are experiencing difficulties? Record a few possible prompts which you could use.

LESSON FORMAT

Depending on your resource setting, whether you are in the classroom with one computer, or in a computer suite or a corridor, how long will the different phases of your lesson last? The three-part lesson may not always be the best model but it is certainly a common one which has gained predominance in recent years. If this is the case and your time with the children is going to be organised in this way, give timings for:

- an introduction outlining the learning objectives;
- development of the lesson through focused activities and integrated tasks;
- a plenary, wherein all the strands are drawn together and children have an opportunity to share successes and problems.

EVALUATING THE LESSON part 1 – OPERATIONAL ISSUES

Good planning includes a space in which to reflect on how the lesson actually proceeded. It only needs to be a few lines, written at the time or soon after, which can give you a perspective on things you needed to change to make the lesson work (and which could, in turn, inform your planning later). Did you need, for example, to alter the timings of the introduction to ensure understanding of what was required for all the children? Did you find that, in fact, you talked too much and the children needed more time and more independence in their working?

EVALUATING THE LESSON part 2 – LEARNING OUTCOMES

How far did the lesson achieve the intended learning objectives? Make a judgement based on your identified assessment opportunities. If it is part of a sequence of activities, how much is there still left to do? Comment on how the lesson went for the children experiencing difficulty or for those children of high ability. How well were you able to meet the needs of those with English as an additional language? Did children with special educational needs have full access to the activity and were they able to succeed?

EVALUATING THE LESSON part 3 – NEXT TIME

Make some brief notes about what needs to happen next on the basis of your comments above. Identify some issues which need to be addressed for the next lesson in the sequence to be successful. What will you do differently next time? What went well?

Auditing

Your college tutor will be able to outline how the audit is carried out in your particular institution. If you feel, in discussion with your mentor, professional tutor or other colleagues, that you have covered aspects of the audit of your development according to the Standards for QTS, then make a note of it, copy the plan, attach any relevant photographs or printouts as further evidence and cross-reference it with your audit in your portfolio of ICT work. Remember that a good plan, a good lesson activity and detailed evaluation may provide evidence that you are operating at a good level within one or more Standard.

ICT as a subject: working with the National Curriculum and its frameworks, schemes and strategies

This section is concerned principally with the curriculum as it is outlined for children entering Year 1 of primary school up to Year 6. The curriculum for the Foundation Stage, from the age of three until the age of five/six, is covered in a separate chapter.

The most recent version of the National Curriculum for schools in England was published early in 2000 and since that time a range of strategies has emerged alongside it intended to provide a set of schemes of work which support its working at school level. At the same time, several websites and resources on disk provide models of how to work with ICT in the different subjects. Frustratingly, sometimes these disk resources are lost or hard to trace in placement schools. Equally frustratingly, sometimes the websites move, are renamed and change their emphasis in response to different strategies. It is worth being proactive in seeking support and searching through Google (UK version) and elsewhere for the latest versions of these documents.

Some of the web resources which follow are correct at the time of going to press and provide essential support in planning with ICT. To begin with, the National Curriculum in Action website has an entire set of pages, inward and outward links for supporting ICT in subject teaching. It announces itself as follows:

> *This website now includes examples of pupils' work with ICT across a range of subjects, with teacher commentary on how the use of ICT enhanced learning in the subject. The work exemplifies the requirements to use ICT in subject teaching.*
>
> (National Curriculum in Action, 2006)

This is a comprehensive resource for introducing planning for the use of ICT in subject teaching from the National Curriculum side which is subdivided into each of the subjects and presented under headings which look at 'ICT learning', 'ICT Statutory requirements', 'ICT opportunities' and 'Hardware and software'. There are very many – too many to list here – sites which address the issue of planning at local level and even at school level with examples of children's work. Some of these may be linked to Teachernet, which is a meta-site for resources to do with teaching (Teachernet, 2007).

You will also be able to locate advice and support at the web pages of Becta, which is the British Education Communications and Technology Agency. Although its emphasis has changed in recent years and moved towards support for management of technology in education, the site has a wealth of ICT advice located within its school pages which bear the tagline 'Improving learning through technology' (Becta schools, 2007). As we have previously stated, we believe that it is people and not technology who improve learning. Semantics aside, this site has a lot to offer you in the way of support and you should add it to your bookmarked resources (see section on using social bookmarking).

Also on the web, with streaming video versions of all of its programming, is the quasi-governmental, but editorially independent, Teachers' TV. You can receive the broadcasts from this station through satellite TV (Freeview or your paid subscription account if you have one). Through a broadband account the web streaming works very well and there are good search facilities on the site which will enable you to find example programming about teachers and learners working with technology (Teachers' TV, 2007).

The website for the Primary National Strategy for the teaching of English and maths is also promoting the use of an interactive planning tool (see relevant sections below on the strategies). The interactive planning tool aims to:

> ...facilitate short and medium term planning with the content from the new frameworks. This will enable:
> * *Searching, finding and selecting objectives*
> * *Building personal planning templates for re-use or choosing a template from a library*
> * *Assigning selections to a template to create the plan*
> * *Saving plans on your computer so they can be edited or completed over time and retrieved at a later date*
> * *Exporting your completed plans so they can be shared within your school and used within your classroom*
>
> (Primary National Strategy site, 2007)

Aside from the many websites (and there are very many more than those above) there is a set of offline disk-based resources which were published to coincide with the new Primary Strategy and associated frameworks in 2005. If you can locate these in a college library or your school staffroom you may well find them extremely useful. They comprised a set of DVD resources for all year groups in the school (and the Foundation Stage years), containing video clips, accompanying notes and so on. You will find them in a blue box or in your classteacher's cupboard. The full reference is at the end of the chapter (DfES, 2005)

The revised National Curriculum responded to the changes in the nature of educational ICT, including the arrival of the Internet and communications technology in schools. It set out the programme of study for ICT under the following headings:

* **Finding things out;**
* **Developing ideas and making things happen;**
* **Exchanging and sharing information;**
* **Reviewing, modifying and evaluating work as it progresses;**
* **(The breadth of study for the above).**

You can find an online version of this subject-by-subject and downloadable (nc.uk, 2007).

You may well have noticed, if you have arrived in teacher training from another job, that the name has changed from information technology (IT) to information and communication technology (ICT). There was much debate around the loss of the old name for the subject, particularly from colleagues in secondary education and in secondary teacher education. Many of the exchanges centred on the fact that IT was an already established discipline with a history and a set of syllabuses in many different educational contexts. Furthermore, as you will have found, IT is more widely understood as a term outside the world of education. However, ICT has become much more widely referenced within education in recent years and, perhaps more than IT, aligns itself with the networked society in which we live and work.

What do the headings of the National Curriculum mean in practice? The headings describe what should be studied by all children in schools in England. This means finding curricular opportunities within ICT in subject teaching and within ICT as a subject in its own right to develop children's knowledge, understanding and skills under the headings of:

- **finding things out;**
- **developing ideas and making things happen;**
- **exchanging and sharing information;**
- **reviewing, modifying and evaluating work as it progresses.**

Additionally, a statement about breadth of study at Key Stage 1 and Key Stage 2 is included to provide a context for teaching and learning about the characteristics and purposes of information and its representation.

Beginning with 'Finding things out', there is a requirement that pupils are taught how to gather information, how to enter and store information, and, how to retrieve information (Key Stage 1). At Key Stage 2, 'Finding things out' develops a more critical sense whereby children are able to discuss the sort of information they need, learn how to prepare it from different sources for development using ICT, and, how to interpret it and verify it. Elements of what used to be 'Communicating and handling information' have become 'Finding things out'.

'Developing ideas and making things happen' is concerned at Key Stage 1 with developing ideas using ICT by means of text, tables, images and sounds as well as adding to that information for a particular purpose. Also at Key Stage 1 is the requirement to plan and give instructions and to explore what happens in simulations onscreen. For Key Stage 2 children working in this area of ICT knowledge, there is a requirement to deepen their understanding of these concepts; in other words, to refine organisational skills, skills of programming and testing, using simulations, etc. Elements of both 'Communicating and handling information' and 'Controlling and modelling' have become subsumed under the heading of 'Developing ideas and making things happen'.

'Exchanging and sharing information' is the element of ICT knowledge which has been added to take account of the use of the Internet in schools. At Key Stage 1 there is a requirement that children begin to share ideas by presenting work using ICT in a variety of ways and presenting it effectively for public display. At Key Stage 2, the use of e-mail and publishing on the Internet has been suggested to meet the requirements to develop children's sense of what ICT can do to help us to communicate to different audiences. Elements of what used to be 'Communicating and handling information' have become 'Exchanging and sharing information'.

Finally, in the targets for developing skills, knowledge and understanding, comes 'Reviewing, modifying and evaluating work as it progresses'. At Key Stage 1 children are asked to develop a sense of reflection about the work produced with ICT which allows them to think about what they might change on a future occasion. At Key Stage 2 this becomes reflecting in detail about the particular effectiveness of ICT compared with other methods for carrying out similar tasks. Elements of what used to be 'Communicating and handling information' have become part of 'Reviewing, modifying and evaluating work as it progresses'.

The breadth of study of ICT in the National Curriculum requires that children become familiar with a very wide range of ICT tools and applications from floor turtles to word processors and from database packages to the Internet and e-mail. All the time, there is the requirement that they understand real and work-related examples and discuss the uses (and occasional misuses at Key Stage 2) of ICT in school and in the outside world.

These are the requirements for ICT in schools in England. They also represent an entitlement and a right for every child to expect to meet the necessary teaching and teaching resources in their school career throughout Key Stage 1 and 2 (and, we will see in a later chapter, there are benefits to using ICT in the pre-school setting too).

Looking briefly at resource provision for planning with the National Curriculum, as a minimum, the table below indicates the kind of resources in terms of hardware and software which you would expect to see provided in order for children to have their entitlement to ICT met.

Area of knowledge, skills and understanding	Resource entitlement for KS1 and KS2
Finding things out	Safe Internet access, DVDs, CDs, videos, TV, databases and data-handling packages
Developing ideas and making things happen	As above with word processors, desktop publishing, multimedia software, digital cameras (still and video), scanners, floor turtles, onscreen logo, monitoring and data-logging equipment
Exchanging and sharing information	As above and including, e-mail, online forums, music composition software
Reviewing, modifying and evaluating work as it progresses	All above with opportunities to print and compare

Working with Curriculum 2000 means the same as the earlier versions of the curriculum, in effect creating opportunities to use ICT to develop subject knowledge in all areas of the curriculum, at the same time as developing ICT itself. The following two sections address planning for ICT itself and for ICT in subject teaching.

Planning for ICT with the QCA Scheme of Work

What is the QCA Scheme of Work?

The Scheme of Work for ICT provides a detailed framework for teaching which combines provision for developing subject knowledge within ICT at the same time as using it as a tool in other subjects. It is possible to find cross-curricular links in virtually every study unit to virtually every other subject.

It is therefore no longer adequate for a teacher to think in terms of putting 'Using the Internet' on a term plan under the heading 'ICT for Spring Term' and hope that this will cover children's developing ICT subject knowledge. There can't be many other National

Curriculum subjects where this might even be considered a possibility. Imagine a teacher's plan for maths which said 'Using Dienes cubes' and nothing else. It indicates nothing about the context or the subject knowledge that is being developed in the ICT lesson. Placing 'Using the Internet' in a plan for another subject as a resource to use, by a detailed list of the learning outcomes in that subject, is, of course, a different matter.

This section is concerned with the use of the QCA scheme of work in planning for children's developing subject knowledge in ICT itself.

The Scheme of Work codified for teachers the stages of development of subject knowledge through which children should be allowed to progress. There is substantial guidance for schools in the document even in terms of the vocabulary to be used with children. Schools must have at least this scheme of work in place (or equivalent; see below) as a fundamental aid to planning, a map of the learning outcomes for ICT in their school and as a statement of intent and entitlement. However, it is worth pointing out that the scheme is guidance only and is not a legal requirement. As the teacher's guide notes at the outset, 'The original scheme of work and the additional units can be used as a basis for work in ICT if a school wishes. However, there is no compulsion to use them and schools may use as little or as much of the material as they find helpful.' (QCA, 2000)

Not all schools are using the QCA Scheme of Work. Some have schemes which are based on the QCA model or are based on a similar, local authority one. Good schools will not be leaving it up to chance. OFSTED has identified a lack of scheme of work (or development plan) as significant in keeping standards in ICT low (see section below on monitoring). A school which is delivering ICT well, on the other hand, will have a clear idea of the model of progression through the curriculum which a scheme can provide. This may well now be aligned to exemplars provided by the government at some of the sites mentioned above or through the local advisory service or local Grid for Learning.

Try to establish early on in your placement school which scheme is in place and use it in your ICT planning. If there is no obvious plan for ICT year on year other than the ubiquitous 'Using the Internet' in the term plan, you need to be proactive and use the QCA Scheme of Work at the right level for your placement. You can find a version of this online which is easier to work with than the published copy. (If you are working in an Early Years setting, see the relevant section on pages 43 and 72 for some starting points to planning using the Curriculum Guidance for the Foundation Stage.)

Using the QCA Scheme of Work for ICT

The document is relatively easy to use once you get used to the different sections. In hard copy, it is set out in a folder with a teacher's guide, an index card linking the various units to the programmes of study contained in the National Curriculum, and a pocket full of the various scheme units in A3 format. At the time of going to press, the most recent version of the guidance was an update, produced in 2003 and available from the Scheme of Work website (DfES Scheme of Work for ICT, 2006). It is a pdf format document which provides useful links to other subjects in the integrated tasks (see below and sections which follow on planning other subjects). It follows the same template as the earlier versions wherein the units of work are related directly to the wording of the programme of study for the National Curriculum. A key is provided which refers the units back to statements in the National

Curriculum which define Knowledge Skills and Understanding under the four headings shown above:

1. Finding things out
2. Developing ideas and making things happen
3. Exchanging and sharing information
4. Reviewing, modifying and evaluating work as it progresses.

Thus, if a particular unit refers to a National Curriculum statement (2a) it refers to statement (a) of Developing ideas and understanding (namely, pupils should be taught *to use text, tables, images and sound to develop their ideas*).

On the Internet, the scheme appears as a hyperlinked list with the National Curriculum year group and topic listed as follows:

Unit 1A. An introduction to modelling
Unit 1B. Using a word bank
Unit 1C. The information around us
Unit 1D. Labelling and classifying
Unit 1E. Representing information graphically: pictograms
Unit 1F. Understanding instructions and making things happen
Unit 2A. Writing stories: communicating information using text
Unit 2B. Creating pictures
Unit 2C. Finding information
Unit 2D. Routes: controlling a floor turtle
Unit 2E. Questions and answers
Unit 3A. Combining text and graphics
Unit 3B. Manipulating sound
Unit 3C. Introduction to databases
Unit 3D. Exploring simulations
Unit 3E. E-mail
Unit 4A. Writing for different audiences
Unit 4B. Developing images using repeating patterns
Unit 4C. Branching databases
Unit 4D. Collecting and presenting information: questionnaires and pie charts
Unit 4E. Modelling effects on screen
Unit 5A. Graphical modelling
Unit 5B. Analysing data and asking questions: using complex searches
Unit 5C. Evaluating information, checking accuracy and questioning plausibility
Unit 5D. Introduction to spreadsheets
Unit 5E. Controlling devices
Unit 5F. Monitoring environmental conditions and changes
Unit 6A. Multimedia presentation
Unit 6B. Spreadsheet modelling
Unit 6C. Control and monitoring – 'What happens when...?'
Unit 6D. Using the Internet to search large databases and to interpret information
(DfES Scheme of work for ICT, 2006)

Written out in full for example, for Year 1, the five units described relate back to the curriculum as follows:

Year/ unit	Title of unit	Related elements of National Curriculum programme of study
1A	An introduction to modelling	From (2c and 2d), Developing ideas and making things happen, pupils should be taught: c) how to plan and give instructions to make things happen [for example, programming a floor turtle, placing instructions in the right order] d) to try things out and explore what happens in real and imaginary situations [for example, trying out different colours on an image, using an adventure game or simulation]. From (4b and 4c) Reviewing, modifying and evaluating work as it progresses, pupils should be taught to: b) describe the effects of their actions c) talk about what they might change in future work.
1B	Using a word bank	From (1a and 1b) Finding things out, pupils should be taught to: a) gather information from a variety of sources [for example, people, books, databases, CD-ROMs, videos and TV] b) enter and store information in a variety of forms [for example, storing information in a prepared database, saving work]. From (2a and 2b), Developing ideas and making things happen, pupils should be taught to: a) use text, tables, images and sound to develop their ideas b) how to select from and add to information they have retrieved for particular purposes.
1C	The information around us	From (1a and 1b) Finding things out, pupils should be taught to: a) gather information from a variety of sources [for example, people, books, databases, CD-ROMs, videos and TV]. b) enter and store information in a variety of forms [for example, storing information in a prepared database, saving work].
1D	Labelling and classifying	From (1a) Finding things out, pupils should be taught to: a) gather information from a variety of sources [for example, people, books, databases, CD-ROMs, videos and TV] From (2b), Developing ideas and making things happen, pupils should be taught: b) how to select from and add to information they have retrieved for particular purposes.
1E	Representing information graphically: pictograms	From (2a) Developing ideas and making things happen, pupils should be taught: a) to use text, tables, images and sound to develop their ideas. From (3a and 3b) Exchanging and sharing information, pupils should be taught: a) how to share their ideas by presenting information in a variety of forms [for example, text, images, tables, sounds] b) to present their completed work effectively [for example, for public display].
1F	Understanding instructions and making things happen	From (2b and 2c) Developing ideas and making things happen, pupils should be taught: b) how to select from and add to information they have retrieved for particular purposes c) how to plan and give instructions to make things happen [for example, programming a floor turtle, placing instructions in the right order].

Like any other scheme used for planning, there is a learning curve. However, the more you use it, the more familiar the language becomes, and the more straightforward it is to adapt to the particular resource setting in which you find yourself. Furthermore, the notes of guidance explain very clearly how to navigate the unit planners which are organised as follows.

On the first page is the unit title (see examples 1A to 1E in the table above). The letters are not there to indicate any particular order in which the units should be taught. Underneath the title is a section labelled 'About the Unit' which gives an overview of the unit. This is followed by descriptions of the unit in relation to other parts of the scheme (WHERE THE UNIT FITS IN), the vocabulary you need to introduce to the children (TECHNICAL VOCABULARY – similar in concept to the *Primary National Strategy for Literacy* vocabulary lists), and, the resources you will need (RESOURCES, both computer based and other forms of technology).

The element of differentiation is supplied in the section labelled 'Expectations'. This is a series of outcomes for 'most children', 'some children (who) will not have made so much progress' and 'some (who) will have progressed further'. These broad statements require much greater fine-tuning at the classroom level, particularly at a time when the concept of 'personalisation' is becoming more widely applied to planning. You will encounter this term often in the literature around planning and in the policies which your school will be adopting. It is often extended into thinking in particular about learners who have been identified as 'gifted and talented'.

The unit descriptions continue under four headings.

- **Learning objectives.**
- **Possible teaching activities.**
- **Learning outcomes.**
- **Points to note.**

'Learning objectives' outlines the steps towards full understanding of the unit. 'Possible teaching activities' are described under three potential headings (see below). 'Learning outcomes' describes the indications of a child's progress and are intended to inform assessment (see chapter on assessment for a much more detailed discussion of this element). 'Points to note' outlines the misconceptions which a child may have and includes suggestions to overcome these issues.

As stated above, 'Possible teaching activities' are further grouped under three different types of teaching activities:

Setting the scene – introducing the unit to the children and taking only a few minutes to do so. Short focused tasks – instructing on a specific IT task and introducing key ideas such as cutting, copying and pasting.
Integrated tasks – more complex projects which build on the shorter tasks and require several sessions to complete. These are linked much more closely to other curriculum areas in the most recent version (DfES ICT handbook, 2003) and we will look at this in some of the sections which follow.

The units of work are adaptable to the range of resource settings discussed earlier and identified in this book as low, medium and high resource settings (see previous section).

Planning example from the QCA Scheme of Work

An example follows of a longer-format lesson plan which is taken from a unit of work from the QCA scheme. It assumes a high resource setting, a school with a networked suite of computers. The context is the unit for year 2A: Writing stories: communicating information using text.

LONGER LESSON PLAN FOR ICT AT YEAR 2
FROM ICT UNIT 2A: Writing stories: communicating information using text:
CROSS-CURRICULAR LINK: English (*Primary National Strategy for Literacy* at Y2 – Creating and shaping text)

LESSON OVERVIEW
The children will work on a pre-prepared file which contains no full stops or capital letters and connects ideas using the word 'and' repeatedly and inappropriately. They will identify where the sentence breaks should be, delete each inappropriate 'and' in question and replace it with a full stop and capital letter. There will be opportunities to extend the work into wider kinds of connectives if this is appropriate.

SCHOOL/CLASS CONTEXT
The school is a large, inner-city primary school with a wide range of ability. Some 20 different languages are spoken, of which the majority speak Sylheti-Bengali. There are 29 children in the class, an average size for the school. The children are all in Year 2.

LEARNING NEEDS OF THE CHILDREN
FOR ICT: Most children are confident at logging on and using the computers in the network suite. The children need experience of dropping into text and changing it using the mouse and the keyboard.
FOR ENGLISH: The aim of the lesson is to back up literacy lessons on improving drafts of writing by looking at changing writing containing too many long sentences (deleting 'and' and replacing with full stop and capital letter of the next word).

GROUPING/TIMING
The lesson will last one hour, not including a 10-minute outline of how to use the software. We will go into the room at about 1.30 and leave at about 2.45 in time for the afternoon break. The class will be split into two groups. Half will log on for 30 minutes then the other half will swap. The middle group, not using the computers, will have work to do which relates to the lesson, correcting drafts from their own written work.

RESOURCES
The computer suite comprises 15 stations arranged around the outside of the room with a central table-based working area for work away from the computer.

THEORETICAL CONTEXT
From Angela MacFarlane's 'Thinking about writing' (Chapter 8 in MacFarlane, 1998): 'The use of word processors helps to present text as something to be experimented with, redrafted and developed as ideas develop, or as the purpose or audience change. It liberates the writer from the heavy burden of manual editing and presentation.

NC/FOUNDATION STAGE CONTEXT
Developing ideas and making things happen (Programme of Study 2a)

---

pupils should be taught to use text, tables, images and sound to develop their ideas
Exchanging and sharing information (Programme of Study 3a), pupils should be taught
to share their ideas by presenting information in a variety of forms [for example, text,
images, tables, sounds]
Reviewing, modifying and evaluating work as it progresses (Programme of Study 4a),
pupils should be taught to review what they have done to help them develop their ideas

SCHEME OF WORK CONTEXT
Lesson ideas from QCA Scheme of Work for ICT, Unit 2A: Writing stories: Communicating information using text

YOUR OWN LEARNING NEEDS
Preparing text in a word processor for the children to work on.
Making sure that I know how to save the work in the children's user areas as a template to work on.
Understanding the context of the work on grammar and punctuation in the Primary National Strategy for Literacy at Y2.

ORGANISATIONAL MEMORY JOGGERS
Can I get into the network room during the lunch hour to make sure that the pre-prepared file is in the right area on the network? Do I have the appropriate access rights to the network in order to do this?
Do all children know how to log on? (See Organisation chapters)
Are there spare USER IDs in case of emergency?

OTHER ADULTS
Assuming a learning support teacher for a child who is experiencing difficulties with writing. Remember to copy the lesson plan and talk to them before the lesson takes place if at all possible.

LEARNING OBJECTIVES

FOR ICT: The key idea that ICT can be used to improve text and make a message clearer by means of onscreen editing. Learning deleting and inserting text to improve readability. (Part of QCA scheme of work Unit 2A)
FOR ENGLISH: The key concept of full stops and capital letters to create sentences and improve sense and understanding of writing. As an extension: the key idea that writing can be connected by a wider range of connectives than just the word 'and'.
(Part of *Primary National Strategy for Literacy* at Y2)

DIFFERENTIATION
For Blue Group (lower ability), a slightly simpler form of the file with highlighted 'and's.
For the Red Group (higher ability), a longer version of the file and extension into creating their own files for each other to correct (if time allows). Other connectives to be suggested for the longer sentences.
For other groups in the class – the basic file and questions.
See also: key questions, below.

LEARNING NEEDS – EAL
Remember that children who have English as an additional language are all at different

stages of acquiring English. Partner the children appropriately according to language needed to access the activity. Consider allowing some pairs to work at the same computer if they are experiencing difficulties. Remember to check and re-check understanding of the task.

LEARNING NEEDS – SEN

For the child with difficulties with motor control, remember to ensure that the Touch Screen driver is loaded and that the support teacher has space to sit with her.

ASSESSMENT OPPORTUNITIES

Complete observation pro-formas on targeted children or on the whole class profile (as appropriate – see Chapter 5).

KEY QUESTIONS

Remember to focus on the language being developed for ICT in the QCA unit, i.e. shift, spacebar, return/enter, insert, backspace, delete. For English, refer questioning to texts and units currently under study during the literacy hour.

Some questions for ICT development, differentiated according to ability, might include:

Which keys do you use to delete or rub out words? (Lower)

How do you change letters from lower case to upper case? (Lower/Middle)

How do you move around in the text and/or how do you place the cursor where you want it to go? (Middle)

Do you know a quick way to locate the word 'and' in the text? (Higher)

LESSON FORMAT

5–10 minutes: Opening with demonstration at the whiteboard. Invite some participation from the children. Ask questions. Check and re-check understanding of the task. Share the learning objective with the children.

20 minutes: Group 1 at the computers, Group 2 at the tables. Allow pairing of children where appropriate and supportive.

5 minutes: Changeover and recap on purpose of the activity.

20 minutes: Group 2 at the computers, Group 1 at the tables. Allow pairing of children where appropriate and supportive.

5–10 minutes: Plenary with contributions/questions from children. Allow the children themselves to demonstrate and talk through their work at the interactive whiteboard. Remember to allow for questions from across the ability range.

EVALUATING THE LESSON part 1 – OPERATIONAL ISSUES

As stated above, note here any changes during the lesson which might affect the way you work on this unit on the future. Issues which might have arisen include:

All children needed more time. Allow the whole class to log on together for longer and share the equipment, or,

The 20 minutes was fine for the activity as it occurred, some children needed to be partnered within the groups to make it work, or,

The pencil-and-paper activity was too short. The children needed more work away from the computers, or,

The plenary was too rushed and there was insufficient time to draw the understanding together and revisit the learning objectives with the children.

EVALUATING THE LESSON part 2 – LEARNING OUTCOMES

Note in this section any particular achievements which children demonstrated. Were you able to carry out the assessments planned for during the session?

EVALUATING THE LESSON part 3 – NEXT TIME
What aspects of this work need to be repeated? How could you deepen understanding of the ICT concepts behind the work? What will you do next time on the light of the organisational changes you had to make?

REFLECTIVE TASK

Planning with the QCA Scheme of Work

Identify a unit of work in the QCA scheme which refers to the age group you are teaching. Find an activity from within the unit which fits in with the current units of work being undertaken in any of the other subject curriculum areas. Follow the pattern for the example lesson plan from above, identifying the cross-curricular links in detail.

LESSON OVERVIEW

SCHOOL/CLASS CONTEXT

LEARNING NEEDS OF THE CHILDREN

GROUPING/TIMING

RESOURCES

THEORETICAL CONTEXT

NC/FOUNDATION STAGE CONTEXT

SCHEME OF WORK CONTEXT

YOUR OWN LEARNING NEEDS

ORGANISATIONAL MEMORY JOGGERS

OTHER ADULTS

LEARNING OBJECTIVES

DIFFERENTIATION

LEARNING NEEDS – EAL

LEARNING NEEDS – SEN

ASSESSMENT OPPORTUNITIES

KEY QUESTIONS

LESSON FORMAT

EVALUATING THE LESSON part 1 – OPERATIONAL ISSUES

EVALUATING THE LESSON part 2 – LEARNING OUTCOMES

EVALUATING THE LESSON part 3 – NEXT TIME

Auditing

After the lesson, discuss the outcomes with your mentor and/or professional tutor. If the lesson has allowed you to demonstrate evidence of achieving parts of any Standards for QTS you could attach the plan and any work examples to your audit and date it. Possible Standards to reference include the following.

Q7

Reflect on and improve practice, and take responsibility for identifying and meeting developing professional needs.

Q8

Have a creative and constructively critical approach towards innovation, being prepared to adapt practice where benefits and improvements are identified.

Q11

Know the assessment requirements and arrangements for the subjects/curriculum areas you are trained to teach, including those relating to public examinations and qualifications.

Q12

Know a range of approaches to assessment, including the importance of formative assessment.

Q13

Know how to use local and national statistical information to evaluate the effectiveness of their teaching, to monitor the progress of those they teach and to raise levels of attainment.

Q22

Plan for progression across the age and ability range for which you are trained, designing effective learning sequences within lessons and across series of lessons and demonstrating secure subject/curriculum knowledge.

Q25

Teach lessons and sequences of lessons across the age and ability range for which they are trained in which they:

(a) use a range of teaching strategies and resources, including e-learning, taking practical account of diversity and promoting equality and inclusion;

(b) build on prior knowledge, develop concepts and processes, enable learners to apply new knowledge, understanding and skills and meet learning objectives;

(c) adapt their language to suit the learners they teach, introducing new ideas and concepts clearly, and using explanations, questions, discussions and plenaries effectively.

Q26

(a) Make effective use of a range of assessment, monitoring and recording strategies.

(b) Assess the learning needs of those they teach in order to set challenging learning objectives.

RESEARCH SUMMARY RESEARCH SUMMARY RESEARCH SUMMARY

Planning Primary ICT

Research on pedagogical issues in literacy and numeracy from the University of Newcastle under David Moseley and Steve Higgins (Newcastle University/TTA, 1999) working in collaboration with the Lynn Newton and the CEM centre at Durham University presents teacher research and case studies of ICT use in classrooms. The study is published under the title: 'Ways forward with ICT: effective pedagogy using information and communications technology for literacy and numeracy in primary schools'. It attempts to identify key elements for successful integration of ICT in teaching and learning by situating the work of the teachers in the context of what they themselves said and thought about the work.

The findings of the team point clearly to the need for precise planning as well as for matching the needs of the children to the tasks themselves. This comprehensive study underlines many of the concepts about planning outlined in this and the following chapter, namely,

> 'Clear identification of how ICT will be used to meet specific objectives within subjects of the curriculum to improve pupils' attainment . . .
>
> A planned match of pedagogy with the identified purpose of ICT activities and learning by outcomes'.
> (Newcastle University/TTA, 1999)

A SUMMARY OF **KEY POINTS**

This chapter has negotiated the area between the National Curriculum for ICT and its associated scheme of work. It has identified a possible model for planning which takes account of the context of the class, the curriculum, the learning needs of all parties and the availability of equipment.

> **The various terms of the curriculum were explained and a further set of contexts from the associated websites was presented.**

Moving on

Consider the wide range of planning opportunities you have seen for primary ICT. In your induction year, how do you think you will work with planning for primary ICT? As you move into your career you will find INSET opportunities relating to new technology, in particular the use of media in the curriculum. Think about how this might impact on the ICT scheme and the Primary National Framework in the future.

FURTHER READING FURTHER READING **FURTHER READING** FURTHER READING

Becta Schools pages (2007) **schools.becta.org.uk/** Accessed 30 January 2007

Cooper, P. and McIntyre, D. (1996) Effective Teaching and Learning, *British Educational Research Journal*, 22 (5) December

DfES (2000a) *National Curriculum Handbook for Key Stages 1 and 2*, London: DfES

DfES Standards site – ICT Scheme (2003 version) **www.standards.dfes.gov.uk/schemes2/it/?view=get** Accessed 30 January 2007

DfES Interactive Planning tool (2007) **www.standards.dfes.gov.uk/primaryframeworks/planningtool/** Holding page Accessed 30 January 2007

DfES Primary Framework homepage (2007) **www.standards.dfes.gov.uk/primaryframeworks/** Accessed 30 January 2007

Kyriacou, C. (1997) *Effective teaching in schools*, London: Routledge

National Curriculum in Action – ICT pages (2007) **www.ncaction.org.uk/subjects/ict/inother.htm** Accessed 30 January 2007

National Curriculum online (2007) **www.nc.uk.net** Accessed 13 May 2007

Primary National Strategy (2007) **www.standards.dfes.gov.uk/primary/**

QCA (2000) *Support and guidance for ICT*, **www.qca.org.uk/downloads/curriculum_support_and_guidance.pdf**

Smith, H. (1999) *Opportunities for ICT in the primary school*. London: Trentham Books

Somekh, B. and Davis, N. (eds) (1997) *Using Information technology effectively in teaching and learning*. London: Routledge

Teachernet (2007) **www.teachernet.gov.uk**

Teachers' TV homepage (2007) **www.teachers.tv/** Accessed 30 January 2007

3
Planning primary ICT in subject teaching

Chapter objectives

This chapter is concerned with planning for the use of ICT in subject teaching, beginning from the subjects themselves rather than the QCA scheme of work for ICT. We have seen in the previous chapter that it is perfectly possible to explore cross-curricular opportunities by beginning with the QCA scheme of work for ICT. However, it is equally important to consider the approach which starts with the National Curriculum Schemes of work and moves towards the relevant ICT applications. The National Curriculum makes many explicit references to, and gives examples of, the use of ICT within the schemes of work for each subject and there are numerous hyperlinked resources within all the government resource and support pages.

The chapters which follow address the context of ICT in subject teaching, beginning with the core curriculum, taking in the national initiatives in literacy and mathematics and moving through to the Foundation subjects. Throughout, while the emphasis is on how the ICT supports the learning in each of these subjects, there is clearly a parallel development going on of the trainees' own skills and the opportunities to look at self-auditing.

Planning ICT in literacy

There is more to the teaching of literacy in the primary school than the programme envisaged when the literacy hour was first set out as part of the old *Literacy Strategy*. Indeed, some early evidence shows that there must be more or children will not have the time in the day to develop their extended writing skills (HMI/OFSTED, 2000). However, the *National Literacy Strategy* (NLS) framework as it was originally issued is now established in most primary schools in the UK and, although often much adapted and changed from its original format, still exists within the newer structures of the *Primary National Strategy for Literacy*. Furthermore, in the National Curriculum it is explicitly stated that the framework 'provides a detailed basis for implementing the statutory requirements of the programmes of study for reading and writing' (QCA, 2000a). In other words, the NLS is a *de facto* scheme of work for some, perhaps not all, of the National Curriculum subject of English. Given that ICT should be used in every subject scheme of work, it must also have a place within a literary session. There is clearly a need to begin to address what ICT can do alongside the framework in helping to raise levels of achievement in literacy.

The framework, with which trainees will become very familiar during their training in English, outlines the activities in literacy by year group from Year 1 to Year 6, over each of the terms of the school year. There are materials for Reception which are also in use in some schools although there has been a change as the curriculum guidance for the Foundation Stage has been adopted and developed in schools. The difference between the earlier version of the strategy and the newest one in the *Primary National Strategy* is that learning is now mapped out in 12 'strands' in two sets as follows:

Speaking and listening for a wide range of purposes in different contexts
- *Speaking*
- *Listening and responding*
- *Group discussion and interaction*
- *Drama*

Reading and writing for a range of purposes on paper and on screen
- *Word recognition: decoding (reading) and encoding (spelling)*
- *Word structure and spelling*
- *Understanding and interpreting texts*
- *Engaging and responding to texts*
- *Creating and shaping texts*
- *Text structure and organisation*
- *Sentence structure and punctuation*
- *Presentation.*

(Primary National Strategy, 2006)

The issue for those attempting to work with ICT in literacy sessions is how to integrate it into the very tight timescales available. The solution to this issue, will, as usual, be different in almost every setting and contingent upon the resources available in all the categories: human resources, hardware resources and software resources.

The outline of the original literacy hour, which exists still in schools as a kind of subtext but not usually as formally organised anymore, was as follows:

The first 10 to 15 minutes outlined the work of the day in terms of word level or sentence level. The next 15 minutes focused on an aspect of word level work (key stage one) and sentence or word level work (key stage two). Up to this point in the basic model of provision, children were to have been sitting on the carpet for up to half an hour. For the next 20 minutes, children undertook group activities at their tables, in fives and sixes, which were related to the overall learning objective. Finally, there was to be a plenary, lasting approximately 10 minutes. This attempted to draw the strands from the hour together and to underline key teaching points with the children.

There is great potential at all the different resource levels for the use of ICT in literacy sessions and good planning can take account of this.

Group activities – low resource setting

To take one aspect of a traditional literacy session, the 20 minutes of group activity lend themselves to the use of the computer. In a low resource setting, with one computer in the corner of the classroom there will need to be some creativity with the planning. Depending on the nature of the task and the nature of the software being used, it could be possible to split a group of six into two lots of three with 10 minutes each. This group would then become part of the working week in the normal way and the whole class rotated through in a week.

In some ways, this is an example of the atomised curriculum at its worst, with children not being able to develop any real ICT skills in such short bursts. It also has high planning overheads because of the need to think of something for the children to do while they are waiting for their turn. On the other hand, there are activities which lend themselves to shorter amounts of time at the computer. In tutorial software from CD there might be short activities and investigations around a particular learning objective, such as learning the sounds of English. The most recent debates in teaching literacy in primary schools has brought to prominence, and back into favour, the teaching of synthetic phonics in a systematic way. Software publishers have not been slow to exploit this and a whole range of titles and online areas is emerging which aim to provide multimedia reinforcement for learning sounds. An onscreen exercise, for example, to identify parts of words and break them down into constituent sounds would be one. Clearly, pointing and clicking on items in a menu or a game in such software is not doing a great deal to advance the knowledge and understanding of ICT. However, literacy provision itself might be enhanced by the regular presence of reinforcement of learning objectives which rely on heard sounds and take children away from the daily provision of photocopied worksheets.

Another idea is to use open-ended software in this situation to create your own short activities. Using a word processor, a document template could be created which allowed children to, for example, search and replace nouns with pronouns. Another could allow children to highlight all the verbs in a sentence in sentence level work and change the font in some way. At this level of resourcing, activities are going to be low level with some element of repetition and reinforcement. However, in this example with open-ended software, the ICT is being used to provide stimulus and variety and one more planning option for the hard-pressed class teacher. It can also legitimately be said to be providing variety for the children and a further opportunity to address pupils' learning styles.

The plenary in a low resource setting

If you have access to presentation software and the computer is accessible to the carpet area, then in a given week, children could be preparing small presentations on the learning objective for the plenary each day. This is potentially the highest-order development of ICT skills, perhaps also of the literacy focus. As the class-teacher familiar with the children concerned, you would be in a position to determine which of the children would benefit from this. It need not always be the most able. In this situation, having an adult helper who is also familiar with the software (see human resources in previous chapters) would allow the children who are struggling with a given concept to reinforce their learning by having to construct a presentation for others.

The situation in this resource setting could be described in the following table.

Activity	Software	Literacy v. ICT potential
Ten-minute onscreen reinforcement of learning objective	Tutorial CD, focused aims, revision in a game-style environment	High literacy Low level ICT skills
Ten-minute onscreen search and replace, reinforcement of learning objective	Word processing	High literacy Higher level ICT skills
Collaborative work on presentation for the plenary about a particular learning objective	Presentation software Word processing software	High literacy High level ICT skills

The literacy lesson in a high resource setting

Looking at the other extreme, where a school has very rich provision for ICT, there is inevitably more room for using ICT in a literacy lesson.

In the simplest example, if there are more computers in the classroom (perhaps three) then a group can work in pairs for the whole of the 20 minutes of group activity, undertaking any of the examples illustrated above at a higher level due to the extended time available.

If the high resource setting manifests itself in the form of a collection of handheld computers, there is very great potential. A group of six children can have access to search and replace activities on the palmtops as well as onscreen templates of various kinds. Children can also undertake guided writing with adult support if this is appropriate. This activity can become part of the cycle of activities during the week, perhaps combined with the uses of the desktop described above.

In a network room, it could be possible to run the entire literacy hour there at regular intervals. Each child would have access to the computers, plenaries could be held using the large monitors, interactive whiteboards, visualisers or screen control software. The opening sections of the literacy hour could be presented to the children using hypermedia resources, perhaps containing scanned parts of books for the big-book part of the session. These activities have a high overhead in terms of staff training and confidence. In a high resource setting where training has taken place which fully integrates ICT into the good practice of the school and where the children are using the network room confidently, ICT has much to offer literacy, specifically:

- **it provides a different resource base for the literacy hour, a break from the classroom;**
- **it allows children to develop ICT skills alongside literacy skills (except in the case of tutorial software);**
- **it reinforces the message that ICT is a medium in which to carry out work of different kinds;**
- **it provides the opportunity for children to combine text, graphics, sound and video in different software packages.**

The following table summarises literacy teaching in the High Resource Setting:

Activity	Software and hardware	Literacy v. ICT potential
Group activity reinforcing learning objective for 20 minutes	Three computers, tutorial software or word processing	High literacy Low level ICT skills (tutorial) Higher level ICT skills (word processing)
Group activity on search and replace, guided writing	PDAs or laptops available for groups	High literacy Higher level ICT skills
Collaborative work throughout literacy hour on learning objective, used on the interactive whiteboard and perhaps published online on the school website	Network room Presentation software, html editors, etc. Word processing software Authoring templates provided by the online supplier (local grid for learning or regional broadband consortia)	High literacy High level ICT skills

The Internet and literacy – publication and exhibition issues

The Internet, in a reliable, high resource setting, is an area of real potential. Very large numbers of teachers and children are already sharing ideas online for lesson plans. Many of these are downloadable without charge and provide a basis for planning, though some require subscription. Other sites provide onscreen activities with immediate feedback, all of them directly related to the literacy objectives within the *Primary National Strategy*.

School web pages or local authority intranets can provide rich sources of material and opportunities for publication, including many examples of good practice in literacy teaching and learning.

Finally, as noted above, the idea that children can now publish their own work within secure online environments means that the distance between objective, idea and final publication is shortened. There is a real meaning in which this publication and the commentaries provided on it allow for a sense of audience and purpose to be built up which motivates and increases children's concept of personal authorship. There is a discussion elsewhere in this book of the potential of web publishing within the world of social software/web 2.0 in the main chapter on the Internet.

ICT and your own planning

Various companies have started to produce resources which specifically address the planning needs of teachers. CDs from the BBC provide lesson examples, and CDs from such companies as the Skills Factory provide complete lesson planners and databases of activities. Downloadable updates provide a way of staying ahead of the guidance as it changes. The guidance itself, the entire literacy programme within the *Primary National Strategy* framework, is available from the DfES standards website.

PRACTICAL TASK PRACTICAL TASK **PRACTICAL TASK** PRACTICAL TASK

Literacy planning

Look at the ***Literacy Framework*** for a given year group and consider the learning objective in relation to the children you are working with:

- **Decide on what level of activity you could aim at according to the tables above, according to whether you are in a high resource setting or a low resource setting.**

- **Design an activity for five or six children for the 20 minutes of group activity.**

- **Remember to consider factors such as individual school variation (some schools are evolving with the way they operate and may have longer for this part of the hour than in the original guidance).**

- **Remember also to discuss the levels of ability of the group with the class teacher and to target the actual content appropriately.**

For example, we consider here one of the activities supporting learning objectives from Year 3, Term 1, for sentence-level work on verbs, namely:

...to use verb tenses with increasing accuracy in speaking and writing, e.g. catch/ caught, see/saw, go/went, etc. Use past tense consistently for narration...

Our context from the NLS is mapped out in the analysis to the planning. For the ICT element in a low resource setting, where there is one computer to the 30 children in the class, consider getting the children to work on a pre-prepared Word template file which contains, say, 10 sentences with verbs in the present tense. Have a series of regular and irregular examples differentiated for ability groups through the week. Ask the children to identify the verbs in the text and change them into the past tense using the features of the word processor.

In a high resource setting, in a network room, prepare templates for the whole class, differentiated according to ability and ask them to search and replace. Alternatively, ask children to investigate the patterns in pre-prepared onscreen texts and prepare a presentation about it. This is going to depend on flexibility of implementation of the strategy in the school. The context is everything. Part of analysing the situation accurately is about taking into account the school, the children, the resource setting and the relevant curriculum and strategy documents as they are being applied in that setting.

Some questions to ask yourself after the activity, some of which form the usual pattern for the use of ICT, some adapted for the purpose of this activity could be:

- **How was the activity integrated into the normal running of the classroom?**
- **What skills did I need in order for the activity to succeed?**
- **What skills did the children need?**
- **How did I ensure that all children had access to the activity?**
- **What were the learning outcomes for the children in literacy?**
- **What were the learning outcomes for the children in ICT?**
- **What assessment opportunities were there?**
- **How does this experience add to my understanding of ICT in Subject teaching?**
- **What will I do next time?**

Planning ICT in English (general and cross-curricular)

We have examined in the previous section how the use of ICT can have an impact in a setting with time-constrained Literacy provision, working a more or less traditional Literacy hour. It is worth spending some time considering briefly how to use ICT in the teaching of English in a wider sense. Beyond the structure of the Literacy Hour, children are using English in a cross-curricular way, for example:

- **publishing a science write-up;**
- **creating a local area guide book in geography;**
- **writing school web pages;**
- **generating a historical account;**
- **writing about their beliefs in RE;**
- **creating rules for classroom and playground behaviour in PSHE;**
- **generating captions to explain findings in maths data handling;**
- **reading for information in any of the Foundation subjects, science and maths.**

The issue for planning for ICT to support these wider uses of English is, as usual, how to operate in the differing resource settings and differing cultures of ICT in UK schools.
Higher resource settings are going to allow for much greater exploration of the provisional nature of information, simply because faster, more distributed Internet access through a

school means that greater numbers of teachers and children can become involved. In lower resource settings, where one computer is still shared between the class, there are still opportunities for engagement with the wider English curriculum; for example, in speaking and listening (encouraging children to defend choices made in simulations and adventure games), reading (whole-class reading sessions from the screen) and writing (using the Word Processor as an aid to drafting materials and understanding the writing process better).

The cross-curricular opportunities for developing English teaching which uses ICT are many and varied and the limit to what is feasible will be determined largely by the access to the software, hardware and the Internet which the children have.

REFLECTIVE TASK
REFLECTIVE TASK

Planning cross-curricular English outside literacy

Consider a curriculum area in which you are expecting the children to write at the computer. It could be taken from the list above, i.e.

- **publishing a science write-up;**
- **creating a local area guide book in geography;**
- **writing school web pages;**
- **generating a historical account;**
- **writing about their beliefs in RE;**
- **creating rules for classroom and playground behaviour in PSHE;**
- **generating captions to explain findings in maths data handling;**
- **reading for information in any of the Foundation subjects, science and maths.**

Create a lesson plan which focuses on the specific areas of development of the writing itself which you are developing using the ICT.

LESSON OVERVIEW
Include here the English element, the ICT element and the element from the other subject. For example, a lesson overview for 'Creating a local area guide book in geography' for Year 4 might describe the ICT element as using desktop publishing software and digital images. The Geographical element could be from the work on localities described in the National Curriculum (see below). The English element is the developing sense of audience and of how to present information in a clear and accessible manner.

SCHOOL/CLASS CONTEXT
As described previously.

LEARNING NEEDS OF THE CHILDREN
Note these in the cross-curricular context.

GROUPING/TIMING
Think about different groupings from the literacy lesson if your class employs ability groups. Children should experience a range of working partnerships and not always be grouped with the same children. We know from our understanding of the ways in

which children learn that they need to interact with one another and learn in the context of talk with a whole range of peers of different abilities.

RESOURCES
Make the most of information collected on local area trips, in particular, digital images, video clips and sound recordings which could be incorporated into the work on the computer. Consider working with a multimedia-authoring package to produce a multi-media version of the guidebook if you are fortunate enough to be in a highly resourced setting.

THEORETICAL CONTEXT
As described previously.

NC/FOUNDATION STAGE CONTEXT
One example for ICT could be from 'Finding Things Out' at Key Stage 2, pupils should be taught how to 'Prepare information for development using ICT'
For Geography: from the programmes of Study for Key Stage 2. In their study of localities and themes, pupils should: 'study at a range of scales – local, regional and national...'
For English: from the programmes of Study for Key Stage 2 the range of purposes for writing should include: 'to inform and explain, focusing on the subject matter and how to convey it in sufficient detail for the reader...'

SCHEME OF WORK CONTEXT
E.g. For ICT: QCA Unit 4a
For English see the *Primary National Strategy for Literacy at Year 4*; for geography, see the scheme of work...

Make notes under the following headings as described previously:
- **YOUR OWN LEARNING NEEDS**
- **ORGANISATIONAL MEMORY JOGGERS**
- **OTHER ADULTS**
- **LEARNING OBJECTIVES**
- **DIFFERENTIATION**
- **LEARNING NEEDS – EAL**
- **LEARNING NEEDS – SEN**
- **ASSESSMENT OPPORTUNITIES**
- **KEY QUESTIONS**
- **LESSON FORMAT**
- **EVALUATING THE LESSON part 1 – OPERATIONAL ISSUES**
- **EVALUATING THE LESSON part 2 – LEARNING OUTCOMES**
- **EVALUATING THE LESSON part 3 – NEXT TIME**

Auditing

After the lesson, discuss the outcomes with your mentor and/or professional tutor. If the lesson has allowed you to demonstrate evidence of achieving parts of any Standards for QTS you could attach the plan and any work examples to your audit and date it.

Planning ICT in the daily mathematics lesson

The guidance for the daily mathematics lesson contained within the published *Primary National Strategy for Mathematics* outlines more explicit teaching opportunities for the use of ICT than the literacy part of the Strategy. Furthermore, there is a more flexible approach to timings and organisation which tends to mean that the different resource levels within schools can address the issues of integration more consistently. The strands in the mathematics part of the *Primary National Strategy* group teaching according to learning objectives in each of the following areas:

- *Using and applying mathematics*
- *Counting and understanding number*
- *Knowing and using number facts*
- *Calculating*
- *Understanding shape*
- *Measuring*
- *Handling data*

(*Primary National Strategy*, 2006)

Put into practice, the suggested format for the opening of the daily mathematics lesson concentrates on the development of mental mathematical strategies. Children are 'warmed up' with questions relating to the learning objectives which enable them to make connections between their previously gained aspects of maths knowledge. The *Primary National Strategy for Mathematics* contains detailed guidance about what to do in the middle section of the daily mathematics lesson in which children are expected to work on what is called 'the main teaching activity'. The settings for this can vary between whole class, groups, pairs or individuals. The final element of the daily mathematics lesson was always intended to be the same as for Literacy, i.e. the plenary, during which the class had an opportunity to consolidate the knowledge gained during the lesson.

The guidance available on the use of ICT in many of the areas quoted in previous chapters (including the DVD resources mentioned – DfES, 2005) suggests that technology can be incorporated into most parts of the lesson and gives suggestions which are related to the level of resource provision. The opening section on mental maths can be varied in its use of resources by the inclusion of an interactive whiteboard (see also Chapter 15 on using the IWB). The same applies to the plenary where the strands of the lesson can be drawn together by the use of electronic media.

Once again, however, it is the central part of the lesson which lends itself most readily to the integration of appropriate ICT. ICT is broadly defined in the guidance to include all of the available audiovisual aids and, of course, calculators. For the computer, several different possible uses are described for this section of the lesson, summarised as:

- **software to explore number patterns, including the use of spreadsheets;**
- **tutorial software for practising a particular skill, with rapid assessment;**
- **data-handling software;**
- **software for giving instructions of movement and turn in order to develop subject knowledge in, for example, measurement of distance and angle;**
- **software for transforming shapes;**
- **software for branching and sorting in order to develop logical thinking and problem-solving.**

Some of these possible uses have the potential to develop high-order ICT skills. There is also a distinct overlap with items from the Scheme of work for ICT. Given the flexible nature of the daily mathematics lesson, it ought to be possible to plan in a cross-curricular way for some of the numeracy framework. However, it is worth remembering that the focus of the lesson has to be mathematics specifically and the lesson succeeds or fails partly by the way in which the teacher can draw the class together in a plenary at the end of the session. If the activity has moved out of the realm of the initial focus and is meeting some other planning requirement, the quality of the mathematical experience will decline.

The potential for ICT skill development and maths together is summarised in the following table, where, as for literacy, it is possible to see little in the way of such skill development in the use of tutorial software.

Software type in the daily mathematics lesson	ICT Skills, knowledge and understanding
Software to explore number patterns (tutorial)	Low-level ICT skills
Tutorial software for practising a particular skill, with rapid assessment	Very low-level ICT skills
Software for transforming shapes	Middle-range ICT skills (depending on the package being used. Some is much more complex than others)
Data-handling software	High-level ICT skills
Using spreadsheets to explore number patterns	High-level ICT skills
Software for giving instructions of movement and turn in order to develop subject knowledge in, for example, measurement of distance and angle	High-level ICT skills (link with programming)
Software for branching and sorting in order to develop logical thinking and problem solving	High-level ICT skills

The impact of the low and high resource settings is felt in a reduced way because of the added flexibility of delivery of the *Primary National Strategy for Mathematics*. However, in a low resource setting it is possible to become dependent on poorer-quality tutorial software of a very basic drill-and-practice type. Where this is focused (on reinforcing a topic which is under development) and targeted (at children who need it), such software is extremely useful. As we have seen in earlier chapters, where this software is used to keep certain children busy or as a reward or sanction, there is little justification for using it in pursuit of real learning objectives.

In a high resource setting, again in a network room or similar, all children could experience some daily mathematics lessons with access to the relevant software and hardware. The whole lesson could be run in the computer suite from time to time (timetabling allowing).

REFLECTIVE TASK

Daily mathematics lesson planning

Consider the framework for Years 1–3 and look at the learning outcomes for Year 3 pupils for the spring term – Handling Data, unit 12.

In a low resource setting, or one where the children's experience of using ICT is limited, collect simple data about the packed lunches brought to school across a given week. Ask children to enter the information and display it in data-handling software. This could be done using a simple graphing tool or using a more complex data-handling package.

For a medium resource setting, where there is regular access to the computer and the Year 3 children have already gained experiences of simple graphing in Year 2, extend their knowledge by building a more complicated database based on the different methods which children use to come to school each day.

In either case, in your planning develop questions which exploit the ICT learning opportunities alongside the Mathematical learning opportunities. The following table characterises some of these sorts of questions:

Example ICT knowledge questioning	Example maths knowledge questioning (adapted from the NNS)
Which graph shows the information best?	Do most children walk to school? How do we know?
What did we have to do after entering each piece of information?	How many more children walk to school than come by car?
How did we add to the file the next day?	What would happen if it were a wet day?

In this way, the ICT supports the subject and the subject supports very important conceptual developments in ICT.

Questions worth asking as a result of the activity include the following.

- **How was the activity integrated into the normal running of the classroom?**
- **What skills did I need in order for the activity to succeed?**
- **What skills did the children need?**
- **How did I ensure that all children had access to the activity?**
- **What were the learning outcomes for the children in literacy?**
- **What were the learning outcomes for the children in ICT?**
- **What assessment opportunities were there?**
- **How does this experience add to my understanding of ICT in subject teaching?**
- **Did the ends justify the means in terms of time costs?**
- **What will I do next time?**

Some example standards from the requirements for Initial Teacher Training which you may address in this activity, from the generic point of view, from the children's subject knowledge in ICT and for your own audit of progress towards the QTS Standards.

Planning ICT in science

Science, as a subject, appears to have had its curriculum time reduced by the emphasis in the Primary National Strategies in the other two core areas of literacy and mathematics, as well as by schools needing to provide curriculum coverage across the Foundation subjects. However, there is concern about science teaching in all phases of education and there is the opportunity to make good use of the very wide potential of ICT to support the teaching of science. There is ample opportunity for both subjects to support each other.

Planning for science with ICT means identifying the sorts of activities where ICT can support and enhance the learning of science. As with the rest of the core subject provision discussed above, some activities develop the scientific knowledge, skills and understanding of children but do not necessarily generate further ICT skill development. There are other activities which develop much higher-level ICT skills alongside scientific skills of enquiry and hypothesis. To take a simplistic example, a CD-ROM or a website which are tutorial in nature and which describe and then question the user about certain concepts do not necessarily advance the ICT skills of the user who is, as in all tutorial software, rehearsing skills of navigation over and over again. On the other hand, an activity which requires that the user set up and maintain a monitoring situation with ICT equipment and software is clearly requiring a higher level of skills in both subjects.

There is considerable guidance in the National Curriculum and in the sites and resources previously described for teachers who are looking for the links between science and ICT. At Key Stage 1, there are two examples of strong linkage between the subjects. The first is the suggestion that in learning how to recognise and compare the main external features of humans and animals, 'Pupils could use multimedia sources to make comparisons...' (KS1, Sc2 Life Processes and Living Things/Humans and other animals). The second is that in examining variation and classification, 'Pupils could use data collected to compile a class database' (KS1, Sc2 Life Processes and Living Things/Variation and classification).

In the first case, quite low-level ICT skills are being employed. In the second case, much higher-level ICT skills are being employed and there are strong links to the ICT scheme of work possible, in particular, Labelling and Classifying (1D) and Finding Information (2C). The decision to make in terms of lesson planning is to focus on the appropriate activities in the whole scheme of work for the children. Is it the case that you need a context for developing their awareness of databases? Have they browsed CDs at length? Do you now need, in terms of the science, to deepen their awareness of subject knowledge in classification by asking them to work with the data they are collecting? The scientific enquiry and the ICT skills development could usefully go hand in hand with these particular units.

There are further planning opportunities described for Key Stage 1 with strong links back to the ICT scheme of work. For 'Materials and their properties', it is suggested that pupils combine words and pictures about materials and objects on the computer. This comes slightly ahead of the unit of work suggested for ICT for Year 3, Combining text and graphics (3A). The other opportunity described is in physical processes, wherein it is argued that 'Pupils could use sensors to detect and compare sounds' in their study of light and sound (KS1, Sc4 Physical Processes/Light and Sound, 3c).

Throughout Key Stage 1 the breadth of study is intended to include ICT-based sources of information and data. At Key Stage 2 this strand of study is extended and developed further and becomes more closely linked to higher-level ICT skills. For example, there is a higher-level database activity described to support statement 2b, 'Pupils should be taught about the need for food for activity and growth, and about the importance of an adequate and varied diet for health' (KS2, Sc2 Life Processes and Living Things/Humans and other animals). It is suggested that children could 'use a database or spreadsheet to analyse data about types of food in school lunches'.

There follow a series of further suggestions all of which amplify the growing links between the two subjects, some examples of which are:

Pupils could use a branching database to develop and use keys (to support KS2, Sc2 Life Processes and Living Things/ Variation & Classification, 4a).

Pupils could use video or CD ROM to compare non-local habitats (to support KS2, Sc2 Life Processes and Living Things/ Adaptation, 5b).

Pupils could use simulation software to show changes in the populations of micro-organisms in different conditions (to support KS2, Sc2 Life Processes and Living Things/ Adaptation, 5f).

If the school you are placed in is using the scheme of work for science, there are numerous opportunities in your planning to use ICT. Similarly, thinking about the ICT Scheme of Work from a science perspective allows you to discover contexts in which children can develop their ICT capability. The following table explores some of those links. It is a starting point for planning links between the two subjects and is not intended to be exhaustive. Reading the two schemes, you will discover many other possibilities.

Science scheme of work: Units with higher-level ICT skills	ICT scheme of work: Units with potential for work in science
Unit 1A Ourselves	Unit 1C The information around us
Unit 2B Plants and animals in the local environment	Unit 2C Finding information
Unit 3D Rocks and soils	Unit 3C Introduction to databases
Unit 4C Keeping warm	Unit 4D Collecting and presenting information
Unit 5D Changing state Unit 5A Keeping healthy	Unit 5F Monitoring environmental conditions and changes
Unit 6A Interdependence and adaptation	Unit 6D Using the Internet to search large databases and to interpret information

There are many ways in which ICT can support science in a more general way, with the use of templates, for example, in write-ups as a form of *aide-memoire* so as to further structure scientific thought and develop skills of planning and enquiry.

Above all, the use of ICT in science should be seen as something in which the scientific learning has the upper hand; it should be a key to opening up the world of scientific development and not an end in itself. There are benefits for both subjects in close integration.

PRACTICAL TASK PRACTICAL TASK **PRACTICAL TASK** PRACTICAL TASK

Planning to use ICT in science

Choose a unit of work from the science scheme of work for which you have access to the appropriate software and hardware. Plan for one session within the unit to have a major input from ICT. Use the links suggested between the two schemes previously in this section to help you.

When you evaluate the session, consider the following aspects:

Make a judgement, in conversation with your mentor and/or tutor, about the contribution of the ICT to the subject knowledge in the sessions.

Did the ends justify the means?

Would you use ICT to work with this particular concept or unit again?

If yes, would you do anything differently?

If no, why would you prefer not to use ICT in this way again?

Auditing

After the lesson, discuss the outcomes with your mentor and/or professional tutor. If the lesson has allowed you to demonstrate evidence of achieving parts of any Standards for QTS you could attach the plan and any work examples to your audit and date it.

Planning ICT in the Foundation subjects

The situation with planning for ICT and the Foundation subjects is similar to the one for science. There is a great deal of pressure of time in the primary school day on the core curriculum subjects of literacy and mathematics. However, with imaginative organisational strategies and access to the appropriate hardware and software, it ought to be possible to ensure both the children's entitlement to the Foundation subjects and to ICT. Planning for ICT in the Foundation subjects, as for the core curriculum, means identifying those activities where ICT provides an essential part of the learning experience. In other words, it means identifying the lessons in the Foundation subjects where, with ICT, the learning opportunities are enhanced in depth, range and quality. The following examples given under the relevant subject headings are by no means an exhaustive list. They are intended to be starting points for planning for ICT in the Foundation subjects. Following this section, a table helps you to negotiate the schemes of work for the Foundation subjects in terms of ICT.

Art and design

Some of the Foundation subjects depend on a sophisticated understanding of how the ICT works and of how it uniquely contributes to the learning in that subject area. One example would be art, where the understanding of what is happening in a graphics package is crucial to understanding the contribution which it makes to the subject.

Image-editing packages, in spite of their onscreen appearance with virtual canvases and paintpots and virtual pencils, represent a different medium for artists. They may look as though they are replacing the physical world of brushstrokes and charcoal marks. The fact is that they aren't. The way that they work is by arranging digital information on screen. Avril Loveless in 'Working with images, developing ideas' (in McFarlane, 1997) builds an argument about helping children and teachers to understand that they are interacting with a new medium, rich with different possibilities. She writes that 'IT has the potential to be a catalyst in the development of new ways of expressing a visual language' and goes on to define the central role that the teacher has in the process,

> *It is the interaction of the facilities of IT, the children's ability to explore and extend their visual ideas and the teacher's pedagogy that can improve the quality of teaching and learning.*
>
> (Loveless, in McFarlane, 1997)

Opportunities for links between subject and ICT are spelled out in the margins of the National Curriculum handbook. For art and design, these are given as the following:

> *At Key Stage 1, while children are being taught about 'visual and tactile elements, including colour, pattern and texture, line and tone, shape, form and space' they could use painting software to explore some of these elements.* (Art and design, knowledge an understanding, KS1 4a in DfES/QCA, 2000)

At Key Stage 2, the use of digital and video cameras to record observations is suggested as part of the strand on exploring and developing ideas (KS2, 1c). There is also a recommendation that children are encouraged to create material for a school art gallery on the school web page. A powerful suggestion is made about the use of the Internet as a medium for children to explore the work and styles of many different genres across the world. This will depend as always on the accessibility of reliable and fast Internet access in the various resource settings in which teachers, children and trainees find themselves. Nevertheless, these are possibilities which are unique to ICT and which significantly enhance the teaching of the subject. With bandwidth and distribution of the Internet around schools improving all the time, virtual art galleries represent a significant contribution to the art and design curriculum. The higher bandwidth (much faster transfer of much bigger files around the Internet) is of particular benefit in this area because the files are so much larger than with other uses of ICT, for example, word processing.

In terms of planning appropriately, the usual judgements apply about how the subject is enhanced and which ICT skills are being utilised and developed. You can find connections between art and ICT in the ICT scheme of work and could usefully situate your ICT content within the Art curriculum. Units such as 1A (An introduction to modelling), 2B (Creating pictures), 2C (Finding information), 3A (Combining text and graphics) and 6A (Multimedia presentation) are all areas which can be approached from the direction of ICT and taken into the area of art and design.

Similarly, it is possible to find examples within the QCA scheme for art which are rich with possible links to ICT. Unit 2A, Picture This!, for example, suggests a unit of work around children recording an issue or event in their lives which 'could also link with Unit 1A "An introduction to modeling", in the ICT scheme, when children create their own representations of real or fantasy situations' of work for art).

Purposeful exploration of painting packages, image-recording devices and websites which bring art into the classroom in ways which were not possible before are all unique to ICT and offer something to children's learning in art and design. The important thing to remember for your planning is the word 'purposeful' and all that implies. Of particular importance is the notion that the ICT is adding to the potential achievement and learning by the children in the given subject.

Geography

History and geography are two subjects in which ICT can make a contribution to the enhancement of the learning process. We have seen, above, an example of a connection between a geographical activity and a unit of work in the ICT curriculum (in the cross-curricular English planning example).

The world wide web brings much potential to the teaching of geography. The subject itself offers a context for developing skills of searching, emailing and publishing. Similarly, early understanding of mapping and routes is enhanced by the use of a programmable toy. The National Curriculum handbook suggests this and others as examples:

- **Routes and maps with a programmable toy (link to 2c);**
- **Using a digital camera to record events outside classroom (link to 4a);**
- **Using the Internet to obtain comparative weather information (link to 3d, 3f).**

Beyond comparative weather data comes the whole series of possibilities raised by e-mail or video conference contact with children and teachers in other localities. E-mailed questions about what you can see from your window on a given day generate vast amounts of interesting information between pupils of the same age, across the world, very quickly.

Geographical resources which were not available before – detailed maps and aerial photographs of most of the world – are now accessible online and offline. The skill in terms of the teaching will be to integrate these resources usefully into planning. You will need to identify opportunities for learning which are uniquely offered by the technology and then allow your pupils to have access to it. As for all areas, if you are in a high resource setting with large numbers of computers and good Internet access your problems are significantly reduced. In some cases the availability of PDAs with mapping software connected to Global Positioning Satellites (GPS) is enhancing the experience of geography.

History

History is brought to life by many of the activities suggested in its own scheme of work for the primary school. The opportunities for ICT are present throughout.

The Internet brings not only art galleries into the school, but also museums and archival resources of all kinds, many of which are free to use in educational settings. Many of these are also present on CD-ROM. Incorporating such work into history lessons, as with all subject areas, becomes an issue depending on the resource setting in which trainees, teachers and children are working.

The National Curriculum handbook makes several references to links between history and ICT. Some of these are simply to the resource capabilities of ICT, as for example the link to finding out about significant people in the past from CD-ROM (link to statement 4a on historical enquiry). Another example of quite low-level ICT use would be in using digitised maps in local enquiry.

Higher-level ICT skills are demanded by the sophisticated use of databases at Key Stage 2 to study patterns of change over time. This falls in the following area for history:

(the capability to) ask and answer questions, and to select and record information relevant to the focus of the enquiry. (Historical enquiry, 4b)

History provides us with an example of the need to be very clear about the sort of order of skills in both a curriculum subject and ICT which are to be developed in a given lesson. This area was explored previously in the section on planning for the daily mathematics lesson where we saw a trade-off between higher-level ICT skills and content browsing.

Design and technology

ICT offers much to teachers of design and technology in the primary school. The area of most potential is probably that of control technology where children learn that they can control devices and models which will respond to instruction and inputs from outside. Children already know that such devices exist. A quick concept map at the start of work on this subject will bring to mind TV recording programmers, washing machine programmes, central heating timers, burglar alarms and a whole host of other devices.

Additionally, when creating or developing ideas for themselves, children could be encouraged to create digital versions of their ideas. The programmes of study make explicit reference to this idea, pointing out the link back to ICT in the following statements:

Pupils should be taught to:
a) generate ideas by drawing on their own and other people's experiences
e) communicate their ideas using a variety of methods, including drawing and making models.
(From KS1, Strand 1: Developing, planning and communicating ideas)

At Key Stage 2 there is a greater level of complexity and a more explicit statement of the need to engage with ICT in order to deliver the subject. There is a further statement about the tools of presentation and onscreen creation available through ICT (see Strand 1: Developing, planning and communicating ideas). There is, however, an understanding that in developing a knowledge and understanding of materials and components children should be taught:

c) how mechanisms can be used to make things move in different ways, using a range of equipment including an ICT control program'.
(From KS2, Strand 4: Knowledge and understanding of materials and components)

It is difficult to imagine being able to meet the needs of young learners in design and technology and their curriculum entitlements without significant levels of ICT use in their school career. Again, the major caveat is whether the resource base is high enough in your placement school to begin exploring this issue in your planning. Although, as we have seen in previous sections, the situation is improving, control technology is often down the list in terms of buying under educational funding arrangements.

A further issue is the availability of support in terms of expertise. Although relatively simple-to-use software is involved, there is something about the number of wires and additional interface boxes involved which deters many people from including this area in their planning. Most teachers who do take it on find that the equipment and software working together are highly motivating for children and stimulate a great deal of interest and creative learning potential.

Music

ICT has for a long time enjoyed a close relationship with music in primary schools. Tape recorders and CD players have been used in schools for many years to:

- **bring children into contact with music from different times and different cultures;**
- **record children's own compositions;**
- **provide resources for learning songs;**
- **provide accompaniment to dance (link to PE);**
- **provide a source of music for assemblies and performances;**
- **provide a resource for budding instrumentalists to record and assess their work.**

Additionally, schools with electronic keyboards have been able to extend the performance aspects of assembly songs. Keyboards with sound modules in which real instrument voices have been stored allow children to explore the different timbres and possibilities of different instruments.

In terms of computer use, there are software packages available which allow children to explore composing. The feedback which they gain from such software is immediate and the 'performing and appraising' aspects of the curriculum are therefore made similarly immediate. As was the case for art and design, there is no suggestion of the computer based musical tools replacing hands-on experience with the whole range of instruments found in primary schools. Instead, the suggestion is that ICT be used to enhance the learning process.

Children learn that computers are capable of storing more than just text and images and that they can be used to record and manipulate sound. To put it another way, they learn that sound itself can be represented and stored digitally, in which form it can be transformed in many different ways.

Computers and hard disk recorders are now the medium of choice in professional and home recording studios for composing and arranging music. Children will be aware of the possibilities of mixing and remixing songs as they hear different versions of their favourite songs produced. Some children may have access to simple tools on mobile phones for music editing (or older siblings with them or at least know of them). The learning curve for teachers and others who are seeking to use music composition software and keyboards at this higher level is sometimes perceived to be quite steep and requiring specialist INSET. However, once the basic concepts are mastered, such devices open up a whole range of possibilities for young composers in both key stages, but particularly the older ages in Key Stage 2 in the primary school and there are increasingly simplified, yet powerful, tools to use for this (see Chapter 17 on Music and Sound).

The links between ICT and the programmes of study for music are many and can be found in statements such as:

> 2. Pupils should be taught how to:
> a) create musical patterns
> b) explore, choose and organise sounds and musical ideas.
> > (From KS1, Creating & Developing Musical Ideas – Composing Skills)

The link here is the use of software for sound exploration.

> 3. Pupils should be taught how to:
> b) make improvements to their own work.
> > (From KS1, Responding and reviewing – appraising skills)

The link here is the use of recording equipment for reviewing work (this could be tape or computer based).

The breadth of study for Key Stage 2 in music requires that children use ICT to 'capture, change and combine sounds'.

The resource setting is one potential obstacle to exploiting fully these links between music and ICT. Another is teacher confidence and appropriate training, as well as access to hardware and software. However, at even the most basic level of using taping equipment, ICT enhances subject teaching in music in powerful ways.

RE, PSHE and citizenship

ICT in terms of its access to resources on the Internet is a major contributing factor to growing subject knowledge and understanding in the interlinked areas of RE, personal, social and health education (PSHE) and citizenship. The diversity of religions over the world can be explored on the Internet and on CD-ROM. Children can have a context for their writing which extends their sphere of personal expression into that of personal belief.

The RE scheme of work links with ICT in many places. Two examples would be:

- **in the unit on Belief and practice** (Unit 1D, where it mentions the resourcing possibilities);
- **in Unit 4D on 'What religions are represented in our neighbourhood?'** (This time, there is more to be made of the capacity of ICT for preparing and representing writing. Digital cameras and the Internet are suggested means of gathering and storing information about local faiths which are then to be represented in children's classwork.)

As for history and RE, the potential of the Internet to link to other cultures and belief systems can engender respect (when taught appropriately). ICT brings these worlds within reach (with all the caveats about connectivity and appropriate Internet use) in a unique way.

For the non-compulsory areas of PSHE and citizenship there are statements of usefulness of ICT in the National Curriculum. One example is that of developing relationships through work and play (for example, communicating with children in other countries by satellite, e-mail or letters).

Children are aware that the school holds information about them from the earliest years (they quickly and routinely give information at the start of each day in the register). They can be explicitly made aware of the uses of ICT in gathering and processing this information. Later, they could discuss the confidentiality issues raised by large databases being held by companies and government agencies full of personal information.

It is as well to raise the issue of ethics in its widest sense with older children. Many will be aware of the fact that not everyone has access to computers and that the world wide web as a phrase refers to circumnavigation rather than connectivity in all countries. Access to websites which map cyberspace will be particularly revealing in this regard. One example would be the Institute of Cybergeography, which has a fascinating collection of atlases of cyberspace (Institute of Cybergeography, 2006).

PE

There is a place on the PE curriculum for ICT, certainly in terms of devices which can help to record movement for pupils to analyse later. Some schemes of work are distributed for INSET using different storage and replay media, whether it is on videotape or videodisc.

The revised National Curriculum from the year 2000 was more enthusiastic than previous versions about ICT and stated linkage between the subjects includes the following:

For Dance and gymnastic activity at Key Stage 1, 'Pupils could use videos of movements and actions to develop their ideas.'
For Dance, gymnastic and athletic activities at Key Stage 2, 'Pupils could use video and CD-ROMs of actions, balances and body shapes to improve their performance'.

Further cross-curriculum opportunities exist in the analysis of the effects of exercise which can be carried out using sensors. Here, the potential link to science has already been outlined above. The potential to link with maths in the exploration of data in spreadsheets is also clearly there. Some bespoke software exists to do this (the 'Five Star' athletics software, for example).

Clearly, it would be unwise to make strong claims for all-day, every-day pervasive links in planning between ICT and PE. However, there will be times, particularly when tackling the issue of assessment in PE, when ICT can make a vital contribution. The contribution of digital video in particular is noted in Chapter 11.

Languages and primary ICT

ICT has great potential to support the teaching of languages in primary schools. The curriculum for Key Stage 2 teaching of European and other languages will be supported and enhanced by the use of high-quality CD and DVD-based resources, which, alongside websites, allow for different learning styles to be incorporated into working.

Some learners will benefit from simpler drill-and-practice vocabulary reinforcement and extension. For others, the opportunity to explore scenarios and solve problems in other languages online and in collaboration with other learners will be highly significant and a genuinely useful context for technology such as video-conferencing

Increasingly the sophisticated operating systems of both Windows and Mac computers have simplified the use of a variety of language fonts both European and worldwide, making multilingual publishing in the classroom a real possibility.

ICT and Foundation subject planning aid

The following table gives you locations of some example units in the various QCA schemes of work for the Foundation subjects with strong links to ICT. It also links the ICT scheme of work back to that subject. The list is not exhaustive. It is intended as a guide for planning from whatever scheme of work document you may have access to in order to incorporate ICT in that subject. There are certainly many other links between the various schemes of work.

Foundation subject	Subject scheme of work: Example units with links to ICT	ICT scheme of work: Example units with links back to the subject
Art and design	Picture This (2A) Investigating pattern (3B) People in action (6A)	An introduction to modelling (1A) Creating pictures (2B) Multimedia presentation (6A)
Geography	Improving the environment (Unit 8) Investigating rivers (Unit 14) The mountain environment (Unit 15)	Combining text and graphics(3A) Multimedia presentation (6A) Using the Internet…6D)
History	How did life change in our locality in Victorian times? (Unit 12) How can we find out about the Indus Valley civilisation? (Unit 16) What can we learn about recent history from studying the life of a famous person? (Unit 20)	Combining text and graphics (3A) Analysing data (5B) Using the Internet…(6D)
Design and technology	Packaging (3A) Lighting it up (4E) Alarms (4D)	Finding information (2C) Combining text and graphics (3A) Controlling devices (5E)
Music	Journey into space: exploring sound sources (Unit 18) Songwriter exploring lyrics and melody (Unit 19)	Manipulating sound (3B) Multimedia presentation (6A)
RE, PSHE and citizenship	Beliefs and Practice (1D) Celebrations (2C) What religions are represented in our neighbourhood? (4D)	Finding information (2C) Email (3E) Using the Internet…(6D)
PE	Dance activities – Unit 1 Gymnastic activities – Unit 5	Finding information (2C) Monitoring environmental conditions and changes (5F)
Languages	Curriculum for KS2 languages as a whole	Finding information (2C) Combining text and graphics (3A) Email (3E) Using the Internet…(6D)

BEFLECTIVE TASK
REFLECTIVE TASK

Planning ICT in your specialist subject

If you are in a course which requires that you develop a specialism, use your specialist subject as the basis for the following activity. Use the school scheme of work in your specialist subject to complete it. Where there is no scheme of work, use the relevant QCA documents as guidance.

Identify a unit of work. Cross-reference it to an ICT unit from the ICT Scheme. Decide on the balance between the two and plan a series of four to six lessons (or activities) which develop the subject knowledge of the children alongside some identified aspect of ICT capability.

At the end of the sequence, address the following issues as an overview of all the sessions:

Were the learning objectives achieved? How?

Which aspects of ICT capability did the children develop (not rehearse, but develop)?

What operational difficulties were encountered (if any) during the activity?

Make a judgement, in conversation with your mentor and/or tutor, about the contribution of the ICT to the subject knowledge in the sessions.

Did the ends justify the means? Once again, consider the time factor.

Would you use ICT to work with this particular concept or unit again?

If yes, would you do anything differently?

If no, why would you prefer not to use ICT in this way again?

Auditing

After the lesson, discuss the outcomes with your mentor and/or professional tutor. If the lesson has allowed you to demonstrate evidence of achieving parts of any Standards for QTS you could attach the plan and any work examples to your audit and date it. Possible standards to reference include:

Q7

Reflect on and improve practice, and take responsibility for identifying and meeting developing professional needs;

Q8

Have a creative and constructively critical approach towards innovation, being prepared to adapt practice where benefits and improvements are identified;

Q11

Know the assessment requirements and arrangements for the subjects/curriculum areas you are trained to teach, including those relating to public examinations and qualifications.

Q12

Know a range of approaches to assessment, including the importance of formative assessment.

Q13

Know how to use local and national statistical information to evaluate the effectiveness of their teaching, to monitor the progress of those they teach and to raise levels of attainment.

Q22

Plan for progression across the age and ability range for which you are trained, designing effective learning sequences within lessons and across series of lessons and demonstrating secure subject/curriculum knowledge.

Q25

Teach lessons and sequences of lessons across the age and ability range for which they are trained in which they:

(a) use a range of teaching strategies and resources, including e-learning, taking practical account of diversity and promoting equality and inclusion;

(b) build on prior knowledge, develop concepts and processes, enable learners to apply new knowledge, understanding and skills and meet learning objectives;

(c) adapt their language to suit the learners they teach, introducing new ideas and concepts clearly, and using explanations, questions, discussions and plenaries effectively.

Q26

(a) Make effective use of a range of assessment, monitoring and recording strategies;

(b) Assess the learning needs of those they teach in order to set challenging learning objectives.

A SUMMARY OF **KEY POINTS**

> **How ICT supports learning in subject teaching.**

> **Planning for ICT in subject teaching.**

> **Development of your own ICT skills.**

Moving on

Consider the wide range of planning opportunities you have seen for primary ICT in subject teaching. In your induction year, how do you think you will work with planning for subjects? As you move into your career you will find INSET opportunities relating to new technology, in particular the use of media in the curriculum. Think about how this might be a way to join subjects together in cross-curricular projects and look for ways to develop this in your professional life.

FURTHER READING FURTHER READING **FURTHER READING** FURTHER READING

Becta Schools pages (2007) **schools.becta.org.uk**/ Accessed 30 January 2007

DfES (2000a) *National Curriculum Handbook for Key Stages 1 and 2*. London: DfES

DfES Standards site **www.standards.dfes.gov.uk**/ Accessed 30 January 2007

DfES Standards site – ICT Scheme (2003 version) **www.standards.dfes.gov.uk/schemes2/it/?view =get** Accessed 30 January 2007

DfES Interactive Planning tool (2007) **www.standards.dfes.gov.uk/primaryframeworks/planningtool/** Holding page accessed 30 January 2007

DfES Primary Framework homepage (2007) **www.standards.dfes.gov.uk/primaryframeworks/** Accessed 30 January 2007

National Curriculum in Action – ICT pages (2007) **www.ncaction.org.uk/subjects/ict/inother.htm** Accessed 30 January 2007

National Curriculum online (2007) **www.nc.uk.net** Accessed 13 May 2007

Smith, Helen (1999) *Opportunities for ICT in the Primary School*. London: Trentham Books

Somekh, B and Davis, N (eds) (1997) *Using Information technology effectively in teaching and learning*. London: Routledge

Teachers' TV homepage (2007) **www.teachers.tv**/ Accessed 30 January 2007

4
Planning ICT in the Early Years: the computer in the Foundation Stage

Chapter objectives

This chapter is about planning for ICT activities in the Early Years setting. Trainees in the Early Years are expected to achieve additional Standards during their training. This chapter will give some consideration to the issues around planning in a very different environment from the mainstream primary classroom.

The Early Years setting

The first and most obvious difference is the environment of the Early Years setting. This is defined as the range of learning environments for young children from about the age of three until they enter the primary school in Year 1. The QCA guidance refers to this stage as the Foundation Stage.

The Foundation Stage has an entirely different structure from the National Curriculum. If you are not an Early Years specialist but you find yourself in a placement which is an Early Years setting you need to familiarise yourself with the very thorough guidance provided. In particular you need to become attuned to a setting which looks at key learning goals for young children, rather than at explicit programmes of study and schemes of work.

The definition of these key learning goals is informed by Early Years specialists' understanding of the ways in which young children think and learn. They are also intended as laying the foundation for the child's future engagement with the curriculum in the mainstream primary setting. The Early Learning goals are mapped out for the Foundation Stage in six developmental areas as follows:

- **personal, social and emotional development;**
- **communication, language and literacy;**
- **mathematical development;**
- **knowledge and understanding of the world;**
- **physical development;**
- **creative development.**

The key issue for practitioners who are seeking to use computers to support young children's development in these areas is how to merge the use of the computer with the philosophy and methodology of planning for young learners.

The adults who work in Early Years settings, planning for and interacting with young children, set out their environment to maximise the opportunities for learning to take place. This is not a simple template for daily use of a space with young learners; it is an environment underpinned by knowledge of how children develop skills, explore and grow in understanding of key concepts. Early Years professionals are trained to plan from the perspectives of child development and the major theories of children's learning. Adults concerned with designing activities and planning for young learners are cognisant of the fact that learning happens both in the opportunity for play and in the interaction between people – all people – in learning spaces.

The theories of Vygotsky are important here as a major component of the theory underpinning the mapping out of Early Years settings. He believed that children are continually refining their growing understanding through a sort of innate, inner speech. Learning potential is enhanced in settings where children verbalise their inner speech and test and re-test it in their interaction with others. This happens in what Vygotsky characterised as the 'zone of proximal development'. Many texts are available which explore these concepts in some depth. One example would be the book by David Woods, *How children think and learn*. Early Years specialists will also be familiar with the work of Sandra Smidt in the *Guide to early years practice* (Smidt, 1997).

Vygotsky's theories and others underpin the Early Years setting. As a result, such environments are rich in opportunities for play (the context for the inner speech of children) and rich in opportunities for interaction (in the zone of proximal development).

Where does the computer fit into this environment? With its associated certainties and appearance of rigidity and non-fluid thinking, the computer appears to contradict this widely held view of the way in which children learn in the zone of proximal development. Some writers (Crook, 1996; Mercer and Fisher, 1997) have, however, attempted to analyse the working of the computer in the zone of proximal development and to look at the key features of talk around children working with computers. Their work suggests that computers are particularly rich in their possibilities for collaborative learning in the zone of proximal development.

This in turn suggests that the best organisational strategies for the Early Years are the same, in many respects, as for the classroom. It means making the computer much more a part of the world of the Early Years setting. At the most basic level this means making the computer more a part of the general experience of play and dialogue alongside the writing area, the modelling, the books, the play equipment. It means making the computer accessible for use in a range of contexts both collaboratively and singly, with an adult, without an adult, in the same way as any Early Years activity might be designed to maximise learning opportunities.

Clearly, giving children and the adults around the computer the space to talk and to play is crucial. Placing the computer in, for example, a role-play situation, building a small office play environment around it and running open-ended software on it could be a starting point for stimulating much of the inner dialogue and talk in the zone of proximal development.

From the planning point of view it is important to be clear about how each of the defined areas of learning can be enriched and enhanced. It means thinking about the computer in each of the six contexts, namely:

- **personal, social and emotional development;**
- **communication, language and literacy;**
- **mathematical development;**
- **knowledge and understanding of the world;**

- physical development;
- creative development.

For 'Personal, social and emotional development' this could mean planning opportunities for any of the following to occur:

- Learning how to share the equipment and take turns (particularly with such a motivating and attractive resource), in other words using the computer to allow children to establish constructive relationships with each other and with other adults.
- Using the computer to encourage collaboration between children, and between adults and children in problem-solving (even at the basic level of switching on, selecting an item from a menu, clicking on a name).
- Using the computer to explore worlds beyond the Early Years setting through the Internet or CD-ROM.
- Using the computer as a tool to encourage collaboration between children who are experiencing difficulties and others in the Early Years setting (using alternative access devices alongside mice and keyboards).

Encouraging children's development of 'Communication, language and literacy' in the Early Years setting with the computer means planning opportunities for children to:

- Write messages, label pictures with their name and otherwise engage with the communicative aspects of ICT. They do not have to get it right in the same way as a writing area doesn't exclude children who can't yet form letters. The uncritical nature of the ICT can prove extremely motivating (particularly when the computer is in a role-play area and the child is experiencing an impetus to try from the imaginative play).
- Experience the notion that computers can communicate words and pictures from books. If an adult helper, parent, older child is present, much useful talk and discussion about books and print, words and sounds, computers and communication can occur.
- Communicate with friends, relatives, peers in other settings nearby and very far away if possible. Children know that the computer is one among many tools for communication over distance and time. If the computer cannot deliver the necessary experiences then other ICT equipment such as a digital camera, video camera, tape recorder may be able to.

For children's 'Mathematical development', the following opportunities might be useful:

- Plan to use software which allows children to experience situations of counting and sharing and identifying numbers, e.g. in counting items for a picnic. The most enduring and widely used Early Years software appears to be amongst the most simple and involves such activities as identifying numbers and counting items.
- Use software which relates a counting song or nursery rhyme known to the children to reinforce early counting concepts and which allows the children to have some free play. If children are working with parent helpers or other adults and making conscious what they understand, much constructive dialogue can take place which takes the child forward.

For the child's developing 'Knowledge and understanding of the world' ICT can develop the skills of enquiry, of building understanding of the world in the Early Years setting in many ways. Some of the following might be used to plan to address this key learning area:

- As mentioned above, set up the computer within a role-play area. Consider settings with which the children are familiar such as libraries, doctors' surgeries, and any kind of office. This creates a powerful context for imaginative play because the computer reinforces the 'reality' of the situation for the child. It is a powerful stimulus for the inner speech and the outer dialogue in the zone of proximal development.
- The computer provides everyone in the Early Years Setting with a means of recording in writing, orally and visually (still and full motion), the children's experiences as learners. Digital cameras are highly significant tools in this context, with their capacity for immediate feedback.
- The capacity for ICT to provide access to activities for many children with special educational needs (including sensory impairment, physical and behavioural problems) allows for activities which promote knowledge and understanding of the world to be planned for all.
- As mentioned in the context of personal, social and emotional development, there is plenty of scope for the Internet and CD-ROMs to bring experiences of other cultures and other worlds into the Early Years setting.

Children's 'Physical development' can be planned for in terms of computer use with the following considerations in mind:

- The use of ICT equipment to promote and develop fine motor skills, in particular, the use of the mouse.
- For children who are experiencing difficulties in fine motor skills across the whole range of severity, access devices such as brightly coloured, larger keyboards, touch windows and trackballs can all be used. Concept Keyboards which contain teacher-defined touch areas, touch screens and big switches which can be wheelchair-mounted and others all allow for inclusion and development within the Early Years setting.

For children's 'Creative development' ICT brings into the world of the Early Years setting, experiences with new media which can be used alongside the range of traditional, hands-on experiences. For example:

- The use of graphics software is an area of great potential in the Early Years setting. The medium in which the learner operates is infinitely editable and scalable. Colours in huge areas of the onscreen canvas can be varied at the click of a mouse. Shapes can be created with and without filled areas. With support from an adult or working with a friend, the child can be encouraged to verbalise their thoughts on the image they are making. Digital cameras allow images of the child themselves to become part of the onscreen canvas.
- ICT also offers the Early Years setting the potential to be creative with sound and with video. Simple musical composition software allows young learners to see that you can do more than just paint and write at a computer. A recording studio is another imaginary scenario in which to explore and develop.

REFLECTIVE TASK

Early Years planning

For those in an Early Years placement or Early Years specialist trainees:

Choose one of the Early Learning Goals.

Identify, with the help of the Early Years team at the school, an appropriate piece of software with which the children are already familiar.

Set up the computer within some kind of role-play context if possible (if space allows and if it fits with the current planning in the setting).

Observe the children working with the software over a period of a few days for a few minutes each day. Ask for one or other of the co-workers in the setting to do the same.

Collate your observations.

How has the presence of the computer assisted in generating talk around the area of learning?

Have you been able to observe any interactions in which peer learning was evident?

Did the children work in the ways in which you expected?

Were there any surprising outcomes?

Were there any overlapping areas of development from the other Early Learning Goals?

Auditing

After the lesson, discuss the outcomes with your mentor and/or professional tutor. If the lesson has allowed you to demonstrate evidence of achieving parts of any Standards for QTS you could attach the plan and any work examples to your audit and date it. Possible standards to reference include:

Q7

Reflect on and improve practice, and take responsibility for identifying and meeting developing professional needs.

Q8

Have a creative and constructively critical approach towards innovation, being prepared to adapt practice where benefits and improvements are identified.

Q11

Know the assessment requirements and arrangements for the subjects/curriculum areas you are trained to teach, including those relating to public examinations and qualifications.

Q12

Know a range of approaches to assessment, including the importance of formative assessment.

Q13

Know how to use local and national statistical information to evaluate the effectiveness of their teaching, to monitor the progress of those they teach and to raise levels of attainment.

Q22

Plan for progression across the age and ability range for which you are trained, designing effective learning sequences within lessons and across series of lessons and demonstrating secure subject/curriculum knowledge.

Q25

Teach lessons and sequences of lessons across the age and ability range for which they are trained in which they:

(a) use a range of teaching strategies and resources, including e-learning, taking practical account of diversity and promoting equality and inclusion;

(b) build on prior knowledge, develop concepts and processes, enable learners to apply new knowledge, understanding and skills and meet learning objectives;

(c) adapt their language to suit the learners they teach, introducing new ideas and concepts clearly, and using explanations, questions, discussions and plenaries effectively.

Q26

(a) Make effective use of a range of assessment, monitoring and recording strategies.

(b) Assess the learning needs of those they teach in order to set challenging learning objectives.

RESEARCH SUMMARY RESEARCH SUMMARY**RESEARCH SUMMARY** RESEARCH SUMMARY

Talk and ICT

A great deal of research has been carried out on the importance of talk around the computer which is of particular interest to Early Years practitioners as they plan for contexts in which young learners express their 'inner speech' (Smidt, 1998).

In Wegerif and Scrimshaw's *Computers and Talk in the Primary Classroom* (1997) a number of projects are outlined which analyse talk in and around computers according to a variety of frameworks. In one example Eunice Fisher reports on the influence of software type on the kinds of talk generated (Fisher, 1997). A pattern of talk emerges in the use of less open-ended software which is quite different from the wide-ranging exploratory talk in evidence when open-ended software is being used by children. Wegerif responds in the chapter which follows, making a case for exploratory talk which is generated around closed software and which actually extends children and 'leads to the educationally valuable combination of directive teaching software with children's active peer learning.' (Wegerif, 1997).

A SUMMARY OF **KEY POINTS**

> The computer is another resource in the world of the Early Years setting.

> Planning for ICT means developing an understanding of the ways in which young children think and learn.

> The talk and play around ICT is as important as any supposed planned outcome.

> Each learning area can be supported with careful planning.

Moving on

Consider the wide range of planning opportunities you have seen for using new technology with younger learners. In your induction year, how do you think you will work with planning for them? As you move into your career you will find INSET opportunities relating to new technology, in particular the use of media in the curriculum. Think about how this might be a way to work with younger learners in the future and look for ways to develop this in your professional life.

FURTHER READING FURTHER READING **FURTHER READING** FURTHER READING

Crook, C. (1996) *Computers and the collaborative experience of learning*. London: Routledge

Fullan, M. (1992) *Successful school improvement*. Buckingham: Open University Press

Loveless, A. (1997) 'Working with images, developing ideas', in MacFarlane, A. (ed.) *Information technology and authentic learning*. London: Routledge

Mercer, N. and Fisher, E. (1997) 'The importance of talk', in Wegerif, R. and Scrimshaw, P. (eds) *Computers and talk in the primary classroom*. London: Multilingual Matters

QCA (2000) *Curriculum guidance for the Foundation Stage*. London: QCA

Smidt, S. (1998) *A guide to early years practice*. London: Routledge

Whitehead, M. (1997) *Language and literacy in the early years*. London: Paul Chapman

5
Assessment and recording in primary ICT

Chapter objectives

The Scheme of Work is intended to provide progression and a possible map of the learning of a child in a given subject. Assessment is a vital part of the process because it allows teachers to track progress and plan appropriately for children to achieve. Without proper assessment and recording in a given subject, there is no real evidence or knowledge of where the children are up to, and planning becomes empty and meaningless. In the worst cases, it leads to the same activities being given out year on year to children who will underachieve because of it. In ICT this means seeing the same basic word-processing activities going on at Year 6 as happened at Year 2. The planning and assessment cycle is incomplete in a school where this occurs and the children make no real progress in the subject (or in its use in other subjects)

Online assessment and profiling

It may well be that the school in which you are working is still working with paper-based assessments of children's work and progress. The suggestions for pro-formas in the pages which follow make this assumption. However, it may also be that you are working in a school which is beginning to store examples of work electronically, possibly with the involvement of the children. It could be that the school is working on developing an electronic portfolio for each child or for a group of children. Either way, the online examples of children's work provided at local level, within the school or LA can be used to help you to make judgements about children's work. There are pages at the government's own National Curriculum in Action website which provide some exemplars (National Curriculum in Action, 2006).

Principles of assessment

The principles which underpin good practice in assessment apply equally to ICT and ICT in subject teaching. As teachers, we are looking for ways to measure achievement which, at the same time, allow us to identify a child's learning needs. These methods of assessment, in turn, will allow us to plan efficiently and appropriately. Ways of assessing children in ICT, as in other subjects, include some or all of the following:

- observing how the child goes about a piece of work;
- diagnosing difficulties which become apparent over a series of lessons;
- observing which planning strategies appear to work and allow the child to succeed in a given area;
- collecting significant pieces of work in a portfolio of development;
- noting the context of the work and any factors which were significant: the grouping, the time taken, the level of concentration etc.;
- noting the views of the child about the piece of work and asking her or him what made the activity so successful/significant;

- feeding the information back into the planning process;
- when appropriate, making a judgement about the child's level in terms of the level descriptions in the attainment targets for ICT in the National Curriculum (at the end of the key stages in the primary school);
- at all times keeping a clear focus on the objective; this is very important as well as having a general awareness of other learning taking place.

Nevertheless, assessment and record keeping in ICT is a complex process. Meaningful work samples are harder to come by in ICT than in most other subjects, with the possible exception of PE and RE. Printouts of work by themselves are not useful. ICT is often used as a tool to present work in its best possible light. Any revealing errors and misconceptions are often lost along the way. The finished product is only the final element of a much longer, more complex process. The process itself is what provides the real assessment opportunities. To borrow an example from another subject, English, a writing sample which contains only the finished ('best') copy is similarly without any real use. Teachers need to go back through the draft book to understand the process the child went through. The child also needs to see and understand this in order to move forward.

Some ICT tools do allow for processes to be explored. Some word processors, for example, allow changes to be tracked and printed out. Others record how many times the child accessed the online help in a particular software package. Browser software tracks the user through the various sites and links they follow. This might provide useful assessment information. In some more forward-looking local authorities, there are systems which allow children to select pieces of work and store them in an electronic portfolio. Taken together, in context, these are useful tools for the teacher assessing a child's achievement and identifying their learning needs. If we add connectivity to the home computer into the equation we have a powerful, fluid record of achievement which is also accessible to parents and to children out of school hours. (Of course, the issue of inequality in computer and network connectivity provision in different areas becomes even more obvious in this context and will need to be addressed by those in positions of power.)

Tutorial software, including software produced as part of an integrated learning system (ILS), can record the units of work which the child has covered and can produce tables, graphs and collections of statistics. These relate to the software itself and closely to the subject being taught. They are of very limited use in assessing the child's ICT capability, however, and should not usually be presented as evidence of attainment in ICT. They record particular progress through an onscreen worksheet or tutorial. As we have seen in the planning chapters, the ability to use tutorial software only demonstrates the ability to use tutorial software. True ICT capability is much more than the ability to follow onscreen instructions and click on the button which says 'Next' or 'Continue'.

The most useful tool in assessment in ICT is the teacher's own observation of the child in all contexts and interaction with them about their work. In all of the resource settings we have discussed in this section, this presents real logistical difficulties and requires systematic planning and the use of other adults in order that it is carried out usefully. Many schools, for example, operate an assessment week with samples being collected across the curriculum at the same time, in each class, in each half term. Extra adults are sometimes drafted in to support the class teacher in this work. Collection of ICT evidence and observation could also be planned for in this way.

However, on teaching practice with all of the course demands being placed upon trainee teachers and their mentors and tutors, any assessment activity has to be focused and manageable as well as useful. The course requirements which follow the prescribed curriculum for initial teacher training will spell out the number of assessments to be made of children and at what particular level in each curriculum area.

It is important to bear in mind that a further difficulty is the collaborative nature of ICT. It is sometimes hard to separate out the individual contributions to a joint project. There will be times when this is irrelevant and unnecessary. However, whilst collaboration itself is usually to be encouraged, there comes a time, at the end of the year and, more formally, at the end of the relevant key stages, when a level of operating within the National Curriculum must be ascribed to an individual. It becomes important therefore to develop skilled observations of individual contributions to partner work in ICT. Developing skills in monitoring the situation in this way protects quieter, less dominant children from being overlooked.

The examples which follow detail two very different forms of assessment. The first, individual profiling, provides a means of systematically tracking an individual child in some detail. The second, whole-class snapshot, provides a means of measuring ICT capability at a very basic level in order to gain a picture of where each child in the class is at a given moment in time. They need to be employed together in order to gain the maximum benefit in terms of the assessment and planning cycle.

It is worth stating at this stage that the level descriptions of capability for a child are intended to be applied at the end of a key stage using a judgement of 'best fit'. That is to say, the teacher reads the descriptions and decides on a numerical level on the basis of observations and knowledge of the children in the class. The level descriptions for all subjects can be located at the back of the National Curriculum handbook. If, all year, there has been a sound, formative assessment process which informs the planning, backed by samples and observations, these end-of-key-stage judgements will be relatively easy to make and have a higher level of accuracy. In other words, they will be more meaningful to the child and her or his teachers and parents.

Individual profiling

Individual profiling of children in curriculum subjects provides a means of mapping their progress through the various work samples collected and observations made. It makes a link to the child's own view of their developing capabilities and a link back to planning, completing the planning and assessment cycle.

The following pro-forma is intended to be completed two or three times in a term and should take no longer than five or ten minutes, once it becomes familiar. Ideally, it should be completed with the child in discussion about a particular work sample. The number of these completed in a teaching practice would need to be negotiated in terms of the overall course requirements for assessment (which in turn depends on a negotiation with the Standards themselves). The questions next to each of the cells provide an *aide-mémoire* of how to complete the form. As you can see, the areas covered include the child's individual progress alongside notes about the school context and an opportunity to record the child's own response to the piece of work. It is intended that the same sheet is used for each child and that the columns are completed for each observation so that it is possible to check progress across the two or three observations made.

Date				
Name of child				
IT context (computer in class/network room, etc.)	Was the child working in the network room or on one machine? What was it?			
Software/web	Using software standalone or on the Internet?			
Type (tutorial CD, office tool, etc.)	If the child was using software, write the type here			
QCA or school unit if app.	Which QCA or school study units if any was the child using?			
Working with partner? Who?	Was the child working alone, with a peer, with the teacher, parent or other adult?			
Length of time	For how long?			
Confidence with hardware, mouse, keyboard	Rate the child's confidence with the hardware listed and/or with printers or other devices. Very, fairly, not very, needing support, etc.			
Software navigation (use of menus)	As above but for navigation within the particular piece of software			
File management... saving, opening, renaming work etc.	As above but for working with files, re-opening them, knowing where to find work, etc.			
Curriculum context. Using computer to support work in English, science, maths	How was the child operating within the curriculum context? Did the computer support the subject? Were there particular difficulties? Did the use of ICT help to improve the outcome?			
Child's view of their ICT	Ask the child about their view of themselves as a user of ICT. Were there significant things about this piece of work that pleased them?			
Give best fit level if appropriate	Using the level descriptors, if appropriate, make a best fit judgement of the child			
Where next?	What activities with ICT would move the child forward?			

The following is a blank copy for photocopying:

Date			
Name of child			
IT context (computer in class/network room, etc.)			
Software/web			
Type (tutorial CD, office tool, etc.)			
QCA or school unit if appropriate			
Working with partner? Who?			
Length of time			
Confidence with hardware, mouse, keyboard			
Software navigation (use of menus)			
File management… saving, opening, renaming work etc.			
Curriculum context. Using computer to support work in English, science, maths			
Child's view of their ICT			
Give best fit level if appropriate			
Where next?			

Whole-class snapshots

To gain a picture of the whole class over a shorter period of time, in order to map out their skills, knowledge and understanding of ICT, it would be useful to complete a very basic skills matrix. This is in no way suggested as a substitute for the detailed profiling and sampling suggested in the previous section. This gives you an overview very rapidly upon which you can build some basic planning. The more detailed observations of individual children will be needed to gauge more accurately the effectiveness of the planning in raising the achievement of the class.

Name	Date	Mouse	Keyboard skills	Switch on or logon	Switch off or logoff	Open	Save	Cut/ paste	Graphics	Indepen- dence	General comment

Make best-guess judgements on a consistent value scale in order to provide a snapshot of the children in the class. Remember that this is merely an *aide-mémoire* to help you write a short comment on the form for the rest of the class. The best practice in assessment is the longer form where curriculum contexts are taken into account alongside technical skill development. Use the longer format for the identified children.

Use a 1–4 scale for, e.g. mouse skills and keyboard skills, switching on/off, opening and saving, cutting/pasting, inserting graphics:
1 (not at all confident), 2 (developing confidence and accuracy), 3 (accurate and confident), 4 (very accurate and confident).

Assessing Early Years ICT

We saw in the separate planning section on Early Years settings that very young children are working in a different context, that of the Foundation Stage. The different areas for planning were mapped out.

The same applies to differentiating assessment for children learning with computers in the Early Years. The criteria will be the Early Learning Goals and the observations you make will be referenced to the six main areas.

- **Personal, social and emotional development.**
- **Communication, language and literacy.**

- **Mathematical development.**
- **Knowledge and understanding of the world.**
- **Physical development.**
- **Creative development.**

The activities which they undertake at the computer are drawn from these contexts. It follows that assessment should also be grounded in that experience.

The individual sheet described in the section above ('Individual profiling') is of potentially greater use in the Early Years setting than the 'whole-class snapshot'. With the more detailed observation sheet, the background to the activity and the grouping become the more significant fields in which to enter any observations. If you are working in this context, you may even find it easier than in the mainstream school since so much assessment and recording in Early Years setting depends on collating team observations of children across a period of time in different situations.

REFLECTIVE TASK

Assessment at Key Stages 1 and 2 or in the Foundation Stage

At Key Stages 1 and 2 or in the Foundation Stage, use the pro-forma for individual observations to look in detail at the work of three children of varying levels of ability.

Complete the pro-forma during a unit of work from the ICT scheme or from a subject scheme with heavy ICT Content (see table in relevant chapter above for ideas). Carry out three observations on each child.

Collect the samples and cross-reference your observations with them.

Did the assessment reveal any strengths and/or areas for development?

How helpful was the assessment?

Were there questions which you wished to see answered which were not on the form? If yes, what were they?

Were you able to track development through the lessons?

How did you differentiate your questioning for those children?

Auditing

After the lesson, discuss the outcomes with your mentor and/or professional tutor. If the lesson has allowed you to demonstrate evidence of achieving parts of any Standards for QTS you could attach the plan and any work examples to your audit and date it. Possible standards to reference include:

Q7

Reflect on and improve practice, and take responsibility for identifying and meeting developing professional needs.

Q8

Have a creative and constructively critical approach towards innovation, being prepared to adapt practice where benefits and improvements are identified.

Q11

Know the assessment requirements and arrangements for the subjects/curriculum areas you are trained to teach, including those relating to public examinations and qualifications.

Q12

Know a range of approaches to assessment, including the importance of formative assessment.

Q13

Know how to use local and national statistical information to evaluate the effectiveness of their teaching, to monitor the progress of those they teach and to raise levels of attainment.

Q22

Plan for progression across the age and ability range for which you are trained, designing effective learning sequences within lessons and across series of lessons and demonstrating secure subject/curriculum knowledge.

Q25

Teach lessons and sequences of lessons across the age and ability range for which they are trained in which they:

(a) use a range of teaching strategies and resources, including e-learning, taking practical account of diversity and promoting equality and inclusion;

(b) build on prior knowledge, develop concepts and processes, enable learners to apply new knowledge, understanding and skills and meet learning objectives;

(c) adapt their language to suit the learners they teach, introducing new ideas and concepts clearly, and using explanations, questions, discussions and plenaries effectively.

Q26

(a) Make effective use of a range of assessment, monitoring and recording strategies;

(b) Assess the learning needs of those they teach in order to set challenging learning objectives.

RESEARCH SUMMARY RESEARCH SUMMARY **RESEARCH SUMMARY**

Assessment and record keeping in ICT

Cook and Finlayson (1999) argue for the involvement of the child in recording progress in ICT. Tunstall and Gipps (1996) place great importance on the need to feed back to young children, identifying it as a 'prime requirement for progress in learning'. Both of these statements imply interaction and active involvement in the assessment process on the part of the child.

A SUMMARY OF **KEY POINTS**

This chapter has mapped out the main issues in trying to evaluate children's learning with ICT and with ICT in subjects. We have tried to suggest that the involvement of children in the process is important. We have provided some additional inputs on assessment in Early Years Settings. We have also explored the link between planning and assessment.

Moving on

Consider the wide range of assessment opportunities you have seen for primary ICT in subject teaching. In your induction year, how do you think you will manage the workload? Are there ways you can see in which ICT might be useful in assisting with formative and summative assessments of children? How might this work in practice? What sorts of equipment and training will you need? As you move into your career you will find INSET opportunities relating to new technology, in particular the use of media in the curriculum. Think about how this might be a way to support your assessment of learners.

FURTHER READING FURTHER READING **FURTHER READING** FURTHER READING

Becta Schools pages (2007) **schools.becta.org.uk/** Accessed 30 January 2007

DfES (2000a) *National Curriculum Handbook for Key Stages 1 and 2*. London: DfES

DfES Standards site **www.standards.dfes.gov.uk/** Accessed 30 January 2007

DfES Standards site – ICT Scheme (2003 version) **www.standards.dfes.gov.uk/schemes2/it/ ?view=get** Accessed 30 January 2007

DfES Interactive Planning tool (2007) **www.standards.dfes.gov.uk/primaryframeworks/planningtool/** Holding page accessed 30 January 2007

DfES primary Framework homepage (2007) **www.standards.dfes.gov.uk/primaryframeworks/** Accessed 30 January 2007

National Curriculum in Action – ICT pages (2007) **www.ncaction.org.uk/subjects/ict/inother.htm** Accessed 30 January 2007

National Curriculum online (2007) **www.nc.uk.net** Accessed 13 May 2007

Smith, H. (1999) *Opportunities for ICT in the primary school*. London: Trentham Books

Somekh, B. and Davis, N. (eds) (1997) *Using Information technology effectively in teaching and learning*. London: Routledge

Teachers' TV homepage (2007) **www.teachers.tv/** Accessed 30 January 2007

6
Researching primary ICT

Chapter objectives

This chapter aims to provide a brief summary of starting points for researching ICT in school and is aimed at those trainees in initial teacher education who may be writing assignments and/or doing some small-scale research project as part of a nested M level module or subject specialism. It covers the various ways in which ICT is monitored at national, school and local levels as a way into thinking about the context from an official standpoint. It then moves into some sources of information and research about learning with technology in order to help you situate your work within the context of some current research in ICT in education.

Sources of government monitoring and research into ICT in education

If you are training as an ICT specialist in primary schools or one day hoping to lead ICT in a primary school, it is worth knowing about the various ways in which ICT is monitored. That is to say, at the various levels, from the Department for Education and Skills to the local level and the school level, it is useful to know how ICT is measured and why and with what results.

The government used to publish an annual survey through the DfES which tracked the trends of ICT use and hardware buying in schools. You can find examples of this up to 2004 online after which point the reports are superseded and subsumed into the Becta annual reviews (see Becta schools and Becta ICT research, 2006).

The spending on educational ICT has been huge in recent years and the various initiatives associated with it have to be accountable and measurable. The 2004 ICT in schools survey found, amongst other statistics, that there was 'on average, in 2004, one computer for every 7.5 pupils in primary schools (as compared with 1 for every 17.6 in 1998)'. Since that time this figure will have reduced still further. In order to continue to have the latest figures on this you should consider adding Becta and DfES to your online bookmarks if you have not already done so.

The role of OFSTED in the context of ICT

The Office for Standards in Education (OFSTED) has a statutory duty to report on standards in education and teacher education across phases and across the curriculum. Every year, Her Majesty's Chief Inspector of Schools produces a summary report and commentary on inspection findings in the previous year which attempts to draw together trends and developments into a picture of education in England and Wales.

Each year in the Annual Report the Chief Inspector reports on different areas of the curriculum. The early reports, from 1996 and 1997 are quite critical of the implementation of teaching and learning with ICT in primary schools. There have been changes year on year but there is still evidence that the use of ICT in schools is highly variable and inconsistent. The report on inspections in 2005-06, for example, notes that:

> *Ofsted found that most schools in the survey made at least satisfactory curricular provision for ICT, including some balance between teaching ICT capability and its application across subjects. However, none of the schools surveyed embedded ICT to the extent that it was an everyday aspect of pupils' learning. Typically, pupils' use of ICT varied from subject to subject or from year to year.*
>
> (OFSTED, 2006)

We have seen the importance of a scheme of work as a map of the teaching and learning. Where schools do not have such a scheme in place, the same low level activities and skills are being rehearsed year on year and OFTSED is reporting that fact. You can find comments on these issues in the Annual Report for most years in some form. Similar comments arise in the 2005 special report by OFSTED, *Embedding ICT in schools*, which looked at the situation in more depth than the annual report and included in its summary the following comment:

> *The project highlighted continuing inconsistencies within and between schools. In particular, there was wide variation in the extent to which ICT was embedded in the work of schools, although ICT as a tool for learning was expanding in all.*
>
> (OFSTED, 2005)

However, the situation is changing and improving. Structures and support are coming into play in many areas which were not there before. There is still a long way to go and on your course you will notice that there are significant differences between schools in which you have been placed during your training, particularly if you move from one local authority (LA) to another. OFSTED have, in addition their criticisms, noted some positive changes taking place. In the same report quoted above you can find the following:

> *There were many good examples of ICT being used well to enhance teaching and learning in all types of school. Overall the schools had made most progress in resources and CPD and least in assessment.*
>
> (OFSTED, 2005)

School-level monitoring – senior managers, ICT co-ordinators

Senior managers have a role in leading and monitoring the curriculum. In most schools this is delegated to the subject co-ordinators. ICT co-ordinators may be given additional time during the week to monitor the curriculum for ICT. We have seen, however, in earlier chapters that there are as many different kinds of ICT co-ordinator as there are kinds of school organisation for ICT itself. It might be useful to carry out the activity in the following section and would be advisable if you are an ICT specialist in the primary phase:

PRACTICAL TASK PRACTICAL TASK PRACTICAL TASK PRACTICAL TASK

Monitoring and co-ordinating ICT in the school

This activity focuses on the people who impact on the organisation and use of ICT in the school. Find out who they are in your particular school situation. Interview them and discover more about their influence on the whole-school development for ICT.

You could ask them, sensitively, if they are considered to be members of the management team of the school (it is not a good idea to ask about salary scales unless this is volunteered).

Try to find out whether they are working solely on developing ICT or combining ICT with one or more of science, maths, technology or, less usually, English or a creative arts subject. It may even be part of a deputy head or assessment co-ordinator's remit.

For ICT co-ordinators or senior managers in charge of ICT, try to discover the following information about them.

Their training.

How they got the job.

What contact they have with their LA advisory team.

Their role in the management structure of the school.

Their budget.

How they pass on their expertise.

What sort of role they take in troubleshooting (Do they take on minor repairs themselves, or do they encourage others to learn more about the ICT in their school?).

Do they report faults or have a system for doing so?

Is there a service contract?

Crucially, is there a development plan for ICT and how was it constructed?

How do they involve parents and carers, classroom assistants, governors and others in ICT in the school?

Have they been or are they about to become involved in a whole-staff training programme for ICT (Did they benefit from an earlier scheme, e.g. the one funded by the NOF)?

What was the outcome of the most recent inspection in terms of ICT and how is the school addressing the issues?

Relate the findings to the development of ICT in your specialist subject (if it is not ICT). Are there policy statements or schemes of work which outline how ICT can be developed in the subject? Is there evidence to suggest that it is happening in the school?

REFLECTIVE TASK
REFLECTIVE TASK

Monitoring ICT in schools

If the above research into ICT co-ordination proves too difficult in terms of the school situation, try the following activity instead.

Browse the OFSTED and DfES websites. Find out about the latest inspection evidence on schools' ICT. Try the main sites for the national picture using a search string such as 'Survey of information technology in UK schools'. Visit your LA inspection report (if it exists) and discover what information there is about ICT support in the area. Then visit your placement school's OFSTED report and see how the school fits into the pattern of inspection evidence. Answer the following questions:

What is the ratio of computers to children in primary schools as measured by the most recent inspection evidence?

What is the trend in English schools' ICT inspection reports by OFSTED? Towards higher or lower standards?

How does your placement school perform in its most recent OFSTED report? Does the report match up with the current state of provision?

Find out about your specialist subject in relation to the ICT (if ICT is not your specialist subject). What does the national and local picture appear to be on the teaching of your subject with ICT?

Auditing

After the lesson, discuss the outcomes with your mentor and/or professional tutor. If the lesson has allowed you to demonstrate evidence of achieving parts of any Standards for QTS you could attach the plan and any work examples to your audit and date it.

Relevant texts: theory and practice and research into ICT in the classroom

The research boxes provided throughout this book provide starting points for identifying relevant critical literature. Your college will almost certainly supply you with a list of texts which give you a critical dimension to your understanding of ICT in the curriculum. Some of these will be books and periodicals. In other cases there are good sources of material on the Internet. The subject has a shorter history than others in the curriculum but has a growing, rich and diverse body of literature.

As the capacity and range of technology have changed over the years, the influence of a number of subject domains which were once seen as different have begun to converge. It was possible once to characterise the study of technology and education as a purely determinist activity which looked at outcomes for learners which have been 'determined' by their use of technology, usually in formal educational settings. This is no longer the case and you will find healthy discussion in the literature researching ICT in education of a range of different aspects of social and cultural factors in the use of technology. Some areas of research activity include some of the following.

- Technology and innovative pedagogy.
- The use by teachers and learners of online environments.
- Creativity, technology and education.
- Politics and technology – the selling of new technology in education.
- The use of computer games in educational settings, formal and informal.
- Digital video in education.
- The uses of social software (or web 2.0) in education.
- Interactive whiteboards and display technologies in education.
- Various emergent forms of literacy, such as media literacy, visual literacy, information literacy.

There is an introduction to research and debates in technology and education in another Learning Matters publication, *Education studies – an issues based approach* (See Potter, 2006 in Sharp, Hankin and Ward, 2006). In addition to these kinds of summaries there have been reports which have attempted to prove a direct causal link between networked technologies in schools and rising standards (Becta, 2002).

Your tutors or supervisors will point you in the direction of research tools which you will have access to through your college or training provider. A number of journals are published which you could explore for articles of use to you in your assignments and small-scale research projects. If you do not have access to the full text of these articles through your college online account, you could use the index of the particular title to search for abstracts and then approach your college for paper copies. Two titles of immediate usefulness are *Computers in Education* and *Technology, Pedagogy and Education*. Open-text searches on Google (UK) will find the index for these journals.

Journals and libraries aside, some useful, simpler online starting points for researching topics of interest in ICT in Education include the Becta research portal and Futurelab. On the Becta site you will find links to many of the research projects which have had direct or indirect input from them. The portal is hidden on the main page at the time of writing behind a link to 'partners'. One of the features of the web, as you will know from researching on it yourself, is that resources move location and you need to update your own links on a regular basis. Using Google (UK), or a similar search engine, you could enter the following string to find the Becta research pages: 'Becta partners – research'. Once there, you will see that it contains a number of useful resources grouped under the following lead line:

> *BECTA develops and disseminates robust evidence of emerging technology, of ICT's impact on education and of what works in the application of ICT to learning and teaching.*
>
> (BECTA research portal, 2006)

The Futurelab site, formerly NESTA Futurelab, promotes the innovative use of technology in education and includes a number of interesting and useful reports. For research purposes, the most useful section is a series of literature reviews commissioned by Futurelab and freely downloadable, the tagline for which is 'a series of reviews into areas such as thinking skills, games, e-assessment, mobile technologies' (Futurelab, 2006). A number of leading figures in research into ICT in education have put together sources which they regard as key to ways of thinking about technology and education and you can use the reviews as starting points for your own enquiry.

A SUMMARY OF **KEY POINTS**

> **OFSTED and other agencies monitor national trends in ICT in education.**

> **The situation is also monitored at ground level.**

> **A number of researchers and writers have tried different perspectives to understand the complex interrelationship between teachers, learners and ICT.**

Moving on

The field of technology in education is in a state of change as young learners begin to use technology in different ways in their own lives. This impacts on teaching and learning and also makes it a particularly interesting field to study within the context of teacher education and it is possible that your assignment or work related to your specialist interest could be of real use to you as a developing reflective teacher in your future career.

FURTHER READING FURTHER READING **FURTHER READING** FURTHER READING

Becta (2002) *ImpaCT2 – The impact of information and communication technologies on pupil learning and attainment*. Coventry: BECTA

Crook, C. (1996) *Computers and the collaborative experience of learning: a psychological perspective (International Library of Psychology)*. London: Routledge

Cuthell, J. (2002) *Virtual learning: the impact of ICT on the way young people work and learn*. London: Ashgate

Daniels, H. (ed.) (2005) *An introduction to Vygotsky*. London: Routledge

Gamble, N. and Easingwood, N. (eds.) (2000) *ICT and literacy: information and communications technology, media, reading and writing.* London: Continuum

Heppell, S. (2001) Preface in *ICT, pedagogy and the curriculum: subject to change*. A. Loveless and V. Ellis (eds). London: Routledge Falmer

Kempster, G. (2000) Skills for life: New meanings and values for literacies in *ICT and Literacy: Information and Communications Technology, Media, Reading and Writing.* Gamble, N. and Easingwood, N. (eds.) (2000) London: Continuum

Loveless, A. (2003) *The role of ICT.* London: Continuum

McFarlane, A. (1997) *Information technology and authentic learning*. London: Routledge

Papert, S. (1993) *Mindstorms (second edition).* Hemel Hempstead: Harvester Wheatsheaf

Selwyn, N. (2002) *Telling tales on technology – Qualitative studies of technology and education.* London: Ashgate

Twining, P. (2002) Conceptualising computer use in education: introducing the computer practice framework (CPF), *British Educational Research Journal, 28(1), 95–110*

Wenger, E. (1999) *Communities of practice: learning, meaning and identity (learning in doing: social, cognitive and computational perspectives).* Cambridge: Cambridge University Press

Section B
Introducing applications and technologies

Generic software is software that is considered to be content-free and consequently has a wide range of applications across the primary curriculum. In the same way a lot of ICT equipment beyond the standard desktop computer is now available at a cost which schools can afford to enrich the children's work in all subject areas. This section explores some key categories of software and hardware that now should be part of every child's experience at primary school.

Each chapter includes:
- a brief introduction and definition;
- reference to relevant sections of the National Curriculum for ICT;
- reference to related units of the scheme of work for ICT;
- background information as appropriate;
- examples of the ways in which teachers may work with the software or hardware;
- details of the specific functions of the software or hardware with which teachers should be familiar;
- examination of the contribution the software or hardware can make to teaching and learning;
- exploration of any limitations of the software or hardware;
- examples of ways in which the software or hardware can be utilised in the teaching and learning of the core subjects;
- references and further reading.

Topics covered are:
- word processing and desktop publishing;
- graphics software;
- graphing programs;
- databases and spreadsheets;
- digital video;
- digital cameras;
- virtual learning environments;
- mobile technologies;
- the Internet;
- sound and music.

The chapters in this section of the book will inform your development towards meeting the ICT-specific aspects of the professional standards. Although, because of the great diversity available, subject-related educational software cannot be treated comprehensively here, it is helpful to recognise how it differs in nature from generic software. Content is obviously a major element of such packages, presented in a variety of imaginative ways: adventure games and other modelling investigations, multimedia encyclopaedias and other reference works all ultimately intended to convey knowledge and understanding of their themes.

Software covered in this section takes on a certain character. Its freedom from a particular context means that the child may well start working with a *tabula rasa*, a clean slate on which she or he must fashion a finished product. The blank page of a word processor or art software epitomises this situation. The child may then go through a creative journey which culminates in an outcome that represents the harnessing of the software's capability to the child's purpose. However, just as with a blank paper page, the child needs support from the teacher. This is necessary not just to set the objective and guide the process, but perhaps also by providing the scaffolding, such as a writing frame, that enables the child to start in the first place.

The hardware that features in this section is similarly broad in its scope, and gives rise to all sorts of creative opportunities, some of which are described in the chapters, some of which you will think of yourself.

You can find the relevant references in *Professional standards for teachers* (TDA/DfES, 2007) as follows:

Q14
(b) Know how to use skills in literacy, numeracy and ICT to support their teaching and wider professional activities.

Q19
(c) Use a range of teaching strategies and resources, including e-learning, taking practical account of diversity and promoting equality and inclusion.

Q19
(d) Provide opportunities for learners to develop their literacy, numeracy and ICT skills.

However, ICT may have a bearing on imaginative fulfilment of many of the other Standards. For example, that trainees should 'Have a knowledge and understanding of a range of teaching, learning and behaviour management strategies and know how to use and adapt them, including how to personalise learning and provide opportunities for all learners to achieve their potential' (Q10) could well be met in part by thoughtful use of ICT to support the individual child's learning needs and interest.

Similarly, ideas from the chapter on mobile technologies could contribute to the requirement that trainees 'Provide homework or other out-of-class work to sustain learners' progress and to extend and consolidate their learning' (Q20) and 'Establish a purposeful and safe learning environment conducive to learning and identify opportunities for learners to learn in out of school contexts' (Q25).

Q19 (b) requires that trainees 'Plan and teach lessons and sequences of lessons that are well-organised, demonstrating secure subject knowledge relevant to the curricula across the age and ability range for which they are trained'. This Standard applies to ICT as much as any subject, and it is hoped that the following chapters will help trainees gain the appropriate subject knowledge to enable them to teach effective ICT to the children in their primary class, as well at to use ICT in appropriate cross-curricular contexts.

7
Word processing and desktop publishing

Chapter objectives

Word processing is a key medium through which we communicate information using ICT. It is also one of the most common uses of ICT globally and probably remains the foremost implementation of ICT in our schools. Developments in technology and the ways in which we communicate have blurred the distinctions between word processing and desktop publishing (DTP) to the extent that there is usually now considerable overlap in functionality between the two types of software. Additionally many word processors and desktop publishing packages have integrated multimedia elements – images, of course, but also sound, video and animation. The implication is that the same software can be used for presentation both electronically and in paper-based form.

This chapter explores the features of these types of software and their contribution to teaching and learning in the primary school. The principal consideration is the scope of current word processing software. Exploration of the desktop publishing features now included in most word processing software is also covered. Teachers' professional use of word processing is reviewed in the context of administration and management as well as teaching and learning.

What is word processing?
Word processing software allows the entry, storage, retrieval and manipulation of text, and increasingly graphics and sound, in an electronic format. It facilitates a variety of processes which can support and enhance communication.

What is desktop publishing?
Desktop publishing software is concerned with the design of documents containing text and graphics, usually with a publication in mind. While obviously content is important, to a greater extent than when word processing, the desktop publisher will have in mind the overall 'look' of the finished document, and the impact that this will create. Hence initially desktop publishing on a computer was primarily the domain of professional designers in the press and elsewhere. However, the accessibility of DTP software, in terms both of cost and user interface, has increased to the extent that DTP is now within the reach of any computer user.

What do the programmes of study for Key Stages 1 and 2 include?

At Key Stage 1 children should be taught to enter and store information (1b), to use text, tables, images and sounds to develop their ideas (2a) and to select from and add to existing information (2b). They should also be taught to share their ideas by presenting information in a variety of forms (3a) and to present their work effectively (3b).

At Key Stage 2, children should be taught how to prepare information (1b), how to organise and reorganise it (2a), how to share and exchange it (3a), as well as consider its suitability for its audience and its quality (3b).

At all stages children should be taught to review, modify and evaluate their work as it progresses (4a, 4b and 4c).

What does the ICT scheme of work include?

At Key Stage 1, word processing features in Unit 1A (An introduction to modelling), Unit 1B (Using a word bank), Unit 1D (Labelling and classifying) and Unit 2A (Writing stories: communicating information using text).

At Key Stage 2, word processing features specifically in Unit 3A (Combining text and graphics) and Unit 4A (Writing for different audiences). Unit 3E (Email) provides opportunities to transfer and apply relevant learning.

What do teachers need to know about word processing?

Teachers apply their knowledge, skills and understanding of word processing in two distinct ways. One is concerned with teaching and learning with and about word processing, and the other relates to the use of word processing to support more general aspects of the professional role.

It could happen that teachers use different word processors for these different purposes. Several word processors have been marketed specifically for primary age children, and feature facilities such as simple, easily modified interfaces, speech facilities and word banks. Alternatively, schools have adopted Microsoft Word, possibly in its adapted form, RM Talking First Word, which enables the teacher (or child) to set levels of complexity for the interface along the same lines as the word processors designed for children. There are arguments in favour of both approaches. Some educators would prefer software designed for children, while others would argue that drawing children into the use of adults' 'industry standard' software has benefits.

Whichever word processing package is used in the classroom, teachers need to be competent and confident users. This does not mean that they need to know the answer to every question. Rather they should have a working knowledge of the software so that they are able to plan, support and assess appropriate activities as well as predict likely difficulties and assist with problem-solving.

Word processing will impact in several different ways in the classroom.

- **Selecting appropriate opportunities – in which word processing software can facilitate, enhance or extend children's learning, such as the importance of presentation in communication. In some instances the focus will be on teaching and learning in ICT (how to enlarge text, make newspaper-type columns or add a border to a poster), in others ICT will be used as a resource in the teaching and learning of another curriculum area (writing for a specific audience).**

- Making explicit links between related knowledge, skills and understanding – word processing is closely associated with literacy and language work at all levels, and as a consequence has a contribution to make across the primary curriculum.
- Modelling appropriate use of ICT – for instance, scribing and amending shared writing with the whole class or a group using the interactive whiteboard.
- Demonstrating or intervening – for example, inserting an image into a word processing document, cutting and pasting, or deciding how and when to use the spell-checker. Explicit teaching of word processing knowledge, skills and understanding requires demonstration and intervention as with any other curriculum topic. Children may gain word processing skills by themselves, but without the guidance and direction of their teacher the acquisition of such capability will be haphazard.

To support their wider professional duties, teachers use word processing in a number of contexts.

- Preparing resources – such as an electronic writing frame to support writing in history, a word bank to support an individual child or a troubleshooting help-sheet or interactive display to improve children's independence when using the spell-checker. Alternatively teachers may use ICT to prepare resources for activities which do not involve children utilising ICT, such as a shared text printed on acetate for use with an OHP, a range of three differentiated worksheets or number lotto cards to support a group mathematics activity. Some of these examples focus on using ICT as a tool for teaching and learning (in another curriculum area), others focus on the teaching and learning of ICT.
- Administering and managing – for example, correspondence with parents, creating and amending schemes of work or school policies, using templates to prepare weekly planning, recording children's progress and producing banners for display boards.

The list below attempts to identify the knowledge, skills and understanding of primary word processing software teachers need in order to teach effectively with and about word processing:

- creating, opening, saving, closing, deleting and printing documents;
- selecting font, font size, colour, style (italic, bold), line spacing and justification;
- inserting, deleting, selecting, cutting, copying, pasting and undoing;
- utilising help;
- inserting bullet points, tables, clip art, borders, shading and columns;
- altering page orientation (landscape, portrait), background colour, page size and margins;
- altering defaults;
- forcing page breaks;
- utilising tabs and indents;
- utilising spelling- and grammar-checkers (including how to switch on and off), thesaurus, print preview, highlighter and talking facilities (including how to switch on and off) and find and replace;
- connecting alternative input devices (overlay keyboards, touch screens);
- constructing and utilising on-screen word banks;
- inserting page numbers;
- inserting text, graphics, tables and documents from other applications.

The list below details additional knowledge, skills and understanding that teachers need in order to utilise word processing efficiently and effectively to support themselves as professionals (it should be read in conjunction with the list above):

- inserting symbols, headers and footers;
- creating macros and templates;
- utilising dynamic links between documents;
- customising the word processor;
- merging documents;
- formatting graphics;
- protecting documents.

What are the key features of a word processor?

Word processing software has become increasingly sophisticated in the range of features offered. Concomitantly the interface has become progressively more user-friendly and accessible. As with any application it is important to have an understanding of the capabilities and limitations of the software in order to use it effectively. This is not to say that it is essential or even preferable to be familiar with all the possible functions of the software. If you consider your personal use of a word processor such as Microsoft Word, it is likely that on a regular basis you use only as small proportion of its functionality, while nevertheless using it as an effective and efficient aid to communication.

Word processors, like any category of software, are defined by their common features. These features could be listed, but it is important to understand that there may be good reasons to restrict the number of functions available. For example, if the software is to be used by young children, not likely to wish to insert footnotes or track the modification of a document over time, then these facilities may not be included, so reducing the complexity of the interface. In different circumstances, in a hand-held portable computer (palmtop) functionality may have to be balanced by available memory.

In general terms the key features of word processing software can be categorised as follows:

Editing. Editing features allow the entry and manipulation of text or images, such as insertion and deletion at any point in the document, cutting, copying and pasting to reorder and reorganise. It is important in the context of word processing for children to grasp the concept of provisionality: that anything created is easily modified or changed.

Formatting. Formatting features allow the utilisation of a range of fonts, text sizes, text styles (such as italicising), page size, page orientation (landscape and portrait), tables, boxes and other graphics options.

Tools. There is a range of tools which complement and enhance the editing and formatting features of word processors. These include spelling and grammar checkers, speech capability, templates and word counting.

As indicated earlier, many word processors now incorporate desktop publishing and even multimedia and web-authoring tools; Textease (from Softease) and Microsoft Word are examples. The advantage of such packages is that children (and teachers) are able to extend their ICT capabilities without the need to learn new software for specific tasks. Instead they can build on their existing knowledge, skills and understanding.

What do word processors have to contribute to teaching and learning?

Children using word processors can utilise the features of the software in two key respects:

- **to develop their ideas and make things happen (to modify their work, try things out and compare alternatives);**
- **to exchange and share information (to edit and review as well as design and present their work).**

Likewise teachers can use word processors to prepare and modify teaching resources, to model effective use of ICT, to demonstrate techniques as well as to facilitate some of the administrative aspects of their work.

Word processing and the writing process

The obvious context through which to explore the contribution word processing can make to teaching and learning is writing. If the writing process is broken down into its elements then we can see what word processors offer at each stage.

The writing process can be considered to comprise:

- **planning and drafting: the initial composition of the ideas, the facts, the emotions being communicated through the writing;**
- **editing: attention will be given to:**
  - **the structural aspects of writing, such as sequencing and style (text level work);**
  - **the technical aspects of writing, such as sentence construction, punctuation, grammar and spelling (word and sentence level work);**
- **proofreading: the final revision to check for errors in spelling, punctuation and grammar, and for any omissions and repetitions;**
- **presentation: formatting the material to offer a neat, clear final copy. At this point – and probably not before – the focus will be on the layout and look of the writing.**

When children write by hand they must be resigned to a number of complete reworkings of their texts, or must address each element of the writing process simultaneously. While this latter is a valuable life skill in certain situations, it can also be a considerable challenge. For example, attention to presentation may detract from attention to the content. That editing on the computer is so easy, and that the software facilitates presentation to such an extent, are key motivations for the use of a word processor in the classroom and beyond. Let's look at word processing's contribution in more detail.

Word processing's contribution

Planning and drafting (developing ideas and making things happen)

Unless carefully guided, children tend to write sentence by sentence with little overview of the text as a whole, rarely re-reading previous sentences to check the progress of the narrative. Indeed many children find difficulty retaining the thread of their thoughts while they also grapple with the physical aspects of writing, be they handwriting or keyboard entry. For some the challenge of re-reading their writing may prove a further distraction. Many of the word processors available for primary age children incorporate a speech facility, for example, Talking First Word (RM), Textease (Softease), Talking Write Away (BlackCat). This can be set to read each sentence as it is completed (the full stop is placed) or to re-read the entire narrative as required (by clicking). The speech facility may thereby enable children to focus on the progress of their writing as a continuous whole, rather than as a series of disjointed statements.

A range of text input strategies may be utilised in association with word processing software to enable children's speed of writing to match better their thought processes. These include overlay keyboards, word banks, and even voice, and are discussed in greater depth below.

Clearly keyboard skills, particularly speed relative to handwriting, are also relevant. It is suggested that children engage in the writing process for longer when ICT is involved, thus producing extended and perhaps more sophisticated narratives.

The use of writing templates (electronic writing frames), an extension of the widely used non-fiction writing strategy, may assist children to produce writing, providing the support which they need in order to embark on the project.

Editing – structural (developing ideas and making things happen)

Once text has been entered into a word processor there is clearly much scope for revision and development to enhance the quality of the writing. Since making alterations will require thought and some manipulative skill, but not a lengthy re-write by hand, children can experiment with a view to improvement. Text can be re-sequenced, re-phrased, extended and enriched. Meaning can be clarified. Attention can be paid to style, structure, genre, audience and purpose. Alternatives can be explored and compared, changes can be reversed. The act of writing becomes a process rather than an end point; a temporal dimension is introduced, with the opportunity for reflection, even research to influence subsequent amendments. Printouts can be a useful record of the stages of the process and can provide a teaching and learning opportunity in themselves. A text thus revised should far better reflect the writer's intentions than a first draft that has not undergone revision. Children will be encouraged to write more when the prospect of subsequent redrafting is not associated with the physical effort of copying out by hand.

However, children may not automatically use the editing possibilities afforded by word processors to improve the quality of their writing in this way. In practice they are easily distracted by the technical editing opportunities associated with presentation rather than content. Refined outcomes depend on focused and explicit teaching and task-setting.

Editing – technical (developing ideas and making things happen)

Perhaps the most obvious contribution that word processing can make to the writing process is the opportunity for children to focus in the initial stages of a writing activity (composing) on communicating ideas, safe in the knowledge that attention can be paid to grammar, spelling and punctuation (as well as structure and style) at a later stage. Word processors now incorporate functions to address each of these phases, but the built-in tools do not even have to be utilised for children to review and amend these aspects of their word-processed work. Frequently a range of such secretarial adjustments can result merely from re-reading the text, again safe in the knowledge that changes will not result in lengthy re-writing or untidy work. Often this re-reading and the selection of items for amendment can be done away from the computer on printouts. This arrangement serves to maximise effective use of computer resources, but equally importantly, it may be easier to see typographical errors on paper than on screen. If word processors are to provide the opportunity for children to write in a sustained and purposeful way, drafting and redrafting work, then children need access to the range of facilities word processing has to offer. This includes printing out and using drafts of writing in progress, rather than printing only when writing is judged to be finished. Pedagogic considerations should not be sacrificed to financial constraints.

Presenting (exchanging and sharing information)

The options for presentation through word processing are practically endless, and nowadays it is in this area that the overlap with what was formerly the province of DTP software is most pronounced. Children can adjust the font and size of their text to be accommodated in the space available, in keeping with the genre of the work, the intended method of presentation (display on the wall, for instance) and the audience. Colour can be added, as can borders, backgrounds and bullet points. Text can be arranged in columns to replicate newspaper or magazine layout. One of the most significant developments in word processing software is the facility to incorporate images, be they clip art, children's compositions in drawing and painting software, digital photographs or images scanned or copied and pasted from other locations such as the world wide web or CD-ROMs (subject to copyright). We live in an age of changing and evolving literacies, in which children are surrounded by presentations of high quality, so it is important that they too have access to the means through which to communicate their ideas. Teachers similarly need to take advantage of presentation features to provide good models as well as visually engaging resources. However, care must be taken to ensure that children realise the value that teachers place on the content of writing relative to its presentation. While good presentation can significantly enhance communication, it is usually not the primary learning outcome of a writing activity.

There is evidence that for some children being able to word-process their writing, at least some of the time, makes a substantial contribution to the development of self-esteem and confidence in their own abilities, a key determinant in children's progress. As previously indicated, the physical effort involved in handwriting at times may be an active deterrent to the creative process. For some children the struggle to provide tidy or even legible work may seem insurmountable. Access to a word processor may allow such children to produce writing which they feel can stand alongside that of their peers. They may also be enabled to communicate what they really want to say, but may not be able to commit effectively to paper by hand.

Progression of knowledge, skills and understanding

We have already alluded to the range of word processing software available, with the most significant contrast being in packages designed for children compared with those intended for adults working in business environments. This diversity in turn leads to there being variety in functionality among different word processors, and so differences in the ease with which particular outcomes are achieved. For example, Microsoft Word has a button to create bullet points which is situated clearly and conveniently on the Formatting toolbar, while finding a command for a bullet point in some children's word processors may be difficult or impossible. It is consequently problematic to attempt to identify skills development, and in particular to link skills development with levels of attainment or year groups.

With this proviso in mind, the following progression broadly corresponds with the ICT scheme of work and may provide a useful point of reference. Notice that the emphasis is on what the children are doing – the process – rather than the outcome.

Reception Year 1	Children begin to enter text and graphics via keyboard, overlay keyboard and on-screen word bank.
Year 2 Year 3	Children begin to edit text using the mouse, delete or backspace keys; to use the shift key; to alter font, font size and colour; to re-size graphics.
Year 4	Children begin to edit text using cut, copy and paste; to use underlining, bold and italicising; to use search and replace; to use spell-checkers; to import text and graphics from other documents; to use tables.
Year 5 Year 6	Children begin to select and utilise the full range of features as appropriate to their requirements independently; to independently utilise on-screen help and other problem-solving strategies.

A possible progression of word processing and desktop publishing skills

RESEARCH SUMMARY RESEARCH SUMMARY **RESEARCH SUMMARY**

Helen Smith (1999) identifies some specific and particular knowledge young children need in order to use word processors. Some of this knowledge is quite different from that needed to write by hand, for instance:

- that a space must be entered after each word, but not before punctuation marks such as full stops and commas;
- that the shift key provides access to capital letters and some punctuation;
- that the backspace can be used to correct errors;
- that text wraps around automatically onto the next line and that line breaks can be forced using the Enter/Return key.

She also details knowledge necessary for the basic editing of word-processed work:

- that the mouse is used to position the cursor (caret) and the importance of this;
- that arrow keys, page up, home, etc. can be used to move around the text;
- the use of strip highlighting for copying and pasting, cutting, etc.

To this should perhaps be added:

- the value of the undo function.

What are the capabilities and limitations of word processing?

Text entry

Currently most text entry into word processing (and other) software is effected by use of the standard QWERTY keyboard. Supplementary technology, such as overlay keyboards, touch screens and word banks, can be deployed to support children entering text. In some circumstances it is appropriate to use adult scribes (amanuenses). Voice input is available, too, and its accuracy has improved greatly of late. These alternatives to the keyboard often have an important role to play, particularly in SEN contexts. However, it remains that the keyboard itself is the predominant input mechanism for text.

Developing keyboard skills which facilitate text entry and other aspects of ICT use would seem to be a worthwhile investment for the future. Yet, despite the self-evident importance of text entry in primary ICT, there is little consensus about how keyboard skills should best be developed. Teachers have expressed concern over the inefficiency of 'hunt and peck' typing and, particularly in the early stages of keyboard use, the relative time required to enter text. It can be argued that children need to learn keyboard familiarity early on in their computer use, otherwise typing will take more time and concentration than handwriting the equivalent text. Timing is crucial because once habits are learned it is very hard to change them. If children do not develop skills which make word processing accessible as an activity they will not be able to take advantage of the opportunities word processing provides to enhance communication. Keyboard skills do feature increasingly in Individual Education Plans (IEPs) of children with statements of special educational needs, particularly where the IEP also provides for the regular personal use of a portable word processor or computer.

Some knowledge, skills and understanding relating to text entry have already been discussed. There is a wide range of software available dedicated to the development of children's keyboard skills. In addition there are paper-based materials which provide keyboard familiarisation exercises. These can be used with word processing software or even paper keyboards for children to practise either in the classroom or at home.

Most of these strategies focus on **touch-typing**, learning to use the full range of fingers to access the standard keyboard, with the aim of being able to use the keyboard without looking first to locate letters. When compared with the commitment required to gain some mastery of a musical instrument, for instance, touch-typing may not appear as such an unattainable goal, and some children will particularly benefit from practice in hand–eye co-ordination. However, touch typing as taught to secretaries and other adults is based on the span and stretch of a full-size adult hand, and for younger children modified strategies will be more appropriate. These include:

- **knowledge and use of the 'home' keys (*asdf* for the left hand and *jkl* for the right; *f* and *j* often have a raised dot or line on the keyboard to help the fingers in locating them);**
- **encouraging the use of the first fingers of both hands, and then of at least two fingers on each hand, the thumb for the space bar and the little fingers for the Shift key;**
- **the use of the number pad, usually located to the right of the keyboard, for the entry of numbers.**

For younger children stickers to replace the standard capital letters of the keyboard with their lowercase equivalents are available, and may simplify early familiarisation.

When schools are devising their schemes of work for ICT, consideration should be given to the enhancement of children's keyboard skills and the identification of progression. Clearly there is an important role for teachers in the diagnosis and remedy of inefficient or ineffective keyboard techniques.

The physical demands that handwriting places on children and the consequent contribution word processors can make to writing when some of these are removed has already been discussed. However, it is worth remembering that some children (and adults) may prefer to write by hand or may prefer to do certain, perhaps more personal, types of writing by hand.

REFLECTIVE TASK

Think about your own use of word processing. Do you edit directly on screen, or are there circumstances in which you prefer to prepare a handwritten draft initially? Talk with other adults about their choice of approach. What implications do the differences you identify have for teaching children?

PRACTICAL TASK PRACTICAL TASK PRACTICAL TASK PRACTICAL TASK

Research the development of keyboard skills and potential teaching and learning strategies.

Evaluate some of the software and paper-based materials designed to assist the development of children's keyboard skills.

Evaluate your own keyboard skills and design a strategy to enhance them if necessary.

Overlay keyboards have been available in schools for many years. Using a serial link the overlay keyboard is an external input device that can be used as an alternative to, or in conjunction with, a standard keyboard. It is programmed such that, when a particular area is touched, a letter, image, word, sentence or paragraph is entered (the same principle is used at some retail tills, for example in fast-food outlets). In the classroom, different overlays can be constructed for different purposes, typically designed on paper or thin card. The overlay is designed and organised into areas representing the effect intended by touching them, and then the keyboard itself is programmed to correspond. For instance, a picture of a horse on the overlay could result in the input of the word 'horse' into a word processor when the area is pressed. Some software comes with pre-programmed keyboard overlays, for example to support writing activities related to talking books. Teachers may also make their own overlays using the editing software that is usually provided with the overlay keyboard itself. This process does take time, though soon it becomes quicker. Designing and making overlays locally allows them to be customised to the requirements of particular activities or individuals. Overlay keyboards are particular well suited to Key Stage 1 to support writing activities and at all stages for children with certain special educational needs.

Word banks provide some of the functionality of overlay keyboards. These are typically integrated within a children's word processor, and, quite simply, facilitate the choice of appropriate vocabulary (and, by association, spelling). Word banks can be quickly prepared by the teacher to support specific activities; equally a graduated range can provide differentiated support. For instance, a word bank of specific vocabulary could be used in the recording and reporting of a geographical enquiry, enabling children to concentrate or articulating their understanding rather than being diverted by the spelling of new words. Equally children may access personalised word banks.

Most primary word processing packages now include a word bank facility and these are generally easier to prepare than keyboard overlays. Another advantage is that they do not require any additional space around the computer by comparison with the overlay keyboard, which might have an A4 or even A3 footprint. On the other hand, word banks are sometimes limited to text entry. Even more important, for some types of special educational need, standard keyboard and mouse input may not be an option for a child.

Clicker (Crick) is an interesting and valuable on-screen alternative to the overlay keyboard, with at the same time greater versatility than a conventional word bank. Unlike a word bank, Clicker is separate software (in fact, a whole suite of software) that can be used in conjunction with a word processor (and some other applications). 'Grids' can be prepared by the teacher (or children) to the same effect as overlays, dividing the workspace into text, images, sound and even video and animations. Crick have also developed a wide range of ready-made grids to support established curriculum activities such as the Oxford Reading Tree materials.

The grid occupies part of the computer screen space, appearing as a separate window, and the children make selections, usually with the mouse.

Touch screens, while still quite expensive and somewhat delicate, can be used in conjunction with word banks or Clicker to assist text or graphic entry. In these contexts, they may be critical in overcoming physical obstacles posed to some children by the standard keyboard and mouse.

Adult scribes are used to assist children with emergent writing and there is no reason why this practice cannot be extended to word processing. This arrangement can provide another strategy to assist children during the composing phase of the writing, allowing them to concentrate on the communication of ideas. Equally an adult scribe (or the teacher) could record contributions from a whole-class discussion, quickly printing and distributing them to groups to facilitate a follow-up activity.

Voice recognition software has been available for some time (and is now incorporated as standard in Microsoft Windows) but has proved difficult to implement in practice, partly because of the necessity for the software to recognise the particular inflexions of individual users. This involves training the software by reading prepared texts and lists of words and phrases. The software builds up a profile of how words and sounds are pronounced by the user.

Although invaluable in some special needs contexts, voice recognition software has yet to arrive in primary schools as a mainstream technology. The need to spend time training the software is one obstacle, but there is also the more mundane concern of background noise which will interfere with the process.

Speaking word processors

Most word processors designed for the primary school now incorporate a speech facility. They are usually referred to as 'talking' word processors. Since talk carries connotations of a dialogue or discussion, 'speaking' may be a more accurate description, but the increased interaction between a child and a word processor which has a speech facility does indeed carry some of the characteristics of conversation, in which the child responds to what is being said.

Speaking word processors can be used to assist children's writing by reading back each sentence as it is completed, or the entire narrative so far, reminding children of what they have written and prompting them to take the writing forward. It is suggested that the writing of children who are still emerging as readers may as a result be more coherent. Similarly, the computer will read back what the children have actually written, as opposed to what they thought or wanted to write, alerting them to opportunities for revision. This support clearly works to provide word level feedback, too.

RESEARCH SUMMARY RESEARCH SUMMARY RESEARCH SUMMARY

Becta (2006a) has drawn together a series of case studies which illustrate how word processing can support early writers, and also those pupils who are struggling with writing for a variety of reasons. Various approaches involving a talking word processor and predictive word-processing are explored. It is worth making the point that the sometimes dramatic impact that technology can make for children with disabilities may also help other children make gains too.

If used indiscriminately, speaking word processors can be a distraction both for children writing electronically and for those working close by. Children need to be clear how the speech can assist them to develop their writing and when and where not to use it. Choosing the appropriate settings (whole words or sentences, individual letters and sounds) is also important. Explicit communication of learning outcomes and classroom protocols is essential for such tools to be used effectively – for instance, completing a first draft and then listening to the computer read the text to assist with the identification of errors and opportunities for improvement. Headphones may also be useful for individual work.

Teachers need to understand and make explicit to children the limitations of the speech facility. Words are uttered through the word processor by concatenating small chunks of recorded sound that correspond to the phonemes represented by letters or short combinations of letters. This can lead to the speech facility occasionally failing to pronounce properly words that are correctly spelled. Greater accuracy is provided when the sound database is extended to the point that it includes whole words, but this obviously increases the database's size (and the production cost). As an aside, talking books, which allow children to click on words to hear them pronounced, work on the same principle, but the publisher's necessary sound inventory is limited to the text used in the books.

Children will enjoy challenging the software with words that it is not programmed to pronounce, and will play games mimicking the robotic-sounding speech, or seeing what happens when they type 'naughty' words.

PRACTICAL TASK PRACTICAL TASK PRACTICAL TASK PRACTICAL TASK

Explore the speech facility of a primary word processing package to find out how to change the settings (when the word processor will speak). Listen to the individual sounds and blends as read by the machine in order to establish its limitations. Plan for a pair or small group to reinforce or extend a stated literacy objective using the speech facility. What are the issues surrounding the use of headphones when using a speaking word processor?

Spell-checkers and thesauruses

Spell-checkers can be useful to draw attention to possible errors, though they are far from infallible. Concern has been expressed about over-reliance on such tools which can act as a disincentive to children to improve spelling. Additionally, used indiscriminately, spell-checkers may not only want to correct spellings which do not require correction (are merely not within the spell-checker's memory) but more importantly provide a distraction to writers in the early stages of the writing process. Much time can be wasted adjusting and readjusting spellings, diverting children's attention from the ideas they are seeking to convey. Most spell-checkers allow for new words to be added and teachers should make use of this facility to ensure that the vocabulary associated with current curriculum work is recognised by the word processor. Some watchfulness should be used in encouraging children to add new words – perhaps these should first be checked by the teacher or learning support assistant, to avoid the obvious difficulties associated with inaccurate suggestions being offered by the spell-checker.

Spell-checkers, like speech facilities, may be easily turned off. It may be appropriate for children to complete their initial writing and only then use the spell-checker. Teachers must employ discretion about when and to what extent these facilities should be used. A child in the early stages of writing development may be undermined by accusatory highlighting or underlining appearing on almost every word. The spell-checker may prove to be no use at all in decoding emergent spelling, or that of children with specific difficulties such as dyslexia. If too many words are identified as misspelled, and some of these may after all not be, there is little real opportunity for the writer to focus sufficiently to improve spelling. On the other hand, there can often be benefit in children independently working to improve their writing before submitting it to the teacher for assessment.

A spell-checker may provide for a valuable learning experience in itself where unfamiliar words are suggested, particular if used in association with a dictionary or thesaurus, enriching vocabulary. Likewise, **thesauruses** can be used as part of a structured learning activity to promote independence.

CLASSROOM STORY

This is a true story. A Year 4 boy, David, was sitting at the computer typing into the word processing program as series of 'j's:

jjjjjjjjjjjjj

His teacher, naturally curious, went up to him and asked what he was doing. The answer came, 'Oh, I'm doing my handwriting practice, but this week I thought I would do it on the computer.'

Grammar- and style-checkers

For similar reasons to those discussed in relation to spell-checkers, grammar- or style-checkers, though generally helpful, need to be treated with some caution, especially in software which originated outside the UK where syntactic conventions may be different. The grammar-checkers in many adults' word processors were originally designed for the business market, and the suggestions made reflect this. Additionally, they are unable to evaluate usage in context. Some grammar-checkers can be customised so that they will pick up particular errors and overlook others, and can be very useful for identifying overlong sentences or inappropriate use of apostrophes.

Portable computers

Word processing software is frequently used in conjunction with portable computers. There is a range of portable machines available, including the following.

Notebooks/laptops. These are portable versions of desktop machines, running from the mains or rechargeable batteries. They run standard software and usually now have multi-media capability. However, users working at speed often find the laptop keyboard less ergonomically convenient as it is not raked. A mouse and standard keyboard can be attached if preferred.

Tablet PCs and slates. Over the last few years educationalists have been showing increased interest in the opportunities to use tablet PCs in teaching contexts. These come in a variety of forms. At their most sophisticated, tablet PCs have all the functionality of a laptop, to which is added the possibility of working with a stylus directly onto the screen. The stylus controls the pointer, but also gives alternatives for text entry. This can be done either by handwriting with the stylus onto the screen, with the handwriting converted to word-processed text by 'hand print' optical character recognition software, or through an on-screen keyboard. Cheaper, but more rugged, tablet PCs are available without the laptop keyboard, and it is these that are more aptly referred to as slates. However, the terms may be seen used interchangeably.

Palmtops, handhelds and PDAs (personal digital assistants). Palmtops are much smaller than laptops. The screen, typically arranged in portrait style, usually incorporates an on-screen keyboard. However, there are now handheld devices which provide a miniature keyboard as part of the hardware design. Handhelds usually also incorporate handwriting recognition software with the input of text being implemented using a stylus.

See Chapter 14 on mobile technology for more information.

Dedicated word processors. There are a number of machines available that function only as word processors, such as AlphaSmart and DreamWriter. They allow the entry, storage, downloading and usually direct printing of documents. They do not facilitate much in the way of text formatting, though they do incorporate a small screen which will allow re-reading and elementary editing. Text can be downloaded into a word processing program on a desktop computer to provide greater options for revisions and printing. Because of the limited functionality, dedicated word processors formerly had a price advantage by comparison with desktop computers, but the fall in computing costs over recent years has eroded that advantage.

Word processing using portable computers can have a range of benefits for schools. Portable equipment by its very nature enables trips, outside, to the hall or music room, even home to be supported. In cramped classrooms the possibility of using computer equipment on standard tables, rather than specially adapted and located furniture, can be attractive.

Portable word processors have proved effective tools for the support of struggling writers, often bringing associated gains in terms of improved behaviour and social confidence, particularly when used to provide differentiated support for children with SEN. Children gain confidence from the privacy and support provided by the technology. Portable machines have also been useful tools in encouraging parental involvement in children's writing, with children taking the equipment home to continue their writing.

Explicit skills teaching

One key area for children (and teachers) is their developing understanding of the scope and range of word processing software – what is possible and what isn't. The swiftly evolving nature of the software means there is no lasting answer, but a developing appreciation of the possibilities goes hand-in-hand with a developing sophistication of use.

The nature of the ways in which we learn about the various functions of word processing (and other) software can lead to inefficient and ineffective practices. Much of the time we learn new skills by experimentation ourselves, by asking our peers or our teachers, by using built-in help, by observing others and by accident when we are trying to achieve something quite different. Some software also allows the same effect to be generated by a range of different strategies; for instance, in Microsoft Word, highlighted text can be copied by accessing the copy command from the edit menu, by using the copy icon on the standard tool bar, by using the keyboard shortcut Ctrl–C and by using the right button to access a mini-menu of options, again including copy. Some of these may work in some other word processing packages and some may not. All are effective. Some are more efficient in terms of time and number of mouse clicks than others. Some suit some individuals and the ways in which they work better than others.

It is important sometimes to watch children working with word processing software and to note and confront inefficient and ineffective practices. For instance, many children access capital letters via the caps lock. This requires them to put on the caps lock, type the letter and take off the caps lock, a three-stage process. Very often children forget the final stage and may have typed several more words before they notice. Changing capitals to lower case letters once typed requires a quite detailed knowledge of some word processing software; it is just not feasible in others. In practice, children tend to delete the offending words and retype them. Time and continuity are lost. Use of the Shift key can be taught explicitly, either informally on a one-to-one basis or demonstrated to a whole class. This alternative makes the capitalisation of letters a two-stage process (Shift and the letter) and avoids unwanted capitals. Similarly, if children are typing in a number of figures, they may find the number keypad at the right-hand side of the keyboard easier than the numbers at the top of the keyboard. Many young children get into the habit of forcing their own line breaks via the Enter key or a mouse click when they notice they are getting towards the right-hand side of the typing area and do not realise that the text will wrap around automatically. This becomes a problem when children subsequently edit their text and the line breaks are not then in the best positions.

A regular 'tips' slot where children demonstrate useful strategies to their peers, or the teacher models a new idea, can easily and fruitfully be incorporated into classroom practice. It should not be assumed that children will learn word processing unaided. As in any subject, they will benefit from explicit teaching and guidance.

Children need to be aware of the limitations of software tools: that the spell-checker is not always right (likewise the grammar- or style-checker); that some words may not be in its dictionary and that some of its suggestions may not be appropriate. Some understanding of the clues that spell-checkers use to offer alternatives may be useful to enable children to make best use of such facilities. Similarly, the talking function may mispronounce words not in its memory, potentially giving children the false impression that something is incorrect.

Document sizes and their implications

Text documents do not on the whole take large amounts of memory for storage. However, the inclusion of formatting features such as page borders, tables and images may considerably increase the size of a word-processed document. This will result in longer saving and retrieval times.

Word processing and the core subjects

The ideas and activities introduced below are intended to give a feel for the range of ways in which word processing can be utilised to support and enhance teaching and learning in mathematics, science and English. They are not intended to be comprehensive, merely to go some way towards illustrating the breadth of possibilities and to provide starting points for the customisation of ideas and the generation of others. Examples introduced under mathematics, for instance, may be just as applicable to one or more of the other areas. Other useful sources include professional journals (such as *Primary Science Review*, *Junior Education* and *Child Education*), websites (such as Becta), and the respective schemes of work.

Word processing and mathematics

Children can use word processing software to present the results of mathematical investigations. Writing can make a valuable contribution to the development and particularly the articulation of meaning and ideas, no less important in mathematics and science than in English-language development work. The word processor allows children to import graphs from graphing or database programs and images from painting and drawing packages or a digital camera. They can add commentary, perhaps to pose questions for their peers or to produce fact sheets to contribute to a whole class reference document.

Of course, many graphing and database packages allow text to be added and amended for the recording and presentation of results. Children need to know that they can transfer their skills from one to the other, but also to recognise the potential limitations of such software; for instance, word banks or bullet points may not be available. Accordingly children, and their teachers, need to make an informed choice.

Word processing and science

The strategies discussed for mathematics can similarly be applied to the teaching and learning of science.

Children at all stages can use word processing software to assist with sequencing and sorting information. The degree of preparation and structuring required may vary with the development of the children. Young children may begin by using an on-screen word bank featuring images with text labels, to sort materials into hard and soft, for instance.

An obvious extension for such an activity may be the writing of a sentence of explanation, with adult assistance as necessary. This could be achieved with the aid of the word processor, or to maximise access to limited computer resources, handwritten on a printout.

Sequencing the stages of an investigation can be supported at a range of levels. Children can use cut and paste to sequence and re-sequence the elements of a prepared text. Children may enter their own text and use the facilities of the word processor to revise and re-order their work until they are satisfied. Activities such as these are appropriate for pairs or small groups, since the associated discussion and decision-making should be a fertile ground for rehearsing explanations, justifying opinions and articulating ideas.

One of the principal conventions of science is the systematic recording of investigations. Children begin early in their school careers to develop this skill and word processing can be used to support this writing in various ways. A word bank can be used to access new or difficult vocabulary, allowing children to concentrate on articulating their developing understanding. Electronic writing frames or templates, prepared files with headings and sometimes questions of a general nature which can be used in a variety of contexts or customised for particular activities, can be useful. The various parts of the template scaffold children in the framing of their ideas under each of the headings and help to ensure that important elements are not forgotten. Children can either use such a framework on screen or make use of a printout to support writing by hand.

Word processors can be useful tools when children are seeking information from databases. Children can make their own notes about what they have found, supplementing these as appropriate with images or text copied and pasted from electronic sources. Children may then use their notes in either an electronic or paper-based format to develop their work further.

The examples given above focus predominantly on using the features of word processors to assist in the development of writing associated with science. Each of these can be taken a stage further by using the tools and facilities to improve the technical and presentational aspects of children's writing in science. The word processing and desktop publishing facilities of the software can be used to good advantage when children produce posters to communicate important facts such as why we should clean our teeth or which foods we need for a healthy diet. Equally, information can be prepared in a word processing document with a view to linking it with the work of others to form a multimedia document, for the school's website or to make a non-fiction talking book or reference guide for younger children. At this point it is particularly important that teachers are clear about their primary learning objectives which might reside in any combination of English, science and ICT.

Word processing and English

Word processing has a range of features which support writing activities, some of which have already been discussed. Editing offers powerful possibilities, and may be structured in ways that develop both English and ICT capability. For example, under a heading such as *All about me* young children can select and enter words, sentences and images from Clicker or an on-screen bank. Alternatively, or as an extension, children could delete descriptions from a prepared text which do not apply to them. Such an activity promotes skills in working with text on the screen.

A wide range of sentence-level literacy activities can be facilitated – for instance, highlighting direct speech from a prepared text. Some children might use the word processor to complete this activity, while others could use a highlighter and a print-out, thus making practical and effective use of classroom resources. Likewise a prepared text can be changed from reported to direct speech. Word-level work can involve inserting punctuation into a continuous narrative to produce sentences or using search and replace to substitute alternatives for *said*.

Shared text-level work on instructions may focus on *How we clean our teeth* with the teacher fielding suggestions and acting as scribe as the class or group look on. The interactive whiteboard provides an ideal medium for this sort of work. A more complex instructional text such as a recipe for Easter biscuits can be supported at different levels according to need – a prepared list requiring reordering for some, a partial list or a blank sheet for others. Word processing allows children to insert, delete, reorder and present their work. It also allows the comparison of alternatives. Such activities carried out in groups and/ or leading to feedback to the whole class can facilitate speaking and listening as children support and refine their ideas. Independent users of word processing can produce a help sheet on how to create a hyperlink in a multimedia document, thus combining instructional text with appropriate images to facilitate communication and formatting to enhance the aesthetic appeal of the help sheet.

Prepared texts can be turned from prose into note form, or notes turned into prose. Interesting comparisons can result if one group of children perform the inverse task on the work of others (once it has been saved or printed). A competitive element can be introduced as children seek to use the fewest number of words while still conveying meaning. Debate on what is and is not considered to be important may ensue.

There are opportunities for work focusing on the importance of layout, for instance in the writing and presentation of poetry. The effects of inserting line breaks and capital letters, centring, illustrating or font selection and size can be examined. Cartoons and newspaper layouts can be supported at various stages. Teachers can prepare paper templates for planning and electronic templates to support some children with the layout of their work. Designing front and back covers and title pages for books can provide an alternative to the book review, although children can make use of a prepared electronic writing frame to support such writing.

Children of all ages can work with tables, to compile ongoing lists of synonyms for common adjectives.

Many of the activities suggested above make use of prepared word-processed documents. Teachers should ensure that they manage the use of these carefully. Always have a back-up copy and agree with the children how the prepared document will be used. Clearly, having the first pair of children making adjustments and then saving their work over the original is to be avoided. Protect the master document so that changes cannot be saved and encourage children to save the document with a new name before they do anything else or to print out their work and then close the document without saving.

Desktop publishing

Software is now available which enables the non-expert to produce high-quality desktop-published documents. Through the use of wizards, birthday cards, invitations, calendars and newsletters can be generated by following the on-screen instructions, inserting the required text or graphics as directed. The software does the rest. Publisher, from Microsoft, is one example. Textease, widely adopted in some local authorities, is another.

Many schools are now using such applications for half-termly newsletters, prospectuses, fliers, display banners and other publicity and display materials. They can also be usefully deployed in the classroom, for instance in newspaper activities. DTP software does not always allow for changes to be made easily, particularly in text. This mirrors the professional DTP process where graphics and text are comprehensively edited and considered to be finished before being incorporated in the layout.

A SUMMARY OF **KEY POINTS**

Word processing can support, enhance, extend and enrich communication in a variety of ways, but only when:

> **it is used with a clear understanding of its potential and potential difficulties;**

> **learning outcomes are clearly defined, explicitly communicated and reflectively evaluated.**

Moving on

Word processing is such a fundamental aspect of ICT that we tend to accept it somewhat unreflectively as a given way in which we work with computers. However, as a primary teacher it is important to consider that the word processing software that you use on a daily basis does not represent the only approach to what we have seen is a complex and involved creative process. Try to test out other word processing software, particularly packages designed for children, and make comparisons with the application that you use regularly. If you were designing a word processor for children, what features would you include?

FURTHER READING FURTHER READING FURTHER READING FURTHER READING

Abbott, C. (2002) *ICT and literacy teaching*. Reading: National Centre for Language and Literacy

Allen, J. (2000) Information and communication technology: investigating new frontiers, in Clipson-Boyles, S. (ed.) *Putting research into practice in primary teaching and learning*. London: David Fulton

Andrews, R. (ed.) (2004) *The impact of ICT on literacy education*. London: RoutledgeFalmer

Archdeacon, T. (2005) *Exciting ICT in English*. Stafford: Network Educational

Becta (2006a) *Improving access to writing*
http://schools.becta.org.uk/index.php?section=tl&catcode=as_chr_02&rid=4324 Accessed 7 January 2007

Becta (2006b) *How to teach keyboard skills* **http://schools.becta.org.uk/index.php?section=tl&rid=538&catcode=as_cu_pr_sub_14** Accessed 7 January 2007

Becta (2006c) *Learning difficulties and ICT*
http://schools.becta.org.uk/index.php?section=tl&catcode=ss_tl_inc_ac_03&rid=1805 accessed 7 January 2007

Bennett, R. (2004) *Using ICT in primary English teaching*. Exeter: Learning Matters

DfEE/QCA (1999) *Curriculum Guidance for the Foundation Stage*. London: DfEE/QCA

DfEE/QCA (1999) *The National Curriculum*. London: DfEE/QCA

Hull Learning Services (2004) *Supporting children with dyslexia*. London: David Fulton

Leask, M. and Meadows, J. (2000) *Teaching and Learning with ICT in the Primary School*. London: Routledge

Loveless, A. and Dore, B. (2002) *ICT in the primary school*. Buckingham: Open University Press

Martin, F. and Asprey, E. (2001) *Double click on word processing*, Oxford: Heinemann Educational

McFarlane, A. (ed.) (1997) *Information technology and authentic learning: realising the potential of computers in the primary school*. London: Routledge

Monteith, M. (ed.) (2002) *Teaching primary literacy with ICT*. Open University Press

Mosely, D. *et al.* (1999) *Ways forward with ICT: Effective pedagogy using ICT for literacy and numeracy in primary schools*. Newcastle: University of Newcastle

QCA/DfEE (1998, revised 2000) *Information and communications technology: a scheme of work for Key Stages 1 and 2*. London: QCA/ DfEE

Smith, H. (1999) *Opportunities for ICT in the primary school*. Stoke-on-Trent: Trentham Books

Wegerif, R. and Scrimshaw, P. (eds) (1997) *Computers and talk in the primary classroom*. Clevedon: Multilingual Matters Ltd

8
Graphics software

Chapter objectives

Images, patterns, shapes and colours are key features of children's early learning. Logos and icons are increasingly important in making sense of the world, from choosing breakfast cereal to operating computer software. Children learn to communicate and interpret visual imagery and ICT has a significant contribution to make to the development of visual literacy.

Recent advances (and cost reductions) in hardware have readily made accessible computers with sufficiently large memories for the storage and manipulation of complex graphics. At the same time graphics software has become more sophisticated in the range of features and functions supported. The continued move towards icons and toolbars for controlling these functions has improved accessibility for children and their teachers. Many generic software applications, such as word processors and databases, now support graphics. Associated peripheral equipment, particularly scanners and digital cameras, is increasingly available in primary schools. This chapter investigates graphics software in the context of primary education. Its application in the core subjects is explored, together with related capabilities and limitations.

What is graphics software?

Graphics software allows the entry, storage, retrieval and manipulation of images and their constituent elements – line, colour and texture – in an electronic format. Generic graphics software is considered to encompass painting and drawing software, although a range of other related software, such as clip art and digitising software for scanners and digital cameras, is becoming increasingly important.

What do the programmes of study for Key Stages 1 and 2 include?

At Key Stage 1 children should be taught to gather information (1a), enter and store it (1b) and retrieve it (1c). They should be taught to use text, tables, images and sounds to develop their ideas (2a) and try things out and see what happens in real and imaginary situations (2d). They should also be taught to share their ideas by presenting information in a variety of forms (3a) and to present their work effectively (3b).

At Key Stage 2, children should be taught to talk about the information they need (1a), how to prepare information (1b), how to organise and reorganise it (2a), how to share and exchange it (3a), as well as consider its suitability for its audience and its quality (3b).

At all stages children should be taught to review, modify and evaluate their work as it progresses (4a, 4b and 4c).

What does the ICT scheme of work include?

At Key Stage 1 graphics software features in Unit 1A (An introduction to modelling) and Unit 2B (Creating pictures).

At Key Stage 2 graphics software features in Unit 3A (Combining text and graphics), Unit 4B (Developing images using repeating patterns) and Unit 5A (Graphical modelling).

What do teachers need to know before using graphics software?

Drawing and painting software

Graphics software can be characterised under two main headings: drawing and painting packages, each having different strengths and limitations. One of the key differences is in the storage mechanism for the images created and manipulated within them.

Painting programs produce bitmap images. Bitmap images are minutely detailed, essentially recording separately every pixel (tiny dot) displayed on the screen, including blank areas. This results potentially in very large documents.

Graphics documents can occupy large amounts of memory

Drawing programs, sometimes called vector graphics programs, operate a completely different method of storing information. Drawings are stored as a series of vectors. These are mathematical descriptions of lines determining their magnitude and direction from the points at which they originate to their ends – and including all the curves and changes of direction in between. This is a more economical way of describing a simple image, and it results in smaller file sizes.

Convergence and expansion

There has, however, been considerable convergence in graphics software. Most graphics programs are now painting programs which also support drawing features, such as lines, arrows and shapes. Drawing features have also been subsumed into other software applications. For example, most word processing software supports a range of drawing functions which enable the user to easily incorporate diagrams and other line art into their documents.

PRACTICAL TASK PRACTICAL TASK **PRACTICAL TASK** PRACTICAL TASK

It is worth exploring the characteristics of different image file types using an adult's image manipulation software such as Paint Shop Pro, Photoshop or Fireworks. Alternatively, the free utility PixResizer (**http://bluefive.pair.com/pixresizer.htm**) is specifically designed to support the resizing of images and their subsequent saving in alternative file formats. Compare the differences in file size. Paste an image into a graphics or word processing program and enlarge it significantly. What do you notice? Could you explain what is happening, and why, to children?

What do teachers need to know about graphics software?

Teachers need to be competent and confident users of primary graphics software in order to facilitate children's learning. This does not mean that they need to know the answer to every technical question, but they do need a working knowledge of the software so as to be able to plan, support and assess appropriate activities. They also need to have strategies to support the children in their discovery of how the software works, as well as to assist with problem-solving.

Teaching with and about graphics software involves teachers:

- *Preparing resources* – such as a worksheet to support early mathematics work, or a prepared graphics document in which children may explore and reinforce early symmetry work, or illustrations to accompany a wall display. Some of these examples focus on using ICT as a tool for teaching and learning (in another curriculum area), while others focus on the teaching and learning of ICT.
- Selecting *appropriate opportunities* – in which graphics software can facilitate, enhance or extend children's learning, such as the importance of presentation in communication. In some instances the focus will be on teaching and learning in ICT (how to make a border for a poem using a repeated pattern), while in others ICT will be used as a resource in the teaching and learning of another curriculum area (matching presentation to audience).
- *Making explicit links between related knowledge, skills and understanding* – graphics software has applications across the range of the primary curriculum and as a consequence may provide opportunities to make explicit links in knowledge, skills and understanding in mathematics and art, for instance.
- *Modelling appropriate use of ICT* – cropping an image from a digital camera and transferring the result into a word processor to illustrate an activity sheet.
- *Demonstrating or intervening* – for example, demonstrating a new skill such as altering the size of painting tools or intervening to assist a child to delete multiple copies of a saved image to save memory space.

The lists below attempt to identify the knowledge, skills and understanding that teachers need in order to teach effectively with and about graphics software. Many graphics programs support only a subset of these functions. This is no reflection on their usefulness – in most instances simplicity is a strength. However, it does signal that teachers must be aware of the capabilities and limitations of any program as these will be significant in the choice of software for any teaching and learning activity.

Painting programs

- creating, opening, closing, deleting and printing documents;
- selecting file type and saving documents;
- selecting page size, margins and page orientation;
- inserting, modifying and deleting background colours and textures;
- selecting, modifying and utilising tools from the tool bar (spray, round brush, draw a circle);
- utilising fill;
- utilising the pipette/choose a colour tool;
- utilising undo/redo;
- selecting, modifying and utilising the text tool (font, font size, colour);
- selecting areas (for cropping, scaling, reshaping, deletion);
- selecting, modifying, utilising and saving repeated images (stamps);
- selecting and utilising more advanced features such as tiling, flipping and rotation;
- switching grid on and off;
- utilising zoom/magnifier and understanding how it differs from image resizing;
- inserting, deleting, manipulating and saving imported images;
- exporting images to other applications;
- clearing the screen;
- utilising help;
- altering defaults;
- customising set up;
- connecting alternative input devices (overlay keyboards, touch screens, graphics
- tablets);
- protecting documents.

Drawing programs

- creating, opening, saving, closing, deleting and printing documents;
- selecting page size, margins and page orientation;
- inserting, modifying and deleting background colours;
- selecting, modifying and utilising tools from the tool bar (line, arrows, shapes);
- utilising fill;
- utilising undo/redo;
- grouping and ungrouping elements;
- selecting, cutting, copying, pasting, cropping, resizing, reshaping, reordering and rotating elements and drawings;
- switching grid on and off;
- utilising zoom/magnifier;
- exporting drawings to other applications;
- utilising help;
- altering defaults;
- customising set up;

- connecting alternative input devices (overlay keyboards, touch screens, graphics tablets);
- protecting documents.

What are the key features of graphics software?

Graphics software makes use of a variety of tools, editing functions and effects for the creation and manipulation of electronic images.

Tools include brushes, lines, shapes and colour filling among many others. The variety of tools supported varies between software. Much painting software includes a selection of drawing features, although these cannot be manipulated in the same way as is possible in drawing programs because once laid down they are converted into pixels in the same way as the rest of the image.

The distinguishing feature of drawing software is that drawings are composed of a series of layered elements (shapes, for instance) and these may be reordered as required. Similarly the elements may be grouped together to be edited. In painting software, editing functions and effects can be applied to a selected area of an image, but it is not possible to isolate the elements of the image in the same way. This is because each pixel is treated essentially independently of its neighbours.

The image overleaf (*top*) was created with the drawing tools available in Word. Objects were reordered to create the desired overlapping circle effect. Elements were grouped so that the image could be copied, the copies then being resized and rotated. Many drawing and painting packages support a range of common editing functions, including, for example, scaling, reflecting, shearing, rotating, cropping and editing. The image overleaf (*bottom*) demonstrates the effect of each of these on a simple image.

Painting software provides a range of artistic effects, the variety and sophistication of these varying between packages. Common effects include a spray can, watercolour, colour blending, stamping (multiple copying), tinting and diffusing.

> **PRACTICAL TASK** PRACTICAL TASK PRACTICAL TASK PRACTICAL TASK
>
> Explore the tools, editing functions and effects of two common painting packages for children. Decide the most appropriate age range for each. If your school were purchasing a paint package, which would you recommend and why? Produce an A4 help sheet to assist children in the use of a few key effects.

What does graphics software have to contribute to teaching and learning?

Finding things out

Use of graphics software provides a quite different aesthetic and kinaesthetic experience compared with traditional art media. The outcomes produced are also different and there is a completely distinct physical experience associated with creating outcomes. Some children may be frustrated at the difficulties associated with using the mouse as a drawing tool; others may delight in the potential to create difficult shapes, such as curves, exactly as they

Shape-based worksheet designed using the drawing features of Word (Microsoft)

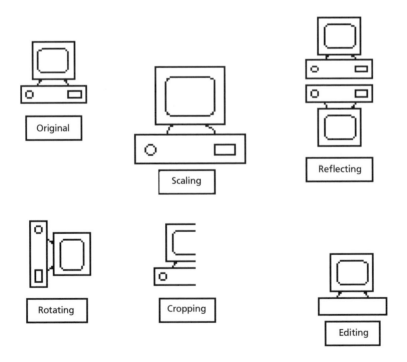

The effects of common editing functions (Microsoft Word)

wish them to look. In order to develop understanding and inform choices, children need a range of experiences on which to base their decisions.

Drawing and painting software facilitates a range of starting points for graphic activities, from a blank screen to a photographic image to be manipulated and developed. Similarly, the sheer variety of tools, editing functions and effects available provide challenges in themselves. The range of tools, editing functions and effects can, however, be limited to promote specific learning outcomes.

Use of graphics software provides an opportunity to introduce and develop children's understanding of related technical issues such as file size and file extensions in a relevant and meaningful context.

Developing ideas and making things happen

Most graphics software allows users to undo the previous action. Many primary packages, though not all, support repeated undoing. This feature allows children to use the software to explore and experiment with effects in ways which are not possible with traditional art media. Comparisons may be made between alternatives to inform choices. Children should be encouraged to take risks. Regular saving of work can provide a similar security, allowing children to return to an earlier stage in their work and follow a different pathway. Graphics software can provide children with access to tools, editing functions and effects which may be difficult or impossible to achieve with other arts resources commonly available in primary schools. Children may be able to develop their understanding of watercolour painting and painters by simulating watercolour effects and similarly of the potential and limitations of pop art.

Exchanging and sharing information

Graphic representation is an important area of communication. Experiencing the creation and manipulation of electronic images assists children to interpret the graphics they encounter, be they sporting goods manufacturers' logos or sophisticated film animations. Similarly, the electronic nature of some graphics enables global sharing and exchange through e-mail and the world wide web.

Graphics software does not in any way replace children working with the traditional range of art media; rather it increases the choices available. In certain situations the software features or even the nature of the outcome, in electronic format for instance, may make it the appropriate selection.

Progression of knowledge, skills and understanding

Graphics work will focus on the development of children's graphical communication and interpretation skills as well as software skills.

Very young children may use touch screens and concept keyboards to control the software, developing their understanding of the relationship between their actions and the effects on the screen.

A range of early language, number and science activities can be supported; for instance, using fill tools to colour in prepared drawings; the boat red, the fish orange and the seaweed green. With adult help children might draw party hats on digital photographs of themselves. With increasing independence children will be able to engage in a range of painting and drawing activities, such as producing a new label for their tray or coat hook.

Children will be increasingly able to make their own choices about the creation, manipulation and presentation of images, extending their repertoire of knowledge, skills and understanding through structured activities and interventions. Older children will be able to make appropriate choices related to the task and its audience. The variations in both software and the intended outcomes make ordering and ascribing particular skills and techniques difficult. Consideration is more appropriately focused on the development of knowledge and understanding which underpin the use of skills. In addition to directly teaching a limited range of skills it is important for a teacher to encourage children to explore the software purposefully for themselves, to think of an effect that they want to create and then discover how to achieve it.

What are the capabilities and limitations of graphics software?

Drawing with graphics software

The features of drawing software enable children to produce shapes and arrows, for instance, rapidly and accurately. An oval can be drawn by selecting the appropriate tool and clicking to locate the centre of the shape or edge of the shape (depending on the program), holding the mouse button down until the desired size and shape are shown. A perfect circle can be achieved by holding down Ctrl or Shift (depending on the program) while moving the mouse. Drawing software also allows objects to be deleted, redrawn and resized. The process is ideal for the creation of diagrams in science, for example, or for simple maps. However, the scope is limited; subtleties of colour and realistic, rather than abstract, representation are difficult to achieve.

Freehand drawing is tricky, requiring a high degree of hand–eye co-ordination. The computer mouse is not a sensitive drawing tool and freehand drawing can be very difficult. There are a number of strategies teachers can use to mediate this problem. Using the zoom or magnifying tool to enlarge the drawing area, drawing the required image, and then reducing the zoom may have the effect of disguising hand-wobble. Some graphics software includes smoothing utilities that provide curves of best fit.

It is possible to adjust the sensitivity of the mouse, but a more effective alternative is to use a simple graphics tablet. A graphics tablet is made up of a small plastic board and a light pen. The light pen allows the user greater manipulative control than is possible with a mouse. Inexpensive graphics tablets are available, such as those from Wacom. Tablet PCs are a much more expensive option, but they have the significant advantage of direct contact between pen and screen which makes hand-eye co-ordination much easier.

Colour handling

Painting software is based on a combination of pixels (derived from 'picture elements'), the 'dots' of an image, which are arranged on a rectangular grid (raster). Each pixel shows a colour, the information about which is stored in the image file. Viewed together, the pixels create the illusion of a picture but in reality they are distinct one from another.

Computers work with colour by mixing different proportions of red, green and blue light – the 'RGB' that gives its name to the cable linking the computer to the monitor. The mix is determined by a scale running from 0 to 255 for each of these primary colours. White, then, is 255, 255, 255, while black – the absence of colour – is defined as 0, 0, 0. All other colours are represented by varying combinations of red, green and blue falling between these values. For example, Red 80, Green 105 and Blue 50 together make a shade of olive. In total 16,777,216 different shades, calculated as 256 × 256 × 256, or 2^{24} (2 to the power of 24) can be defined in this way – more than are discernible by the human eye. It is from this calculation that the term '24-bit image' derives. A bit (binary digit) is either 1 or 0, with current in the computer switched on or off accordingly. Each pixel on which the computer needs to hold information is allocated 24 bits, eight bits (2^8, or 256) for each of the red, green and blue components. In the example given above, the amount of Red (80) is understood by the computer in binary as 01010000, the amount of Green (105) as 01101001 and the amount of Blue (50) as 00001110, together making up twenty-four pieces of information that together generate the olive colour.

Compression and resolution

Graphics software, particularly packages designed for image manipulation, should enable the user to make choices about the resolution at which an image is saved, and the amount of compression that is applied.

It is usually helpful to identify the width and height of an image. Accordingly an image that is 2048 pixels wide and 1536 pixels high holds altogether 3,145,728 pixels, which can be expressed alternatively as 3.1 Megapixels – the unit by which digital cameras are often described.

An image of this size is very big. Let's consider why. Our computer screens are also set at a particular resolution. This might range from an older 17″ monitor set at 800 × 600 pixels to a larger (19″ or more) high quality screen set at 1280 x 1024 pixels. However, our 2048 × 1536 image will not come close to being viewable in its totality on even this more highly specified equipment. A scroll bar or the software's zoom-out facility will have to be utilised. Similarly, if an image is to be incorporated into a PowerPoint slide it will only take up a relatively small proportion of the displayed area. It is sensible to import the image at that optimum size, by using image manipulation software to reduce the size. Given that the monitor has a limit to the number of pixels per inch (PPI) of display (sometimes known as the pixel density) that it offers, if the images that are created are essentially for use on screen, then there is no need for them to be larger than the pixel dimensions that they occupy. Larger files occupy more storage and memory space, which may be a significant factor on school computers if they are not built to a high specification. Similarly, large image files are slower to transfer on the web or by e-mail.

Resolution takes on a different shade of meaning when printing is involved. The instruction to the printer is given to render a specified number of dots per inch (dpi). Accordingly an image that is 800 × 600 pixels printed at 200 dpi will result in a printed picture measuring 4 inches × 3 inches. In this way the same file could be used to create different-sized pictures. Printing the same file at 96dpi will produce a larger picture than if it is printed at 200dpi, but the latter will probably appear to be better quality. 200 dpi is considered a minimum for prints of reasonable quality.

The basic file used by painting programs is the bitmap (file extension: .bmp). The term derives from the organisation, or mapping, of the pixels (composed of bits) which we examined earlier. However, another format, jpeg, which is pronounced 'jay-peg', and has the file extension usually .jpg, sometimes .jpeg, is now a popular alternative option. This is because jpeg files can be compressed, so reducing their size. Painting or image manipulation software usually effects the compression through a slider tool at the point of saving the file. There is a trade-off between quality and file size, though, as the compression technique necessitates some loss of graphical information. However, judicious use of jpeg compression can substantially reduce file size without compromising quality unduly.

The .jpg format follows standards set by the Joint Photographic Experts Group, and is particularly useful when dealing with photo-realistic images. The file type is not so well suited to images containing large areas of flat colour such as cartoons and maps. Here the preference will probably be for GIFs (file extension: .gif), which are economical files in terms of size, because they use a maximum of only 256 colours. In consequence they take up much less storage and memory space. The appropriate limited range of colours is identified as a palette and attached to the file. GIFs also support transparency, allowing one of the palette's colours to be defined so that the background appears through wherever that part of the GIF appears on a page.

In summary, determining the variables of resolution and compression will depend on the way in which the image is to be used. The size of files is not as critical as it used to be, given the increased storage and memory capacity of the computers sold today. Nevertheless it is good practice to be aware of the implications. Generally, images to be displayed on screen, in PowerPoint or other presentations, or in web pages can be saved in lower resolution or compressed format. Graphics which are to be enlarged or which require high-quality printouts such as photographs should be high resolution or uncompressed – or both. Low-resolution images which are subsequently enlarged often become 'blocky' or pixelated.

By contrast, despite occupying less memory, drawing images do not suffer quality reductions when they are enlarged. The vectors which describe the drawing images can be scaled to any size.

Schools without access to a network server, or with older computers, may have difficulty in saving and storing quantities of large graphics file. Teachers should ensure that children avoid saving multiple copies of large documents and that documents which are no longer needed are either deleted or saved in a way which will not occupy large amounts of memory. CD writers have become commonplace and these allow documents to be quickly and permanently stored on CD-ROMs.

Sourcing graphics

In addition to drawing and painting their own graphics images, children can source prepared images from a variety of locations. Sites on the world wide web, CD-ROMs, and scanning are common sources of images produced by others. Similarly pictures can be downloaded from digital cameras. Children often find it daunting to begin with a blank screen and the manipulation of an existing image can be a useful starting point, or a teaching and learning activity in itself where the emphasis is on exploring the features of the software. It is important to remember that any image other than clip art is likely to be subject to copyright.

Clip art

Clip art, which is widely used in primary schools, is usually copyright-free artwork, although it may come as exemplar material as part of a program and so be licensed within that. Clip art is typically simple in execution and offered as GIFs or Windows Metafiles (.wmf) in order to minimise file size. Most word processing software now comes with a range of clip art. There are also sites on the world wide web from which free clip art can be downloaded, though these should be mediated by an adult as they frequently need some negotiation of pop-up advertising. Publishers of educational software also produce CD-ROMs of associated clip art images, e.g. Oxford Reading Tree Clip Art.

Clip art may be used for a range of purposes, such as illustrating notices around the school, computer room and wet play area. Clip art images may also be a useful starting point for children to practise image-manipulation techniques in painting packages. However, clip art is to a certain extent a short cut to create visual impact; its originality lies with the artist who created it rather than with the child who imports it into his or her work.

Scanners

Scanners allow digital images to be made of hand-drawn diagrams, existing photographs, autumn leaves and everyday (flattish) objects such as scissors. Scanners also come with software which enables images to be captured and saved in a range of file formats. The software will conduct a preliminary scan of the original and allow the user to select and save just the parts of the image that are required. Scanners all accommodate images, and usually now are provided with optical character recognition (OCR) software which enables printed pages of text to be converted into digital format that can be fed into word processing or text-editing applications. This technology has become very accurate, but it is not infallible, so documents must be carefully checked.

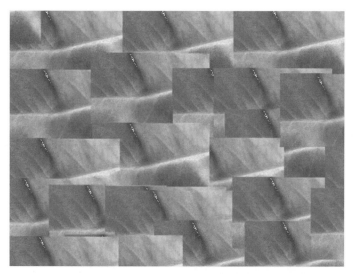

Image created with a scanned leaf and painting software effects (Dazzle, Granada Learning)

Scanners are useful for translating children's artwork, for instance, into an electronic format to allow it to be displayed on the school website. Similarly, scanned images can be the starting point for a range of activities. Children may scan leaves, import them into a graphics package and manipulate them to produce a border for a poem. Alternatively they could attempt to replicate a leaf using the drawing and painting tools in an activity designed to increase facility with these, displaying the scanned and the drawn images side by side. Due caution must be exercised to ensure that scanning does not breach copyright.

REFLECTIVE TASK

Use a scanner or a digital camera to produce a resource to support a science activity. How will you use the resource? How will you differentiate? How will you assess the resource's effectiveness?

Printing

The large size of many graphics documents has implications for printing. Printers have memories into which documents are sent from the computer. Documents which are too large for the printer's memory will not print out. They will also prevent the printing of other documents sent subsequently to the printer until the problem document has been cleared from the print queue. Children may be disappointed to find that importing a number of graphic images into a word processing document, for instance, renders the file size too large to print. Problems with memory are usually associated with older printers.

REFLECTIVE TASK

Find out how to delete jobs from the print queue. NB Sometimes switching the printer off and on again will not be effective.

Images, particularly those which are uncompressed or high resolution and therefore contain the most detail, take a long time to print out on conventional inkjet printers. Waiting for printing can be frustrating and time-wasting if such eventualities are not anticipated. Further, if a backlog of print jobs accumulates in the print queue because documents are taking time to print, the printer's memory may become overloaded, causing it to crash.

Although the price of printers has fallen in recent years, colour printing is expensive. Inkjet cartridges have only a small ink capacity and cost a lot. Colour lasers have become more affordable but again their maintenance is not cheap. If very high-quality images are required, photographic-quality paper is available, but this too is expensive. Nevertheless, if children are to work with images then the likelihood is that at least some of their work should be printed, and schools need to take the consumables involved into account with their budgeting.

Graphics software and the core subjects

The ideas and activities introduced below are intended to give a feel for the range of ways in which graphics software can be utilised to support and enhance teaching and learning in mathematics, science and English. They are not intended to be comprehensive, merely to go some way towards illustrating the breadth of possibilities and to provide starting points for the customisation of ideas and the generation of others.

Examples introduced under mathematics, for instance, may be just as applicable to one or more of the other areas. Other useful sources include professional journals (such as *Primary Science Review*, *Junior Education* and *Child Education*), websites (such as Becta), and the respective Schemes of Work.

Graphics software and science

Children may use painting software to produce images which illustrate the effects of light sources, such as street lights at night, fireworks in the sky, sunlight reflected in water. The particular qualities of graphics software, which enable light colours to be easily imposed on top of dark ones, make ICT a suitable medium for such representations, allowing children to create an artistic effect otherwise only accessible to very practised artists.

Very often science work at all levels requires illustration to aid communication. Graphics software enables images to be created, imported and modified as required. It also supports the addition of labels to aid identification and explanation. Posters may be designed to illustrate scientific understanding – the importance of a healthy breakfast or regular cleaning of teeth, for instance. Such posters can be created using traditional media, although graphics software allows revision and reorganisation to maximise presentational impact. It also enables children to incorporate images from a range of electronic sources.

Experience with graphics software in the manipulation of images, resizing or cropping for instance, is an important skill which can be applied to the incorporation of graphics across the range of generic applications, most notably word processing and desktop publishing.

Graphics software and mathematics

Graphics programs can be used to produce repeating patterns for wallpaper or wrapping paper. The stamping facility in many paint packages enables a design to be rapidly dupli-cated and arranged. The suitability of various shapes for geometric sequences can be explored – an investigation that can be extended into consideration of Islamic art.

Drawing programs may be used to support mathematical modelling activities. A teacher may prepare an electronic file containing a plan view of the classroom and the outlines of a range of furniture to be included. Children could explore possible arrangements. Extension activities might include conditions (the computer cannot be located by a south-facing window) or additions (two new children are starting on Monday; where should the extra table and chairs be located?).

Graphics software sometimes includes a grid which can be switched on and off. Grids may help children use graphics software to develop their mathematical understanding of shape. A teacher may prepare graphics files incorporating a grid, lines of symmetry and shapes in one quadrant. Children can make use of the grid to help them draw the shape reflected or rotated (see image on page 120). Similarly, a teacher may use a regular shape on a grid to demonstrate rapidly and effectively the effect of increasing perimeter on area. The incor-poration of images into mathematics work mediated through the interactive whiteboard presents particularly rich opportunities, simply because of the greater visual impact that an image commands by comparison with text.

Graphics software and English

The design of logos is a popular activity supporting work on interpreting methods of communication. Drawing programs in particular facilitate the production of bold, easy-to-reproduce images.

PRACTICAL TASK PRACTICAL TASK **PRACTICAL TASK** PRACTICAL TASK

Collect together a range of examples suitable to support a project on the design of logos. Use a drawing package to design a new logo for a common product. What are the difficulties children are likely to encounter with such a project? How can you support them?

Images are frequently used to communicate information in newspapers and magazines. Children can select and manipulate images from a wide range of sources, digital cameras, scanners, the world wide web, to illustrate news stories. Possible challenges include manipulating a photographic image, or creating a photo montage, to give a misleading or contrary impression.

The communication of information in cartoon-type format can be particularly enhanced using graphics software. A common background may be prepared and used as the basis for six or eight images telling the story of the child's journey to school or the adventures of a cat. A series of digital images may be sequenced and captioned to provide an account of the class's visit to the fire station or a record of a drama production.

REFLECTIVE TASK
REFLECTIVE TASK

The impact that ICT use has had on the way that we perceive the world is enormous. Use the world wide web to research the covers and layouts of magazines dating from before the computer was widely used in print production e.g. the immediate post-war period. Notice differences in the quantity of images used, and their manipulation for effect. What implications do these differences have for the way in which children perceive the world around them now, compared with then? Is the world now a more interesting place?

Moving on

The best way to understand graphics software is to work with it. With a particular project in mind, develop your personal capability with graphics software by trying to make it do what you want it to, perhaps replicating something you have seen.

A SUMMARY OF **KEY POINTS**

> **Graphics can be incorporated in a wide variety of electronic documents.**
> **Sources of graphics include images composed in painting and drawing software, as well as scanned images, digital camera pictures, clip art and (copyright permitting) CD-ROMs and the world wide web.**
> **Graphics occupy large amounts of computer memory space relative to text documents, which can cause difficulties in file management and printing.**
> **Graphics software complements more traditional art media; it does not replace them.**
> **The functions, effects and tools incorporated in graphics software provide exciting opportunities for image creation and manipulation.**

FURTHER READING FURTHER READING **FURTHER READING** FURTHER READING

Becta (2006) *Intellectual property, copyright and school internet use* Becta **http://schools.becta. org.uk/index.php?section=is&rid=9983** Accessed 16 January 2007

DfEE/QCA (1999) *Curriculum Guidance for the Foundation* Stage. London: DfEE/QCA

DfEE/QCA (1999) *The National Curriculum.* London: DfEE/QCA

Leask, M. and Meadows, J. (2000) *Teaching and learning with ICT in the primary school*. London: Routledge Falmer

QCA/DfEE (1998, rev. 2000) *Information and communications technology: a scheme of work for Key Stages 1 and 2*. London: DfEE/QCA

Somekh, D. and Davis, N. (eds) (1997) *Using information technology effectively in teaching and learning: studies in pre-service and in-service teacher education.* London: Routledge

9
Graphing programs

Chapter objectives

Graphical representations of data are everywhere: in newspapers, magazines, books, on television programmes, on websites. Children are constantly exposed to information communicated in this manner. If they are to interpret this in any meaningful way they need to develop appropriate knowledge, skills and understanding. The ICT schemes of work from Year 1 onwards make specific reference to the contribution graphing programs can make to the development of children's data-handling skills.

Graphing programs have been available in primary schools for many years. Recent developments, particularly the move towards the use of icons rather than keyboard commands to access common functions, have improved the accessibility of such software for children and teachers. The range of features and functions supported by many graphing programs has also been significantly enhanced.

This chapter explores graphing programs and their potential for the enhancement and extension of teaching and learning in the primary classroom. Cross-curricular applications are explored and links made to other generic data-handling software.

What are graphing programs?

Graphing programs facilitate the communication of information through graphical representation. Thus they enable data to be entered, stored, presented and interpreted graphically in an electronic format. Some allow the rudimentary sorting of data, into ascending or descending order of frequency, for instance. Graphing programs do not, however, support sophisticated sorting, searching or modelling. Such data-handling activity requires database software.

What do the programmes of study for Key Stages 1 and 2 include?

At Key Stage 1 children should be taught to enter and store information (1b), to use text, tables, images and sounds to develop their ideas (2a) and to try things out and explore what happens in real and imaginary situations (2d). They should also be taught to share their ideas by presenting information in a variety of forms (3a), as well as to present their work effectively (3b).

At Key Stage 2 children should be taught how to prepare information (1b), to interpret information and check its relevancy (1e), to organise and reorganise information (2a), how to share and exchange it (3a), as well as consider its suitability for its audience and its quality (3b).

At all stages children should be taught to review, modify and evaluate their work as it progresses (4a, 4b and 4c).

What does the ICT scheme of work include?

At Key Stage 1 graphing programs feature in Unit 1E (Representing information graphically: pictograms) and Unit 2E (Questions and answers).

At Key Stage 2 graphing programs feature alongside databases in Unit 4D (Collecting and presenting information: questionnaires and pie charts) and in the context of monitoring and sensing in Unit 5F (Monitoring environmental conditions and changes).

What do teachers need to know before using graphing programs?

In order to teach with and about graphing programs teachers need to be confident about their subject knowledge related to the handling of data. In this area there is a substantial and obvious overlap in terms of subject knowledge between science, mathematics and ICT. Relevant issues include:

- choice of variables;
- types of data;
- grouping data;
- collecting and recording data;
- presenting data.

Many data-handling activities begin with consideration of what data to collect. In science the choice of variables is often a key teaching and learning objective. For instance, the growth pattern of a seedling may be explored by comparing its height at 9.00a.m. each day over a three-week period. Two variables are involved here: seedling height and time. Alternatively, the investigation could be limited to one variable by measuring the height of a number of seedlings once only three weeks after sowing. The exploration would, in this instance, focus on the distribution of heights achieved.

There are three types of data: categorical, discrete and continuous. Categorical data fall into distinct named categories which do not overlap and cannot be ordered. For example, children's eyes may be blue, brown, hazel, green or grey. Where discrete data are concerned, the classes are defined by discrete whole numbers. An example might be the number of siblings class members have. Continuous data cannot be so easily segregated. The height of seedlings is measured on a continuous scale and each seedling's height is, potentially at least, slightly different from that of the others. The type of data collected influences how it is collected, recorded and presented.

Before data are collected and recorded, decisions should be made about grouping. In the case of categorical and discrete data the categories or classes will usually be quite obvious. Where continuous data are involved there is a choice: either to record (and then plot) each individual item, each seedling's exact height, or to attempt to group the data into classes, effectively translating continuous data into discrete. For instance, rather than recording a seedling's height as 8cm, another as 8.5cm, another as 6cm, each of these three seedlings could be entered into the category 5.0–9.9cm, with other categories for 10.0–14.9cm, etc.

Decisions about the grouping of data will affect recording and presentation. To continue the example above, further decisions about accuracy, number of decimal places and use of rounding will be required, and a suitable recording format must be chosen. Data may be collected and recorded in a number of ways, counting and tally charts being the most common for categorical, discrete or grouped data.

Once data have been collected and recorded, consideration can be given to presenting them graphically. It is important that the choice of graph is consistent with the data type. Categorical and discrete data are conventionally represented by bar charts, with each bar representing one discrete category or number. Bar charts can be arranged horizontally or vertically or as bar line graphs. Pie charts are also suitable for the presentation of categorical or discrete data, particularly where consideration of relative proportions is important – for instance, in comparing the ways in which members of a class travel to school. However, caution should be exercised in the use of pie charts, especially where there are two or more categories containing similar or equal amounts of data, since it may be difficult to distinguish their relative size by eye. The representation of data sets where one or more category has a value of zero is also problematic, since these will not be represented on the pie chart.

How we travel to school

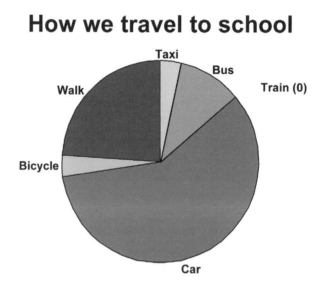

Pie chart with one category (Train) having a zero value

Line graphs and scatter graphs are suitable for the presentation of continuous data. Continuous data may include two variables, for example the growth of a plant may be measured over time, with its height plotted against the day on which each reading is taken. Such graphs are sometimes called *xy* graphs. A scatter graph represents the actual data in this instance, whereas a line graph may be used to join the individual points to give some indication of rate of growth over time. However, children need to understand that joining such plots by a line represents an approximation. If data had been collected at intermediate points they would not necessarily fall directly on the line. Further, if some data-collection opportunities are missed, for instance over the weekend or half-term, the graphing program may interpret no data as having a value of zero. In this case the line graph will return to the *x*-axis. Spreadsheets, which also enable graphs to be plotted from such data, may cope better with this situation.

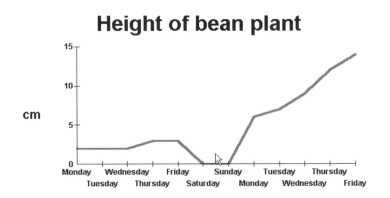

Line graph showing the effect of a break in data collection (CounterPlus, BlackCat)

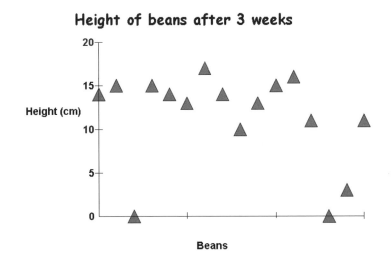

Scatter plot showing distribution of seedling heights (Counterplus, BlackCat)

Plan a sequence of lessons to introduce the concept of tally charts for the recording of data. Choose a suitable subject context. Note how and why ICT can be used, making reference to assumptions about the availability and location of resources. Note prerequisite knowledge, skills and understanding with respect to mathematics and ICT.

What do teachers need to know about graphing programs?

Teaching with and about graphing programs involves teachers:

- *selecting appropriate opportunities* – in which graphing programs can facilitate, enhance or extend children's learning, such as exploring the impact of graphically representing one set of data using a range of scales. In some instances the focus will be on teaching and learning in ICT (how a graphing program can facilitate such an investigation), while in others ICT will be used as a resource in the teaching and learning of another curriculum area (the effect of choice of scale);

- *exploring the full range of data-handling activities* – it is important that data-handling work does not always end with the production of a graph. In many instances data-handling work will begin with a graphical representation and learning will be focused on interpretation and analysis;
- *making explicit links between related knowledge, skills and understanding* – data-handling has applications in many areas of the primary curriculum; teachers thus have opportunities to make explicit and reinforce the links between children's previous experiences and new learning across the range of contexts;
- *modelling appropriate use of ICT* – for instance, the joining of individual plots of data by a line graph to assist in the analysis of the pattern or trend the data represent;
- *demonstrating and intervening* – for instance, intervening to assist a child to export a graph to the appropriate place in a word-processed record of a science experiment; similarly, demonstrating and discussing the potential difficulties of interpreting data represented in a pie chart.

The list below attempts to identify the knowledge, skills and understanding of graphing software teachers need in order to teach effectively with and about graphing programs. Many graphing programs support only a subset of these functions. This is no reflection on their usefulness – in most instances it may be a strength. However, it does signal that teachers must be aware of the capabilities and limitations of any program as these will be significant in the choice of software for any teaching and learning activity.

Graphing program knowledge, skills and understanding:

- creating, opening, saving, closing, deleting and printing documents;
- adding, modifying and deleting data;
- plotting and replotting graphs; selecting and displaying graph types, including more than one graphical representation of the same data;
- selecting and modifying constituent elements of graphs, such as changing the colours of bars in a bar chart to correspond with the data represented;
- selecting, resizing, cutting, copying and pasting graphs;
- selecting and modifying graph scales and autoscaling;
- selecting two-dimensional or three-dimensional representations;
- inserting graph titles, axes labels, key and text;
- selecting font and font size for graph and axes headings;
- exporting graphs into other applications;
- importing information from other applications, such as clip art;
- utilising help;
- altering defaults;
- customising the graphing program, switching off functions not needed;
- utilising alternative input devices (particularly data-loggers);
- selecting appropriate colours or patterns depending on printer availability (black and white or colour);
- protecting documents.

There will be occasions on which other data-handling software, such as databases or spreadsheets, will be more suitable. Teachers need to be confident in making decisions about the most appropriate application for a particular situation.

What are the key features of a graphing program?

Graphing programs:
- **produce graphs directly from data entered;**
- **offer a range of graph types;**
- **usually automatically select the scale;**
- **provide opportunities to reinforce the relationship between numerical and graphical representation of the same data;**
- **allow children to focus on using the information contained in a graph rather than the process of construction;**
- **do not replace children constructing graphs manually – this is an important developmental stage in the process of understanding;**
- **facilitate a range of learning outcomes – for instance, emphasis may be on data collection (planning, organising, recording, entering), or on interpretation, or on the effect of scale;**
- **facilitate work on equivalence and differences between graph types, such as bar charts, pie charts, bar line charts, line graphs, scatter graphs;**
- **facilitate work on progression in graphical representation.**

Graphing programs can be divided into two categories:
- **pictogram programs, which support early graphing activities and usually allow for the representation of data only as pictograms or block graphs;**
- **more sophisticated graphing programs, which support a range of graph types and functions.**

In order to facilitate the exploration of the features and contribution of each of these, they will be referred to as pictogram programs and graphing programs respectively.

What do graphing programs have to contribute to teaching and learning?

Finding things out

One of the key advantages of working with graphing programs to handle data is that much of the time-consuming work of planning and plotting graphs is automated, allowing the user to focus on the information contained in the graph. Which is the most frequently owned pet in Year 3, and how does this compare with pet ownership of children in Year 6? Other questions may then be raised, such as what might be the influences on choice of pet? What constitutes pet ownership where there is more than one child in a family? How is double-counting avoided? The emphasis should be on investigation and analysis as much as on representation.

An important aspect of work in handling data surrounds choosing the most appropriate graphical representation. Graphing programs facilitate immediate comparisons between the different graph types. Would pie charts be the most suitable method of representing the pet ownership information? What if some animals are owned by children in Year 3, but not by children in Year 6? Using graphing programs enables children to make independent choices of graph types, safe in the knowledge that the graph can be redrawn speedily if necessary.

When hand-drawing is involved there may be a tendency for the teacher to direct children towards a shared class decision in order to avoid wasting time.

Most pictogram and graphing programs also enable data to be sorted at a simple level, for instance, into ascending or descending order of frequency. This can be a very useful facility, especially if there is a wide range of categories, or the scale is marked in intervals of two, or five, or ten. Using a sorting function does not obviate the need for children to be able to read information accurately from graphs; it can provide another opportunity for teaching or reinforcing that skill.

Developing ideas and making things happen

Graphing programs can be used to demonstrate the relationship between data, their recording in a frequency table and their representation as a graph. Most programs allow the frequency table to be shown alongside a graph. Making these connections is vital if children are to handle data in a meaningful way.

Developing children's understanding of the equivalence of information represented in different graphs can be facilitated by showing, for instance, a horizontal bar chart, a vertical bar chart and a bar line graph side by side.

Graphing programs have autoscaling features which choose the scale of the graph, usually depending on the highest value or frequency. Most programs replot graphs each time new data are entered. In this way the development of a graph and the effect of each new piece of data can be powerfully demonstrated. Autoscaling often results in graphs where scales are marked in intervals of 2, 5 or more. The construction and interpretation of such graphs are important stages in the progression of children's understanding of data handling. Sometimes the autoscaling feature can be disabled to enable children to make their own selections as appropriate.

Similarly the connection between choice of scale and the effectiveness or impact of a graph can be explored. There can be valuable learning associated with attempting to 'misrepresent' information, choosing a scale such as to make a small variation look large or a large variation look insignificant. Almost any newspaper, magazine, website or TV news programme will contain some graphical representation of information. Making links with real-life applications of knowledge and understanding which children could otherwise view as quite abstract in nature can be a powerful learning tool.

Exchanging and sharing information

Many of the issues discussed above, such as choice of graph type, equivalence, comparison and scale, also have relevance for the exchange and sharing of information. Additionally, if a group of children presents the results of a science investigation for display on the classroom wall, decisions need to be taken not only about the most suitable type of graph for the data but also about its readability at a distance. The advantages of a horizontal bar chart over the more common vertical, where the labels might more obviously correspond with the data, might also be explored. There are instances where two or more graph types may be equally appropriate and children can justify their personal selections and discuss the merits of each (see below).

Copying and pasting a graph into a report or other document is a useful function and many pictogram and graphing programs support this. Graphs can usually then be moved and resized as any other image. It is important that children know that they can transfer their skills in this way within and between applications.

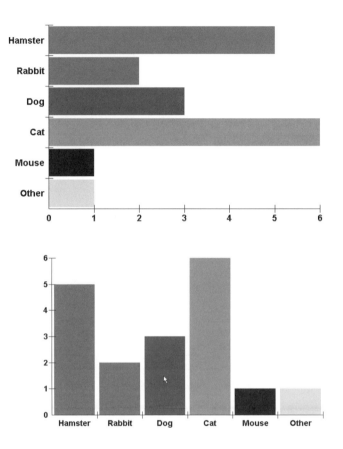

Horizontal and vertical bar charts showing the same data (CounterPlus, BlackCat)

Progression of knowledge, skills and understanding

Early data-handling activities will relate closely to children themselves and their own experiences. 'Ourselves' is a common theme and many pictogram programs such as Counting Pictures (BlackCat) and Pictogram (Kudlian Soft) have a predetermined range of relevant topics to select from, e.g. pets, favourite foods and hair colour. Having chosen a suitable focus, such as children's eye colour, and discussed the likely alternatives, the teacher can call up a blank pictogram on screen and ask each child in turn their eye colour. The children may need to consult with a friend and the teacher (or a child) can click or drag the appropriate icon to include the information in the graph. The pictogram will be built in front of the children and the connection between each child's answer and the appearance of an icon in the relevant column made explicit. This method of data collection is appropriate for young children and the immediate building of the graph reinforces the connection between the data (the answer the child gives) and the graphical representation of the data.

Building a pictogram (Counting Pictures, BlackCat)

At its simplest a pictogram drawn with a graphing program will consist of columns of icons indicating a one-to-one representation. The teacher can lead the children in counting to establish how many children in the class have blue eyes. There is no need for text labelling as each category is identified by an icon, although the software usually allocates a title based on the subject selected.

Pictogram programs have a variety of features which facilitate their use at various stages in supporting children's knowledge and understanding of data-handling. These might include:

Adding a scale. Reading from a scale requires a more sophisticated understanding of number than does counting icons.

Adding axes. The addition of *x* and *y* axes represents a stage in the development from a straightforward pictorial representation of data towards the more abstract model generally recognised as a graph.

Transforming the pictogram into a block graph. Again, this is a development from the straightforward pictorial representation of data, towards something more abstract in nature. Each block in a block graph clearly represents an individual piece of data, which distinguishes it from a bar chart in which the divisions between the data are not distinct. Pictogram (Kudlian Soft) also supports bar charts, representing a further progression.

REFLECTIVE TASK

Following the compilation of a Year 1 class pictogram of favourite foods, what questions would you ask to probe and develop the children's understanding? How would you follow up the activity?

Programs such as DataPlot (Kudlian Soft) and Counter (BlackCat) facilitate more sophisticated data-handling activities. Data are entered through a frequency table and a graph is drawn and redrawn as new data are added. Text labels are transferred from the frequency table to the graph and these are necessary to identify and interpret the graph. There is a range of graph types to choose from, allowing children to experiment and select the most suitable. Scales marked at intervals greater than one can result, although such graphs can also be drawn in some pictogram packages. Options for saving, adding text and exporting to other applications are easily accessible. A further level of sophistication (DataPlot and CounterPlus) enables each axis to be separately titled and choices to be made about colours and/or patterns. Two- and three-dimensional representations are often possible and selection can be made from a wider range of graph types. Negative and decimal numbers are usually supported. Effective utilisation of graphing programs may facilitate the development of children's knowledge, skills and understanding of handling data independently of the motor skills required for the hand-drawing of graphs.

What are the capabilities and limitations of graphing programs?

Selecting appropriate graph types

Graphing programs do not automatically select the most suitable graph type to represent data. The choice remains with the user. Nor will the software warn against unsuitable selections. Teachers will need to ensure that children make appropriate choices based on the data. Many graphing programs automatically represent data as vertical bar charts unless another graph type is specifically selected. This default risks reinforcing the use of this most common graph type at the expense of consideration of alternatives.

CLASSROOM STORY

A trainee teacher had carefully prepared an ICT lesson on graphing programs. His teaching objectives were appropriately described in terms of ICT. He was familiar with the software and had selected data related to current geography work. He took the class to the ICT suite and proceeded to introduce the activity, describing the process. The children were required to access a graphing program, enter into it data relating to average temperatures across a year in a distant place and the UK, and produce pie charts for comparison.

The trainee teacher provided each pair with a help sheet he had prepared and the lesson proceeded. After 35 minutes, each pair had produced two pie charts. These were printed out and the class returned to the classroom. Questioning the children, however, suggested that they had little understanding of the information the graphs represented. Although the data had been chosen to relate to a current geography study, the links between that and the ICT session had not been made explicit to the children. Further, there was little examination of the finished pie charts in order to interpret the data. This would in any event have been difficult using the graph type selected.

Frequency tables and tally charts

Most graphing programs allow data to be viewed through a frequency table as well as a graph. In many, the data are entered through the frequency table. This feature provides an opportunity for teachers to reinforce the correspondence of the information represented in these different ways. Counting Pictures (BlackCat) also has a tally chart function which can be used to facilitate the progression from simultaneous data collection and entry, as in the eye-colour example described previously, to recording and subsequent entry, for which the tally chart is the most frequently used mechanism.

3D graphs

Most graphing programs have the facility to display graphs in three dimensions as well as two. The third dimension allows children to produce sophisticated-looking representations which compare with those they see on television or in the press.

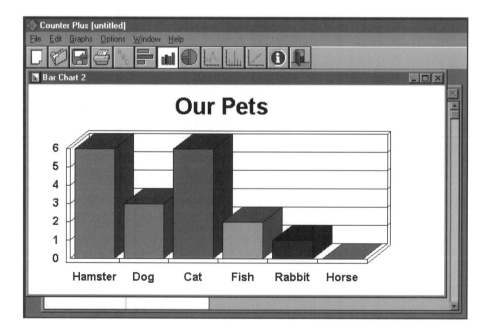

3D bar chart showing category with zero value (CounterPlus, BlackCat)

However, the 3D effect can be problematic for children when reading information from scales. This concern is particularly apparent in respect of bar charts. Children may experience confusion in deciding which lines to follow to read off information. Similarly a bar with a zero value will still contain a block of colour. The interpretation of 3D graphs may thus require explicit teaching. There is an argument for avoiding them altogether as strictly speaking the 3D perspective distorts the areas that should represent the individual fields, so that they no longer comprise an accurate proportion of the whole. This problem is most clearly evidenced by 3D pie charts.

Pictogram packages

Pictogram packages tend to have a limited range of possible graph subjects, such as pets, journeys to school or favourite colour, determined by the icons available. It is entirely appropriate that young children's data-handling experiences involve data which have some relevance to them, rather than the rainfall patterns in a distant location, for instance, and most of these are catered for. Some packages provide the opportunity for the range to be extended although this involves drawing appropriate pictures using the tools provided. Within each graph subject there is also a limited range of categories; 'hamster', for instance, may not always appear as a pet choice, although 'horse' often does. Again these can be customised and software houses enhance their products over time, most welcoming feedback on such issues.

Similarly there may be restrictions on the amount of data that can be entered. With class sizes even in Key Stage 1 of around 30, such a limitation on numbers can be important as the result might be that it is impossible for a record to be entered for each child.

Selecting colours

Graphing programs often allocate predetermined colours to bars in bar charts; thus the first bar may be blue, the second green, and so on. Clearly this may be problematic if the data have some link to colour – for instance, children's favourite colours, hair colour or eye colour – and there is a mismatch. A graphing program will not be helpful if it represents the number of people with blue eyes with a red bar. Better software will allow colours to be changed once the initial graph has been drawn up, but there is some software in which this option is not available.

Teachers need to ensure that they explore such issues when selecting software for particular tasks. The writers of the DataPlot (Kudlian Soft) software saw this as a potential difficulty and incorporated some programming that ensures that if data are identified by colour (e.g. eye colours, blue 6, green 3, brown 7) it is represented by those colours. The software also identifies hair colours such as ginger, fair and blonde and makes appropriate choices (assuming the colours have been spelt correctly).

Printing considerations

Most graphing programs make extensive use of colour. This helps children differentiate between different groups of data and aids the visual engagement with the graphic representation. However, when graphs are to be printed out this may become an issue. Colour printing is slow and expensive. Printing a coloured graph in black and white usually results in various shades of grey. These may be difficult to distinguish. There are two potential solutions available to teachers and most graphing programs will support at least one of these.

Sometimes it is possible to choose to print out a graph without any colour, enabling the children to colour in by hand. DataPlot (Kudlian Soft) provides an option to switch off the colour function. Alternatively it may be possible to change the various colours to white, producing the same effect when printed out. Secondly, some programs provide a range of pattern options which can be selected instead of colours.

Links to other generic data-handling software

CounterPlus (BlackCat) allows multiple columns of numeric information to be incorporated and thus represented on the same graph, enabling comparisons to be made. This type of function is usually only possible using a spreadsheet.

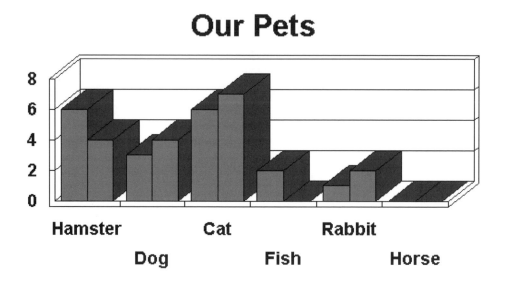

Block graph and frequency table demonstrating comparison between two sets of data (CounterPlus, BlackCat)

Many software houses have linked ranges of data-handling programs, so that the transfer of children's skills from one to another is facilitated by familiar icons and functions. Kudlian Soft produce Pictogram and DataPlot facilitating progression from one to the other. Additionally, DataPlot is a constituent of DataSweet, which also includes the spreadsheet DataCalc as well as database software. Similarly, Counting Pictures uses the same icons as Pick a Picture, BlackCat's early database program.

Common errors and misconceptions

Although using graphing programs reduces some of the demands on children involved in graphical representation of data, it is important to ensure that emphasis is placed on inter-pretation as well as presentation. The graph is not the end product. Children need to be able to analyse, discuss and summarise what the graph means. A display of the children's graphs alone indicates that this process may not have happened. The display will be far more convincing if it includes a record of the children's commentaries.

The scale of data-handling activities deserves consideration. The availability of ICT might prompt the collection of far more data than would otherwise be contemplated. This might be its advantage, for instance in the monitoring of environmental conditions. However, caution should be exercised to ensure that the time taken to collect data does not distract from the teaching focus. On the other hand, especially for older children familiar with the basic principles of data-handling, it is important for the challenge to be authentic. Entering the colours of ten cars from the staff car park into graphing software to establish which shade is the most popular is poor use of the power of ICT to handle data.

Autoscaling can often be disabled to allow children to select their own scale and consider the implications of differing intervals.

Graphing programs and the core subjects

The ideas and activities introduced below are intended to give a feel for the range of ways in which graphing programs can be utilised to support and enhance teaching and learning in mathematics, science and English. They are not intended to be comprehensive, merely to go some way towards illustrating the breadth of possibilities and to provide starting points for the customisation of ideas and the generation of others. Examples introduced under mathematics, for instance, may be just as applicable to one or more of the other areas. Other useful sources include professional journals (such as *Primary Science Review*, *Junior Education* and *Child Education*), websites (such as Becta), and the respective schemes of work.

There is extensive overlap between science, mathematics, English, ICT and other subject knowledge, skills and understanding in this area of data handling. Teachers need to be clear about their primary teaching objective for any particular task or sequence of activities and maximise the opportunities for making explicit links between learning in the various curriculum contexts.

Graphing programs and science

Graphing programs have many possibilities in science for the recording and representation of experimental data. A number of possibilities have already been discussed. Most graphing programs allow text to be entered and displayed alongside graphs and graphs can usually be copied and pasted into other applications, such as word processing software.

Some activities will involve the collection, entry and representation of data, while others may start with prepared data looking for patterns, causal links and evidence to test hypotheses.

Environmental monitoring and sensing

Data-logging is the process of monitoring and recording environmental data such as temperature, light, movement and sound using sensors. The data are displayed through software which can be considered to be a special application of a graphing program, having many common features and functions, such as choice of graph types and scale.

Sensors are linked to the computer through a buffer box interface (for example from Deltronics) or through more portable equipment such as the LogIT Explorer, which provides an integrated interface between the sensors and the computer. The software, which is often supplied with the hardware, or may be purchased separately (such as Junior Datalogging Insight from Longman Logotron), is used to set the timescale for the logging of the data, which can be very short or very long, and the intervals at which data are collected are automatically adjusted. Data-logging can take place with the interface connected to the computer, enabling the results to be simultaneously displayed on screen, or, with LogIT, remotely (even outside) and subsequently downloaded.

Data-logging offers a variety of possibilities both inside the classroom and beyond. Key Stage 1 children can hold temperature sensors in their hands and watch the screen as the sensor warms up. Similarly, they can observe the instant and dramatic effects of clapping, singing or being very quiet near a sound sensor. Recording the sound levels in a classroom over the school day can provide interesting discussion as teacher and children attempt to identify peaks and troughs and relate these to particular activities or incidents.

Older children may insert a temperature sensor into a defrosting bread roll and record data over a 24-hour period. (Temperature sensors fall into two broad technical categories and not all are appropriate for contact with damp conditions.) Two temperature sensors connected to the buffer box can record the temperature inside and outside a window overnight. Similarly, away from the classroom the temperature in the school pond may be monitored night and day over a week or even longer. Another long-term project might involve placing a movement sensor in a pot with a bulb while it sprouts, flowers and dies.

Data-logging can make a valuable contribution to children's data-handling experiences. Its principal advantages are:

- **speed – data can be recorded more quickly than by hand;**
- **electronic data entry – the data recorded are automatically entered into the software, removing the time-consuming manual entry of data;**
- **memory – large amounts of data can be stored;**
- **persistence – data can be logged over extended periods.**

Data-logging can be used to facilitate children becoming more scientific in their experimental technique:

- **enabling the realistic repetition of experiments to achieve consistency in results and appreciate the concept of experimental error;**
- **enabling the testing of variables over greater ranges of values and similarly wider ranges of variables to be tested.**

PRACTICAL TASK PRACTICAL TASK PRACTICAL TASK PRACTICAL TASK

Find out how to:

- **connect the sensors to the data-logging interface and the interface to the computer; select the duration and/or intervals of data collection;**
- **collect data remotely and download to the computer;**
- **save and retrieve collected data.**

Briefly outline activities involving the logging of environmental data suitable for Year 1, Year 3 and Year 5 children. Relate these to the science National Curriculum.

Graphing programs and mathematics

Graphing programs should contribute to the development of children's understanding of the graphical representation of data. Almost any activity involving graphs draws on children's existing mathematical knowledge and provides opportunities for reinforcement and extension work. As already indicated, graphing programs can make a substantial contribution where the speed and automatic function of the software enable teachers and learners to focus more specifically on a particular mathematical objective, be it choice of appropriate graph type or scale, the grouping of data or recording technique.

Teachers can also make use of graphing programs to provide prepared documents as starting points. Children might use printouts for work away from the computer or complete activities involving data that has been pre-prepared. Such strategies maximise the contribution of limited ICT resources.

Graphing programs and English

All media make extensive use of the graphical representation of data to communicate information. On at least some occasions there is an element of selection, either of the data themselves or of the means by which they are presented, in order to persuade the audience to reach a particular conclusion. If children are to engage with information critically they need a range of opportunities through which to explore the issues of selection and presentation of data – taking information presented in a local news story and reinterpreting it to support an alternative slant, for instance. This might involve the selective omission of data, choice of scale, even choice of graph type to accentuate or mask certain aspects.

PRACTICAL TASK PRACTICAL TASK **PRACTICAL TASK** PRACTICAL TASK

Find out how to switch the autoscaling facility on and off. Represent one set of data using a range of scales and comment on the selection of the most appropriate. Collect a range of graphical representations of data from the media. Plan a speaking and listening activity to explore the issues associated with the impressions conveyed.

Children can develop and apply their knowledge of genre and the classification of literature by analysing the books in the class library. A range of data-handling questions arises relating to the selection, grouping and presentation of data. Similarly children will be involved in prediction, articulating their ideas, supporting their views and decision-making. The results can be considered in the light of children's preferences. Further exploration might focus on the similarities or differences in girls' and boys' tastes.

RESEARCH SUMMARY RESEARCH SUMMARY **RESEARCH SUMMARY**

Children, graphs and computers

Phillips (1997) reviews three experiments conducted by others into Key Stage 2 children's abilities to interpret graphical representations of information where ICT is involved.

In the first, children were asked to interpret a car's journey on a distance/time graph. They were able to identify when the car was travelling rapidly forwards, when stationary, when going slowly backwards, although very much more difficulty was experienced with associating these movements to time. In the second study, children were readily able to distinguish and interpret data-logging sensor readings for light, sound, movements and temperature on a time graph, telling the story of the various features of the data. The last involved children investigating paper spinners to determine the optimum length of wings to maximise distance travelled. Scattergraph plots were discussed and a line of best fit used to identify the v pattern in the data and consequently the optimum wing length.

Phillips contrasts these results with data which show poorly-developed graphical interpretation skills amongst secondary children. He concludes that it takes time for children to develop graphical interpretation skills and that the increasing use of ICT for data-handling in primary schools is likely to increase the children's exposure to graphic representations with consequent positive effects. He cautions against well-presented but meaningless graphs which are all too easy to produce with ICT, highlighting informed decision-making in this respect as a key issue for intending teachers.

REFLECTIVE TASK

Work that children undertake with graphing programs in the classroom will become more meaningful if it can be related to examples of the use of graphs in the world around them. Try to collect instances that the children may have encountered, for example voting on a TV game show or graphs in a newspaper. Discuss these with the children. Why are graphs used rather than text? Talk about how graphs can be manipulated; an example of breaks in a bar chart which results in differences in the bars being exaggerated is a good starting point.

A SUMMARY OF **KEY POINTS**

> **Effective teaching with graphing programs requires careful consideration of the selection, collection and recording of data.**

> **Graphing programs enable learners to focus on the interpretation of graphical representations of data.**

> **Graphing programs facilitate work on the equivalence and differences between graph types.**

> **Data-logging software can be considered to be a special application of graphing.**

> **Graphing programs have very specific features. For some data-handling activities, spreadsheets or other types of databases will be more suitable.**

Moving on

As we have seen, there are both a significant number of graphing programs for primary age children, and noteworthy differences among them in terms of the functions and facilities that they offer. Try to gain familiarity with several different packages so that you are confident in making decisions about which might be appropriate in particular contexts.

FURTHER READING FURTHER READING FURTHER READING FURTHER READING

Bennett, R. (2006) *Learning ICT with maths*. London: David Fulton

Briggs, M. and Pritchard, A. (2002) *Using ICT in primary mathematics teaching*. Exeter: Learning Matters

Becta (2006) *How to use ICT for data handling in the foundation stage* **http://schools.becta.org.uk/ index.php?section=cu&catcode=ss_cu_skl_02&rid=647**

Byrne, J. (2002) *Using ICT in primary science teaching*. Exeter: Learning Matters

Clark-Jeavons, A. (2005) *Exciting ICT in maths.* Stafford: Network Educational

DfEE/QCA (1999) *Curriculum Guidance for the Foundation Stage*. London: DfEE/QCA

DfEE/QCA (1999) *The National Curriculum*. London: DfEE/QCA

Fox, B., Montague-Smith, A. and Wilkes, S. (2000) *Using ICT in primary mathematics: practice and possibilities*. London: David Fulton

Frost, R. (2006) *Dataloggerama* **www.rogerfrost.com**/ Accessed 17 January 2007

Higgins, C. *et al*. (2002, 2003) *ICT Connect* (Years 1–6). Oxford: Harcourt Education Limited

Jarvis, G. (2003) *Using ICT in primary humanities teaching.* Exeter: Learning Matters

Leask, M. (ed.) (2001) *Issues in teaching using ICT*. London: Routledge

Leask, M. (ed.) (2000) *Teaching and learning with ICT in the primary school*. London: Routledge

Loveless, A. and Dore, B. (2002) *ICT in the primary school*. Buckingham: Open University Press

Meadows, J. (2004) *Science and ICT in primary education: a creative approach to big ideas*. London: David Fulton

Phillips, R. (1997) Can juniors read graphs? A review and analysis of some computer-based activities, *Journal of Information Technology for Teacher Education*, 6(1), 49–58

QCA/DfEE (1998, rev. 2000) *Information and communications technology: a scheme of work for Key Stages 1 and 2*. London: DfEE/QCA

Way, J. and Beardon, T. (2002) *ICT and primary mathematics*. Buckingham: OUP

Williams, J. and Easingwood, N. (2004) *ICT and primary mathematics*. London: RoutledgeFalmer

Williams, J. and Easingwood, N. (2003) *ICT and primary science*. London: RoutledgeFalmer

10
Databases and spreadsheets

Among the first purposes to which computers were widely applied was the systematic handling of data. That the modern world is so information-rich in so many ways is largely due to the facility with which computers can store and process large amounts of data. Through understanding the concepts underlying data-handling, children will not only develop ICT skills, but also will become familiar with key principles through which knowledge and information are now managed.

What are databases and spreadsheets?

Databases are structured stores of information. They allow large amounts of data to be stored, organised, sorted, searched and retrieved quickly and easily. They provide for more sophisticated interrogation than the graphing programs that we explored in the previous chapter. Databases as repositories of information abound, from the school library catalogue to television listings to government records, and almost all are now in digital format. In order to access, analyse, synthesise and interpret information, children need to develop appropriate knowledge, skills and understanding. The electronic databases used in school take a variety of forms from branching tree identification keys to multimedia CD-ROMs and websites.

Spreadsheets are another kind of data-handling software that is widely used by adults. While they may share some features with databases, spreadsheets are usually not as adept for sorting and searching data, nor are they as effective for storing long text strings. However where they come into their own is in the manipulation of numerical data, which makes them well suited to mathematical calculations and modelling.

As software development continues, the distinctions between many generic categories blur and fade. Spreadsheets are data-handling software which may share many of the features and functions of databases. Similarly, many databases also incorporate spreadsheet functions. This chapter explores the variety, features and functions of databases and spreadsheets and their potential contribution to teaching and learning in the primary school. Clear links are made to other generic aspects of data handling.

What do the programmes of study for Key Stages 1 and 2 include?

At Key Stage 1 children should be taught to gather information (1a), to enter and store it (1b) and to retrieve it (1c). They should be taught to use text, tables, images and sounds to develop their ideas (2a), to select from and add to information (2b) and to try things out and explore what happens in real and imaginary situations (2d). They should also be taught to share their ideas by presenting information in a variety of forms (3a), as well as to present their work effectively (3b).

At Key Stage 2 children should be taught to talk about the information they need (1a), how to prepare it (1b) and to interpret it and check its relevancy (1c). They should be taught to organise and reorganise information (2a), to evaluate the effect of changing values and to identify patterns and relationships (2c). In addition, they should be taught how to share and exchange information (3a), as well as consider its suitability for its audience and its quality (3b).

At all stages children should be taught to review, modify and evaluate their work as it progresses (4a, 4b and 4c).

What does the ICT scheme of work include?

At Key Stage 1 data-handling features in Unit 2C (Finding information) and Unit 2E (Questions and answers).

At Key Stage 2 data-handling features in Unit 3B (Manipulating sound), Unit 3C (Introduction to databases), Unit 4C (Branching databases), Unit 4D (Collecting and presenting information: questionnaires and pie charts), Unit 5B (Analysing data and asking questions: using complex searches), Unit 5C (Evaluating information, checking accuracy and questioning plausibility), Unit 5D (Introduction to spreadsheets), Unit 6B (Spreadsheet modelling) and Unit 6D (Using the Internet to search large databases and to interpret information).

What do teachers need to know before using databases?

Vast amounts of data are collected, from the various meanings of words, to the amount of rain that falls in a particular location, the daytime telephone numbers of families with children at a particular school and the school's annual repair budget. In order for these data to be of any use, they must be organised and stored in some way, usually as an electronic database. The choice of a database is important to ensure that information can be accessed and manipulated as required.

The types of data-handling software utilised in some primary schools can appear quite distinct from those employed in the world at large. However, there has also been a contrasting tendency for educational ICT to move towards 'industry standards'. The argument, used particularly in secondary schools, is that pupils should be encouraged to learn the software that they will encounter in the world of work. As an example, the RM spreadsheet Number Magic has many features which will be familiar to users of Excel. It is important to remember, though, that data-handling software used in schools is designed to facilitate learning about the processes and possibilities of data-handling as well as for the retrieval and manipulation of information. An important contrast is that educational databases usually incorporate presentation capability – the capacity to generate graphs – which may not be so critical for commercial or governmental databases.

A number of different types of data-handling programs are commonly used in schools, including:

- **branching tree or binary databases;**
- **flatfile or tabular databases;**
- **relational databases;**
- **spreadsheets.**

Each of these is structured differently to support different functions.

Branching tree or binary databases

Branching tree or binary databases facilitate the identification of objects, people or plants, for instance, by the posing of questions relating to attributes which must be answered 'yes' or 'no'. The answer to any question leads to a further question to be answered similarly until only one possible outcome remains.

Flatfile or tabular databases

Flatfile or tabular databases are perhaps the type of database that most readily come to mind when primary data-handling activity is considered. A datafile comprises a number of records, each containing data arranged in fields. Children will be able to relate to football cards as an analogy. The pack of cards is the datafile and each card is a record. In addition to the player's name, football cards usually include a photograph, the player's age, the name of the club they play for, the position they play, as well as dates of participation in major championships and national representation. Each of these categories is a field. Data are usually entered into a flatfile database through a form, which resembles a questionnaire and essentially prompts for data to be added to each field.

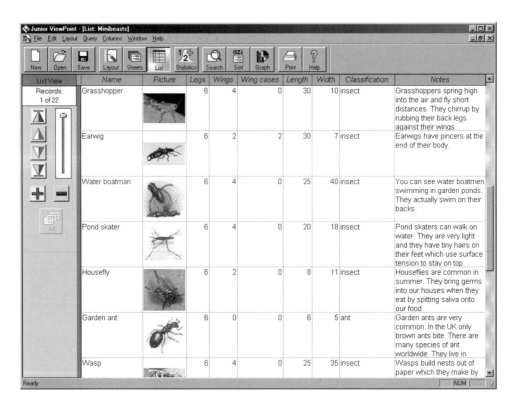

Flatfile database displayed in tabular format (Junior ViewPoint, Longman Logotron)

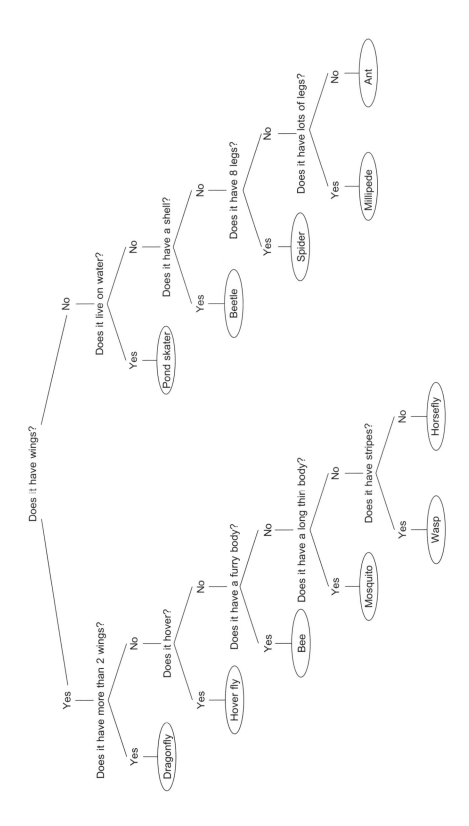

Minibeasts branching tree database

Individual records can be viewed on screen. The entire database can usually also be viewed in tabular format with each column representing a field and each row a record. Sometimes this is called a spreadsheet view. However the term is misleading as the tabular format does not offer all of the functions of a spreadsheet. 'Table' or 'List' are better alternatives.

Relational databases

Relational databases have more complex structures than flatfile databases. Rather than data being organised as it is, then entered into records and fields, which then determine the types of interrogation activity the database will support, information is tagged. The tagging inter-relates the information in the database. This organisational structure supports greater flexibility in interrogation. Some CD-ROM encyclopaedias and reference works are relevant examples of relational databases used in primary schools. They often feature menus, indexes, keywords and hyperlinks as ways of navigating substantial amounts of related information. It is unlikely that in a primary school the need will arise for teachers to teach and children to learn about the technical aspects of relational databases, but they will need to use them.

Spreadsheets

A spreadsheet appears as a grid made up of cells arranged in rows and columns. Each cell is identified by a co-ordinate conventionally comprising a letter for the column and a number for the row – A3, D4, for example. The column reference is given first. Data, often numeric, are entered into each cell by clicking and typing. The data can be searched, sorted, rearranged and presented in graphical format. More importantly, however, individual cells can be programmed to make and display the results of calculations. In the spreadsheet on p152, the cell B12 has been programmed with a formula which instructs it to add 17.5 per cent VAT to the value in cell B10 and display the result.

Spreadsheet showing entry of formula (Number Magic, RM)

What do teachers need to know about databases and spreadsheets?

Teaching with and about databases and spreadsheets involves teachers in the following activities.

Selecting appropriate opportunities – in which data-handling can facilitate, enhance or extend children's learning, such as through a research project that involves interrogating a database, or exploring number patterns and rules with a spreadsheet. In some instances the focus will be on teaching and learning in ICT – how a database can facilitate an investigation. In others ICT will be used as a resource in the teaching and learning of another curriculum area, for instance, using a CD-ROM to research the eating habits of minibeasts.
Selecting appropriate resources – a search tool which enables safe searching of the world wide web or a CD-ROM which supports beginning readers with audio and graphic clues. Both teachers and the children should also make informed choices about when it is worth going through the preparatory work to set up a database, rather than resorting to the quicker option of setting up a spreadsheet.

Preparing suitable resources – although it is instructive for children to construct a database by determining their own fields and records, it may alternatively be appropriate for them to interrogate prepared resources. Many datafiles are commercially available, and may be supplied with the database software, but sometimes teachers will wish to prepare their own or customise existing ones to meet their objectives. Similarly, teachers will sometimes design databases in which children can then enter information they have researched or collected.

Exploring the full range of data-handling activities – databases and spreadsheets are not just about the storage and retrieval of information, they facilitate hypothesising, decision-making, organising, analysing and synthesising.

Making explicit links between related knowledge, skills and understanding – knowledge, skills and understanding of databases and spreadsheets have relevance across the primary curriculum. Teachers thus have opportunities to make explicit and reinforce the links between children's previous experiences and new learning across the range of contexts.

Modelling appropriate use of ICT – for instance, how producing a branching tree database in electronic format enables modifications to be made quickly and easily, or how spreadsheet formulae can be replicated using the 'fill down' function.

Demonstrating and intervening – for instance, intervening to assist a child to identify the tallest child in a class by sorting height data in descending order, or demonstrating the effect of changing the price of sausages in a spreadsheet budget.

The list below attempts to identify the knowledge, skills and understanding of database and spreadsheet software teachers need in order to teach effectively with and about these software packages. The list reflects the features of common software under each of the categories identified. Some software packages may support only a subset of these functions. This is no reflection on their usefulness – in most instances it is a strength, as it may not be helpful for the children to encounter a cluttered interface. However, it does signal that teachers must be aware of the capabilities and limitations of any program as these will be significant in the choice of software for any teaching and learning activity.

Branching tree or binary databases:
- creating, opening, saving, closing, deleting and printing documents;
- adding, modifying and deleting data and questions;
- plotting and replotting branching tree keys;
- inserting titles;
- selecting font and font size;
- exporting branching tree keys into other applications;
- importing information from other applications, e.g. clip art;
- utilising help;
- altering defaults;
- customising the branching tree program, e.g. switching off functions not needed;
- utilising alternative input devices, e.g. overlay keyboards;
- protecting documents.

Flatfile or tabular databases:
- opening, closing, deleting and printing existing datafiles;
- navigating through records using forwards and backwards;
- simple and complex sorting (more than one condition);
- searching to retrieve data;
- plotting and replotting graphs/reports, including:
  - adding text, title, etc.
  - selecting graph type
  - selecting and modifying colours
  - saving
  - exporting graphs to other applications;
- entering data into a prepared datafile, including:
  - selecting a new record/answer sheet
  - entering, modifying and deleting data
  - saving;
- designing a new datafile, including:
  - opening a form/questionnaire designer
  - selecting font, font size, font colour, background colour
  - inserting and modifying questions, including making appropriate selections for style and format of answer supported:
  - words numbers dates;
  - yes/no multiple choice;
- inserting text, images, borders, arrows;
- saving.

Relational databases (e.g. CD-ROMs):
- loading, including installation prior to first use;
- modifying computer display and volume settings;
- opening and closing;
- navigating using menus, hyperlinks, forwards, backwards, home;
- searching and retrieving information using menus, indexes, keywords and hyperlinks;
- playing audio and video;
- copying and pasting text and graphics into other applications;
- selecting and printing information;
- utilising help;
- critical evaluation.

Spreadsheets:
- creating, opening, saving, closing, deleting and printing documents;
- selecting worksheet and cell size;
- selecting font and font size;
- inserting, modifying and deleting row and column labels;
- inserting, modifying, moving and deleting textual and numerical data;
- inserting, modifying and deleting formulae and functions;
- using fill down and fill right functions to replicate formulae;
- inserting and deleting cells, rows and columns;
- formatting data, e.g. left alignment, centring around decimal point;
- searching and sorting data;
- adding, modifying and deleting borders and shading;
- selecting, modifying and displaying graph types;
- formatting graphs to include axes labels, key and text;
- exporting graphs and spreadsheets to other applications;
- importing information from other applications, e.g. clip art, data;
- utilising help;
- altering defaults;
- customising the spreadsheet program, e.g. switching off functions not needed;
- utilising alternative input devices, e.g. data-loggers;
- protecting cells and documents.

There will be occasions on which other data-handling software, such as graphing programs, will be more suitable. It may also happen that a data-handling project that, on a large scale, would be tackled through a database, could in the context of a classroom activity be more easily implemented through a spreadsheet. Teachers need to be confident in making decisions about the most appropriate application for a particular situation.

What are the key features of databases and spreadsheets?

Branching tree databases:
- support sorting and classification activities at all levels;
- support data-handling activities across a range of subject areas;
- provide opportunities for developing and refining questioning techniques;
- do not replace children using paper- or book-based branching tree keys;
- facilitate the creation, revision and extension of branching tree databases;
- often support images as well as text.

Flatfile or tabular databases:
The structure of a flatfile database is determined by the choice of fields and the type of information they contain. These design issues in turn determine the ways in which the database can be used.

Flatfile databases:
- support searching to retrieve information, e.g. the names of the children in the class with blue eyes;
- support more sophisticated searching, on two variables, e.g. the names of girls whose favourite food is pizza;
- support sorting by field, e.g. to see the distribution of hair colour across the class;

- support sorting and ordering a field, e.g. into descending order to find the name of the child with the smallest feet;
- provide graphical representation of enquiry results where this is appropriate, often called a report;
- support sorting and classification activities at all levels;
- support data-handling activities across a range of subject areas;
- facilitate the development of knowledge and understanding across a range of subject areas;
- provide opportunities for developing and refining searching and sorting techniques;
- often support data held as images as well as text;
- support the rapid retrieval of information.

Relational databases:
- support searching by keyword, index and menu;
- support complex or Boolean searching (see Internet chapter);
- support data-handling activities across a range of subject areas;
- provide opportunities for developing and refining search techniques;
- do not replace children using traditional reference sources;
- facilitate the development of knowledge and understanding across a range of subject areas;
- often support video, audio and animations, as well as images and text;
- support the rapid retrieval of vast amounts of information.

Spreadsheets:
- support data held as text or numbers;
- display and process numerical information;
- enable automated calculations and recalculations;
- support the graphical representation of information;
- support the organisation and reorganisation of data to identify patterns, gaps and correlations;
- support the use of graphs to identify errors in data;
- provide opportunities for developing and refining searching, sorting and modelling techniques;
- support the rapid retrieval of information;
- support rapid calculations;
- sometimes support searching to retrieve information, e.g. chocolate bars available for less than 40p;
- support sorting, e.g. displaying chocolate bars in order of unit cost;
- support data handling activities across a range of subject areas;
- sometimes support images for illustration purposes.

What do databases and spreadsheets have to contribute to teaching and learning?

Finding things out

In the wider world, the key characteristic of databases is that they facilitate the rapid retrieval of information. This feature is worth discussing with children as the link between the databases they use in the classroom and a commercial database may not be apparent. A pause to consider how a record is found on the database of a bank or the NHS is important.

Databases support the development of questioning skills in practical situations. Branching tree databases require very particular types of questions, to which the answer can be only 'yes' or 'no', but at the same time they call upon children to apply their subject knowledge as well as skills of sorting and classification. Similarly, if children are to interrogate flatfile or relational databases effectively and productively they need to devise effective questions. Again, these are dependent on experience, knowledge and understanding of the data and structure of the database as well as of the subject itself.

Developing ideas and making things happen

An attribute of spreadsheets is their potential to support 'what if' questions. If the price of every item in the tuck shop is raised by 2p, will profits increase? The answer may appear obvious at first sight, but the children will quickly realise that other variables, such as the effect of the price increase to deter sales, will come into play and the model will need to be modified. Spreadsheets provide opportunities for children to make predictions and hypotheses and test them. For instance, is the cheapest way to buy fruit in large pre-packed bags? A spreadsheet can be used to compare the costs of different fruit bought singly, loose and pre-packed from different shops.

Decision-making is involved in all sorts of data-handling activity. Continuing the example, decisions must be made on which to frame the investigation. Is cost per piece of fruit to be considered or cost by weight? How many different outlets are to be compared? Are the cheapest apples to be sought from each outlet, or is the focus to be Granny Smith apples only?

Similarly, children may consider what is the best way to interrogate a database to retrieve information. Will keyword searching lead to the required information most quickly? Would using the index lead to information which may not be found by a keyword search?

Exchanging and sharing information

Databases are organised stores of information. Information collected by one individual or group is of value to others only if it is accessible. The preparation of data for entry into a flatfile database requires children to order and organise and classify material around the database fields. Structuring information has many applications and is a key skill in effective communication. Children can consider the audience for their data and associated tensions, such as quality versus quantity.

Data retrieval is rarely the final outcome of data-handling activity. Often it is the start. Data retrieved from any type of database can be analysed, interpreted, synthesised and presented.

Many educational database programs have features which support these activities. Relational databases, such as CD-ROMs, often have electronic notepad facilities in which children can make notes, perhaps copy and paste images or short extracts of text and subsequently print off or transfer to a word-processing document. Flatfile databases and spreadsheets support the presentation of data graphically. Very often these graphs can be transferred to other applications or annotated within a report section of the database software.

The presentation of data graphically is often the first stage in analysis and interpretation. It can also support the identification of relationships and potential errors and inconsistencies.

Progression of knowledge, skills and understanding

Branching tree or binary databases

Identification keys for plants and animals are the most obvious example of branching tree databases. The creation of branching tree databases which are as all-encompassing as this is a very sophisticated activity, requiring high levels of subject knowledge and understanding together with well-developed questioning skills. It is more appropriate to use a finite set of, perhaps, minibeasts and explore questions which will progressively lead to a positive identification. Does it have six legs? Does it have a hard, shiny shell? Does it fly?

Children need to use examples of prepared branching tree databases, electronic or otherwise, before they can consider designing their own. It is useful to begin by laying out the objects, or cards representing them, on a table or the floor for children to arrange and rearrange as they select and trial questions. Even with only eight minibeasts to contrast with each other, this may take some time. Children may also need to draw upon reference material to facilitate their sorting. A considerable amount of work may be involved before the children are ready to use a branching tree program on the computer.

Some of the primary packages, such as FlexiTREE2 (Flexible Software Ltd), come with prepared examples. Children can test these and will soon realise that their datasets are restricted. Increasing the range of minibeasts will require more questions. An extension activity could be to try to reduce the number of questions necessary to differentiate between the minibeasts.

Flatfile or tabular databases

Early database activity often focuses on children themselves. Pick a Picture (BlackCat) has four predetermined topics: ourselves, homes, weather and minibeasts. Each topic contains a range of images, and children make selections from these to build up records. Graphs can

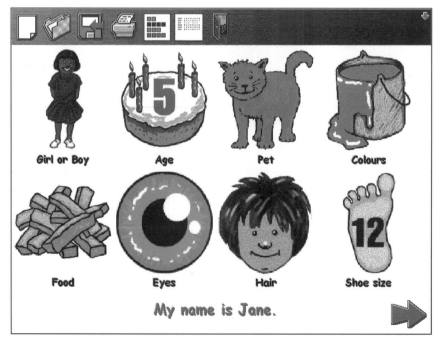

'Ourselves' record from Pick a Picture (BlackCat) which supports early database work

be produced in the form of pictograms or block graphs to display the data graphically. The contents of a datafile can also be displayed in tabular format. This software provides an accessible introduction to flatfile database activity for Early Years and Key Stage 1 children.

ALL ABOUT ME

1. What is your first name? | Daniel |

2. Are you a boy or a girl?   ☒ Boy   ☐ Girl

3. What colour is your hair?   ☐ Blonde   ☐ Black   ☒ Brown   ☐ Ginger

4. What colour are your eyes?   ☐ Blue   ☐ Grey   ☐ Green   ☒ Hazel   ☐ Brown

5. How tall are you?   142 centimetres

6. How much do you weigh?   28 kilogrammes

7. What did you weigh when you were born?   4.0 kilogrammes

**An 'ourselves' questionnaire making use of multiple-choice data entry
(Junior ViewPoint, Longman Logotron)**

Junior ViewPoint (Logotron) is truly generic software which can be used across the curriculum. The example above provides an appropriate model for work with younger children as the amount of information to be entered of a textual or numeric nature is minimal, with some fields requiring selections to be made from multiple-choice lists by pointing and clicking.

In this example children will enter their own data, perhaps with assistance, into a prepared structure. Then, as a group or class, they can interrogate the data to answer questions (how many people have blue eyes?) or test hypotheses (taller people weigh more).

As with graphing, it is not always necessary or appropriate for children to collect and enter their own data into a flatfile database before they interrogate it. They can also work productively with prepared datafiles. A number of software publishers sell prepared datafiles to support a range of curriculum areas. These have advantages which include effective design, accuracy of information, large numbers of records and saving teacher preparation time.

Children will need plenty of experience with databases before they can begin to design their own. Designing and preparing a database is a time-consuming activity and due thought should be given to long-term outcomes. A class may begin a database of plants and animals living within the school grounds, which could be monitored and expanded by subsequent classes, building into a valuable record of diversity and change over time. Trialling the design and checking the entries for errors are vital stages of the process. Such activity is generally recommended for the latter part of Key Stage 2.

Spreadsheets

Children can be introduced to spreadsheets through the functions they perform. For example, RM's Number Magic spreadsheet software comes complete with a number of prepared examples. These will support a range of activities, mainly mathematics-focused across Key Stage 2.

Children can enter numbers into a spreadsheet set up as a function machine to determine what function the machine supports. The teacher may then draw the children's attention to the formula determining the function and encourage them to experiment with modifying the formula.

Another route into spreadsheet activity is making the link with calculators, placing emphasis on a spreadsheet's potential for supporting and facilitating calculations, especially those of a repeated nature. Children may begin by entering a number and choosing an operation to perform on that number, for instance adding 3. This process can be repeated focusing on emerging patterns, predicting and checking. At this level, spreadsheets have a number of advantages over calculators, the most pertinent being that they are easily checkable, by reviewing the formula for a calculation, or by graphing results to identify anomalies. It is important that the copying and pasting of formulae is not offered as a solution too soon, before the purpose and process of formula-writing has been understood.

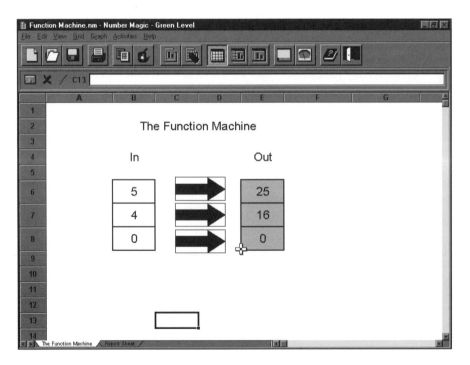

Function machine, a prepared file in RM's NumberMagic

Children will need opportunities to become familiar with the navigation of spreadsheets, the entry of numeric and textual information, the display of numeric and graphical results, saving and printing.

Spreadsheets can then be used to extend children's knowledge and understanding of number facts and arithmetic laws, supporting mental calculation as children predict and check results as well as deriving generalisations, supporting early algebra work.

As we have seen, spreadsheets are ideal for modelling 'what if?' scenarios. These can be applied to mathematic and scientific situations, particularly in Key Stage 2. Budgets are a popular focus as are modelling the effect of changing variables in science work. Graphical representation of spreadsheet data can be particularly powerful in this respect.

CLASSROOM STORY

A Year 6 class was applying their mathematical understanding to the comparison of data from their school weather station with national information for the same period. In order to make comparisons they needed to calculate some weekly and monthly averages from their own data recorded on a daily basis. The teacher reminded the class that, anticipating making eventual use of it, the data had been recorded in a spreadsheet as they were collected. She reminded the children how to enter a formula to calculate the arithmetical mean rainfall over one week in March. The children carefully programmed formulae into other cells to determine median and modal values. The teacher then intervened to demonstrate how formulae could be copied and applied to other cells using the fill handle. A while later the teacher was intrigued to notice that some of the children were busy checking the spreadsheet's calculations with calculators. Questioning determined that this checking regime had been a group decision to ensure that formulae copied from one location to another were actually performing the intended operation.

Relational databases

Dictosaurus (Oxford University Press) adds new dimensions to the traditional concept of the dictionary for children. They can click to hear words spoken to confirm graphophonic relationships. Each word is presented through text, images and sound. Children can also use thesaurus facilities to find synonyms and insert them directly into their word processed text.

Most CD-ROM databases make use of multimedia to a greater or lesser extent and whole new concepts in terms of resources have been developed in consequence. *Magic Grandad's Seaside Holidays* (Sherston) supports history teaching at Key Stage 1 by integrating text and images, together with spoken narration and historical video clips, to enable today's children to contrast holidays now with those experienced 50 or 100 years ago. This database requires some quite sophisticated information-handling skills if children are to search in it independently, although the format and navigation are clear and the teacher can control which resources are accessed.

To some extent classroom use of CD-ROMs has inevitably been overtaken by the 'free' access that schools enjoy to the world wide web. However, the authenticity of CD-ROM material, the sharp focus it gives through its content to the children's learning, and the safe environment that is provided all serve to make CD-ROMs preferable to the world wide web for certain purposes. CD-ROM databases are subject to editorial control by their publishers, in the same way as traditional media. No such quality monitors are exercised by the authors of most world wide web sites and information retrieved from these should be treated with due caution.

PRACTICAL TASK PRACTICAL TASK **PRACTICAL TASK** PRACTICAL TASK

Design an A4 help sheet to help children navigate successfully in a specified CD-ROM. What are the key features of effective help sheet design?

What are the capabilities and limitations of databases?

Selecting appropriate databases

The different types of database discussed in this chapter support different types of data-handling activity. Teachers and children will need to make informed decisions about the most appropriate tool for a particular purpose. Again, this is no reflection on the suitability of a particular piece of software as no single program supports all the features and functions discussed.

Keyword searching

Effective keyword searching relies on the choice of appropriate keywords. For most children such selections will require thought, discussion and practice. Some words which have a wide range of applications may not be suitable. Effective keyword selection implies some background knowledge of the search subject. Refining techniques can be used to further narrow the focus of a search.

> **CLASSROOM STORY**
>
> A group of Year 5 girls had been charged with researching and presenting some information on the planet Earth as part of a class science study on the Earth and beyond. Two of the group decided that a CD ROM encyclopaedia might be a good place to start. They input 'earth' into the search tool and a high number of matches were found. Beginning to explore these in a systematic manner the girls became confused as the first two hits related to soil types and electrical circuits. They had not considered that, even in science, the word 'earth' can have different meanings in at least three contexts: planet Earth, electrical earth and soil.

Spelling is another issue in keyword searching. Incorrectly spelled words are unlikely to prove effective in retrieving the desired information. Some CD-ROMs and websites provide support for children, to help them check their spelling before conducting a search.

One of the strengths of relational databases is that one particular item may be retrieved by searching for any one of a number of keywords. Flatfile or other databases may be more restricted in this respect.

Hypertext literacy

Reading hypertext documents requires a range of skills – many of these have parallels with those associated with traditional texts, while some are different. Many relational databases are navigable by index as with traditional reference material. The presence of hypertext links, however, means that children's reading of these texts is not linear – they may dart about from one narrative to another to another. Retaining a task focus throughout such a process can be demanding. Similarly, hypertext documents give no sense of geographical location within a text. Children may never know whether they have accessed everything on a particular subject.

CD-ROMs

CD-ROM databases should not be confused with:

- *CD-ROM talking books* – these make use of multimedia but their structure mirrors more closely the linear nature of traditional books. The subject focus of a talking book may be fiction or non-fiction (Oxford Reading Tree, Sherston and Living Books, Broderbund).
- *CD-ROM software* – CD-ROMs are used for the storage and transfer of software. Often when a school buys new software this comes in the form of a CD-ROM. The software is then copied onto the school's computer or network as appropriate and used from there.
- *CD-ROM games and resources* – some games and other resources also come in the form of CD-ROMs. These are not necessarily designed to be copied onto the computer's memory; if space is short the resources may often be used direct from the disk. Tizzy's Toybox (Sherston) and Mighty Maths Number Heroes (Riverdeep) are examples.

CD-ROMs and world wide web sites provide access to almost unlimited quantities of information. Sometimes this can be quite daunting as making appropriate selections to satisfy the needs of the task demands that children judge whether particular information is relevant to their enquiry as well as thinking how they might use it.

Copying

Many data-handling activities involve children retrieving information with a view to synthesising or applying it in some way. Teachers have long struggled with children copying information retrieved from reference sources, apparently without engaging with the material. One likely reason for this is that children have difficulty in making sense of the information. Often reference texts are designed with an adult audience in mind and make use of complex sentence structures and sophisticated vocabulary. Information can be useful only if children are able to read it. They also need to deploy associated higher-order reading skills, such as skimming and scanning text.

CLASSROOM STORY

A Year 5 teacher was encouraging her class to make use of CD-ROM databases to support research across the curriculum. She was discouraged to note that many children merely copied down the text as it appeared on the screen or printed it off. She discussed this issue with the children and suggested a new strategy. Children could print entries or copy and paste them into a word processor, but must then read them through away from the computer, highlighting or underlining words that they did not fully understand, and then looking them up. The children then replaced these elements of the text with their own words to form a narrative that had meaning for them. Some time later she drew one child's attention to the presence of the word 'tectonic' in his work, and was told that it was okay because he now knew what tectonic means.

Data accuracy

Effective interrogation of a database relies on the data held being accurate. It also relies on data being entered in a format in which they can easily be searched or sorted. If a child enters data on the number of brothers and sisters he has into a flatfile database as text, they could appear as '2brothers' or '2 buthrs'. The data would require considerable checking and modification before it could be used. The phrasing of questions as multiple-choice or yes/no wherever possible minimises the chance of such errors.

Flatfile databases and types of data

Flatfile databases can support data entered in a variety of formats, including:

- **text, e.g. the name of a minibeast;**
- **numeric, e.g. the number of legs the mini beast has;**
- **dates;**
- **yes/no, e.g. does the minibeast live the the UK?**
- **multiple-choice, e.g. the life expectancy of a minibeast:**
  - **a day**
  - **a week**
  - **a month**
  - **3 months, and so on.**

Where text entries are concerned it is usually possible to limit the length of answers to a specified number of characters. Numeric entries can similarly be limited to a predetermined number of digits, to reduce the chances of inaccurate data being entered in error. In large commercial databases the limits also serve to minimise the storage space needed – a factor which in the past was significant, but which is not so critical now. The use of multiple-choice and yes/no answers further reduces the risk of inaccurate entries or entries that are difficult to search or sort. Multiple-choice answers rather than open-ended text also make analysis easier.

Spreadsheets and the = sign

Teachers will need to ensure that they make explicit the role of the equals sign in spreadsheet formulae. It does not balance the equation, showing that one side is equal to the other, but provides a function, effectively instructing the software to perform the calculations that follow it. This may also be explained as 'the contents of this cell are equal to'. This is slightly different from the use of the equals sign with calculators when the calculations are entered first and the = sign instructs the calculator to perform the functions.

Written algorithm:
10 + 4 = 14 (balance, both sides of the equation are equal)

Spreadsheet:
= B3 + B7 (function, add the contents of B3 to B7 and display)

Calculator:
10 + 4 = (function, now add 10 to 4 and display)

Professional use

Spreadsheets have various possibilities for teachers' professional use. Many teachers make a class list at the beginning of the year which they are able to use and reuse many times as mark sheets or for other records.

Data protection

Personal data are governed by the provisions of the Data Protection Act 1998. Although this legislation was not formed with primary school data-handling activities in mind, teachers must ensure that they comply with its requirements where applicable. The key issues are ensuring that data are secure and cannot be accessed by unauthorised individuals and that they are not held any longer than necessary. See Chapter 18 on the professional use of ICT for further information.

Privacy

The collection and interpretation of personal data about children raise issues of privacy and sensitivity – children's height and weight, for instance. Teachers have devised a number of strategies in this respect. Ourselves-type data can be collected for young children's teddies, while with older children it may be appropriate to discuss some of the issues raised.

Software selection and advice

Often software and ICT-related resources, such as talking books or non-fiction CD-ROMs, can be obtained from their publishers or software wholesalers on approval. The school usually has between 10 and 28 days to evaluate the resource and decide whether to keep it and pay the account or to return it. Obtaining software on approval will probably incur the cost of return postage if the decision is taken not to purchase it. However, with limited budgets and an ever-increasing range of products to choose from, the costs of mistakes can be higher financially and professionally. Software should be evaluated for content and for compatibility. Some software does not sit well with particular operating systems or other software items. It is important to determine whether a software package will cause such problems and, if so, whether the benefits of the software outweigh the problems of overcoming compatibility issues.

Local authority ICT advisers should be a good source of advice and support when purchasing software. In some instances they may have negotiated discounts on recommended titles. TEEM maintain a very helpful educational software database, also containing independent reviews and supplier information. This is available online at **http://www.teem.org.uk**

PRACTICAL TASK PRACTICAL TASK **PRACTICAL TASK** PRACTICAL TASK

Select a range of non-fiction CD-ROMs on a specific curriculum area. Aiming to identify resources that would support the teaching and learning of that subject across a primary school, critically evaluate the resources.

Is one age range better catered for than others? Why might that be?

How might you customise and refine the evaluation criteria suggested to reflect your own:

- **subject specialism?**
- **age range specialism?**

Printing issues

It is all too easy with some data-handling programs to print accidentally the entire file rather than the portion intended. Children may decide that it would be useful to print out the information they can see on the screen, without considering that that may be a subsection of a very large document. Often it is necessary to detail exactly what is to be printed and to check it with Print Preview if such as facility is available. Sometimes copying and pasting into a word processor or other document may be useful.

Teaching and learning

Although using database programs reduces some of the demands on children involved in the manipulation of data, it is important to ensure that value is placed on interpretation and understanding rather than on the presentation of professional-looking graphics. Similarly, use of a database does not ensure successful teaching and learning. This will depend on appropriate task-setting, differentiation and intervention, as in any other teaching and learning situation.

Data-handling and the core subjects

The ideas and activities introduced below are intended to give a feel for the range of ways in which databases can be utilised to support and enhance teaching and learning in mathematics, science and English. They are not intended to be comprehensive, merely to go some way towards illustrating the breadth of possibilities and to provide starting points for the customisation of ideas and the generation of others. Examples introduced under mathematics, for instance, may be just as applicable to one or more of the other areas. Other useful sources include professional journals (such as *Primary Science Review*, *Junior Education* and *Child Education*), websites (such as Becta), and the respective schemes of work.

There is extensive overlap between science, mathematics, English, ICT and other subject knowledge, skills and understanding in the area of data handling. Teachers need to be clear about their primary teaching objective for any particular task or sequence of activities and maximise the opportunities for making explicit links between learning in the various curriculum contexts.

Data-handling and science

Databases are used extensively in primary science. Data can be collected from children's own observations ('Ourselves' is a good starting point) and experimental results, and then recorded for analysis. Alternatively, a spreadsheet might be used to predict and explore the effect of making changes to variables – for example, recording plant growth measurements against differing quantities of water, light and warmth.

Spreadsheets, and particularly graphs generated from them, can be equally valuable in highlighting errors. The concept of experimental error is often difficult to explore effectively in primary schools owing to the lack of opportunity for repeated experimentation. However, data from a whole class's results entered, compared and analysed might highlight anomalies, leading to discussion and prediction of possible causes and perhaps improvements in experimental technique – the same group member operating the stopwatch each time, for instance.

The properties of materials could be a research topic for the compilation of a class datafile resource. Fields might include what the objects are, where they come from and what we use them for, the field structure of the database providing a framework for the children's research. Such resources can be accessed for information later and added to by other classes to build enduring resources over which children have ownership.

CD-ROMs and websites can provide access to high-quality multimedia data. When the USA has a space shuttle on a mission, images are available to children in classrooms around the world as quickly as they are to NASA scientists. Such databases also provide a breadth of resources which would not be available otherwise – slow-motion video of spiders walking or animations of the way the bones or muscles in the leg move as humans walk.

Data-handling and mathematics

Spreadsheets can be used to generate arithmetic and geometric sequences rapidly. Teachers may generate and print these to use away from the computer. A range of problem-solving activities can be supported in this way. For instance, using a hundred square, colour in all the cells containing 7s. What do you notice? Now colour all those with numbers ending in 3. What do you notice?

Using the number pattern function (Number Magic, RM)

A branching tree database incorporating pictures may be used to support the sorting and classification of shapes with younger children. Does the shape have corners? Does it have four sides?

Mathematical investigations such as the shape of the farmer's field can be modelled using spreadsheets – creating the maximum area with the minimum fencing materials, exploring different shapes of field, working towards generalisations and early algebra.

Data-handling activities which have real relevance for children can be derived from school sporting activities. Recording the results from the netball or football league matches week by week can provide opportunities for statistical analysis: average goals scored per match; comparison of home and away results. Children can be charged with determining the placings of athletics competitors on school sports day: calculating the overall winner based on the average of three long jumps or rounders ball throws.

Databases and English

Effective use of a range of databases in the primary school provides opportunities for the teaching and reinforcement of a range of higher-order language skills, such as keyword selection and the skimming and scanning of text.

A class database of book reviews searchable by author, subject matter and reading level may be a valuable ongoing resource. In a whole-school context children may be involved in the process at varying levels. Older children may be called upon to design and trial the structure of the resource. All children could be involved in adding records, with support varying from adult scribes to older children checking the entries for errors and inaccuracies. Similarly, all children might use the database to assist their selection of reading material.

Electronic dictionaries and thesauruses provide alternative reference sources. Some children find these easier to use than paper-based sources because of the combination of audio, images, text and hyperlinks. Most word processing packages have their own built-in dictionaries and thesaurus.

REFLECTIVE TASK

To provide, in your own mind, a context into which children's work with databases might be lodged, make a list of the databases managed by national and local organisations (commercial, governmental, educational, leisure) that hold data about you. Its length may surprise you!

Moving on

A good way to explore the potential of software is to make it do something you want, rather than simply following a tutorial or manual. See if you can construct a spreadsheet which will allow you to track children's progress during a term. You may not be using numerical marks; what other possibilities are there (for example letter codes or colouring in cells)? Is the average mark over a whole term useful, or might it hide improvement (or decline) as the term progresses? Can you make the spreadsheet sophisticated enough to reflect these trends?

A SUMMARY OF **KEY POINTS**

> Databases enable interaction with data to explore meaning through relationships, patterns and modelling.

> There is a range of types of databases and spreadsheets commonly found in primary schools. These include:
>   – binary or branching tree databases;
>   – flatfile or tabular databases;
>   – relational databases;
>   – spreadsheets.

> Good database design is essential if the data contained is to be used effectively.

FURTHER READING FURTHER READING **FURTHER READING** FURTHER READING

Bennett, R. (2006) *Learning ICT with maths*. London: David Fulton

Briggs, M. and Pritchard, A. (2002) *Using ICT in primary mathematics teaching*. Exeter: Learning Matters

Byrne, J. (2002) *Using ICT in primary science teaching*. Exeter: Learning Matters

Clark-Jeavons, A. (2005) *Exciting ICT in maths*. Stafford: Network Educational

DfEE/QCA (1999) *Curriculum Guidance for the Foundation Stage*. London: DfEE/QCA

DfEE/QCA (1999) *The National Curriculum*. London: DfEE/QCA

Fox, B., Montague-Smith, A., and Wilkes, S. (2000) *Using ICT in primary mathematics: practice and possibilities*. London: David Fulton

Frost, R. (2006) *Dataloggerama* **http://www.rogerfrost.com/**

Higgins, C. *et al.* (2002, 2003) *ICT connect* (Years 1-06). Oxford: Harcourt Education Limited

Jarvis, G. (2003) *Using ICT in primary humanities teaching.* Exeter: Learning Matters

Leask, M. (ed.) (2001) *Issues in teaching using ICT*. London: Routledge

Leask, M. (ed.) (2000) *Teaching and learning with ICT in the primary school*. London: Routledge

Loveless, A. and Dore, B. (2002) *ICT in the primary school*. Buckingham: Open University Press

Meadows, J. (2004) *Science and ICT in primary education: a creative approach to big ideas*. London: David Fulton

QCA/DfEE (1998, rev. 2000) *Information and communications technology: a scheme of work for Key Stages 1 and 2*. London: DfEE/QCA.

Way, J. and Beardon, T. (2002) *ICT and primary mathematics*. Buckingham: OUP

Wikipedia (2007) *Database* **http://en.wikipedia.org/wiki/Database**

Wikipedia (2007) *Relational database* **http://en.wikipedia.org/wiki/Relational_databases**

Wikipedia (2007) *Spreadsheet* **http://en.wikipedia.org/wiki/Spreadsheet**

Williams, J. and Easingwood, N. (2004) *ICT and primary mathematics*. London: RoutledgeFalmer

Williams, J. and Easingwood, N. (2003) *ICT and primary science*. London: RoutledgeFalmer

11
Digital video

Chapter objectives

The aim of this chapter is to introduce the reader to the various uses of digital video in educational settings. It introduces some of the key concepts and theoretical perspectives and some of the relevant tools.

Introducing video production in schools

Video production in schools has been made possible and accessible in recent years thanks to the proliferation of affordable equipment and software. Cameras of all sorts and simple editing software have given non-specialists access to areas which were previously in the domain of media professionals. As seen in Chapter 17 on music and sound, a further set of possibilities has been opened up by the ease with which productions can be shared and exchanged through the medium of the Internet or by swapping commonly formatted media files.

For formal educational settings, the production of digital video images of children and their work raises ethical considerations and Internet safety issues. Sensible discussion of these issues with school governors, parents, children, teachers and all stakeholders, together with an agreed protocol for making and distributing these productions, can result in children being given access to the very powerful medium of digital video within a school context. There are schools that regularly publish their children's work within password-protected areas in their local authority online learning environment. Others distribute material to parents on DVD. Some make sure that children can safely use the medium without being identifiable but that they can still engage with work such as animation or simple video production.

Whatever the means by which the obstacles raised above can be overcome, there is little doubt that digital video production of all kinds brings huge benefits in a number of areas of the curriculum. There are a growing number of studies which show a whole range of exciting possibilities in this country and elsewhere of the potential benefits from the Becta DV pilot in this country, covering 50 schools, to the work in Australia involving large-scale teacher–pupil case studies and finally into smaller-scale case studies of individual school projects (Reid, Burn and Parker, 2002; Schuck and Kearney, 2004; Pearson, 2005; Potter, 2005).

Some uses of digital video in schools

Some of the potential sites of this work in school settings include the following.

- **Curriculum-based projects which allow for children to make media productions of project work, either for assessment purposes (e.g. in their portfolios) or for use within the school setting with other age groups ('Make a movie which tries to explain gravity to a younger class').**

- Autobiographical and/or creative productions which allow exploration of the medium in a more creative context, including the use of sound assembled for the project (see also Chapter 17).
- Shorter clips produced with assessment in mind, e.g. for movement within a PE lesson. Shorter unedited pieces used to review movement on a shared space in the classroom (interactive whiteboard).
- Self-produced clips used to explore popular culture and emergent media literacy concepts, through parodies or references to popular programming on TV or online (in areas such as YouTube). Also used to reinforce ICT concepts around media filetypes and simpler skills applicable across all digital media (cutting and pasting and so on).
- Comparison of different tools of production from digital video cameras through to solid-state recorders (see below), mobile phones and PDAs.
- Animations produced using stop-frame software or similar, capturing the image step by step and changing its position over time.

Some of these ideas are summarised, alongside notions of exhibition and consumption in the following diagram:

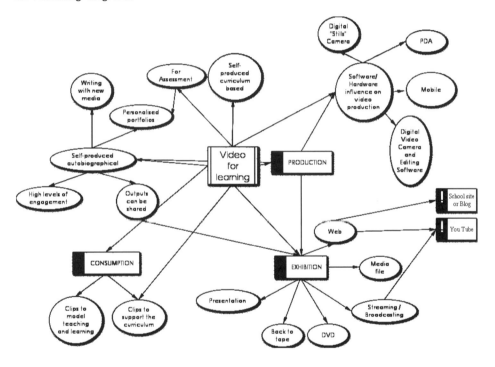

Mind map of possible issues around the use of Video for Learning

It should be apparent by now that the applications of Digital Video to the school curriculum are potentially wide and varied and offer something to all subjects of the National Curriculum. One example would be Literacy, where engagement with this sort of technology allows for an exploration of story and narrative structure at a sophisticated level, not least in the consideration of audience. The notion of literacy in the curriculum is undergoing change with the increasing influence of a developing concept of media literacy as defined by the relevant government agencies (OFCOM, 2005).

Starting points for working with digital video

In order to undertake video production in the classroom there are a number of starting points. Digital still cameras often include the facility to make short movies which can be quickly reviewed and used in a spontaneous way in an unedited form. This could be useful in lessons which require the facility to go back and review live action to make a learning concept explicit (a Science experiment, a piece of classroom drama or performance – see classroom story below – or a PE lesson on making shapes).

Smaller solid-state digital video cameras are available which shoot a small amount of material for downloading directly to the computer for editing via a USB connection. One such is Digital Movie Creator (for the PC), a small blue plastic camera with no moving parts and a viewfinder through which children can capture real or animated scenes. A simple editing interface allows children to add effects and to export a finished version.

Digital Move Creator editing interface (PC software)

CLASSROOM STORY

A teacher has distributed lines from a poem to a Year 4 class, two to each of five tables in the classroom. The task is interpreting the lines in a rhythmic way, to perform them to the rest of the class. The teacher reminds them to think about each word and how it contributes to the whole, to think about how the overall pattern of the piece reflects a particular form (in this case, Calypso). The class comes out table by table after a short time rehearsing and the children record each table's two-line performance in turn. The whole thing is played back on the interactive whiteboard in sequence and the children appraise the overall class performance in terms of its communicative and dramatic aspects. This has been a literacy lesson which has featured a huge amount of excitement, allowed for speaking and listening activities exploring aspects of the *Primary National Strategy* for literacy at Year 4 around poetry and performance. Motivation has been high. There have been no worksheets. Nothing has been recorded in a written form, but the movies can be saved as part of the class portfolio on the network drive and the teacher has had time to review contributions for her own record keeping.

Developing digital video work further

The next, and slightly more complex but more flexible, stage of video production involves the use of a digital video camera to capture the material for editing. Your school may have one or your college may be able to lend you one. These relatively inexpensive pieces of equipment can, nevertheless, produce high-quality moving images ready for editing after they have been downloaded to a computer with editing software. This is achieved using a cable known popularly as a Firewire cable to connect either to a Mac or a PC (provided the latter has been fitted with a Firewire card). They are standard on all Macs and almost always – but not always – available on a PC). Once inside the computer, the software allows for the scenes to be trimmed to appropriate lengths and joined using a variety of transitions simply by dragging them and dropping them onto a timeline. If you have used the free music editing software Audacity, recommended in Chapter 17, you will be familiar with the timeline concept and also the idea that because, like the sound, the video is stored digitally, it can be cut and pasted in the same way. Effects such as titles can then be added and the whole production can be exported as a finished file for exhibition on the Internet, the LA or school network, or for distribution home on disk.

It is worth mentioning at the outset that sound is a big problem in video production by learners. An audience will put up with poor camerawork (to an extent) over poor sound. Sound quality, whether in the form of a soundtrack or speech to camera, is closely bound to an audience's ability to construct meaning from a video production. You should draw attention to this and investigate the possibility of using microphones in noisier settings to record crucial speech or dialogue. Using Audacity, it might be possible to clean up poorer audio but in the interests of keeping the process simpler it is a consideration at the beginning of any project.

There is free software available to edit on a PC (Windows Moviemaker, standard in almost all versions of Windows Vista). On a Mac, as part of the same suite of software which provides Garageband for music production (see Chapter 17) there is also free and powerful video-editing software called iMovie.

The iMovie workspace, showing the clips arranged at the bottom along a simple timeline view

As suggested in Chapter 17, a teacher must have a view of the pedagogy, a reason for using the particular software. There are mappings onto all curriculum areas for digital video production which lend it to cross-curricular work in school. At the same time there are powerful reasons for using it as a way to extend learner knowledge of ICT in a powerful and motivating context and in a form which is culturally significant and authentic for them.

Another factor which you must consider is the extent to which you will enable improvements in the quality of children's work by engagement with the language and techniques of film-making. There are excellent resources available which allow you to introduce important concepts around film-making and one of the very best is that produced by Media Education Wales called *Making movies make sense* (Barrance, 2004).

REFLECTIVE TASK

Children's digital video production

Using Google (UK) search online for Dingwall Primary School's weblog. Here you will find videos made by children at Dingwall School in Scotland. If you cannot locate this resource, search on BAFTA – BE Very Afraid. Here you will be able to view work produced by students and exhibited on the web – with permission – by Stephen Heppell, who has been actively involved in championing children's creative use of technology – including digital video production for a number of years (see also Heppell.net, 2007).

Once you have some examples of children's video, try to respond to the following questions:

- **Which curriculum area, or areas, is represented?**
- **What genre is the film operating in?**
- **Has the teacher given the students input into film-making?**
- **What do you think the plan for this activity looks like?**
- **What skills would you personally require to carry out work like this with children?**

A SUMMARY OF **KEY POINTS**

> **Introduction to uses of digital video.**
> **Key concepts, theoretical perspective and relevant tools.**

Moving on

As you move into your career you will find INSET opportunities relating to new technology, in particular the use of media in the curriculum. Think about the ways in which this will impact on you as a professional, not only on the children as learners. In what ways will media in the classroom support your professional role(s)?

FURTHER READING FURTHER READING FURTHER READING FURTHER READING

Barrance, T. (2004) *Making movies make sense*. Media Education Wales

OFCOM (2005) *Ofcom's strategy and priorities for the promotion of media literacy – A statement*. Available at: **http://www.ofcom.org.uk/consult/condocs/strategymedialit/ml_statement/** Last accessed 20 May 2005

Pearson, M. (2005) Splitting clips and telling tales. *Education and Information Technologies,* 10 (3), 189–205

Potter, J. (2005) This brings back a lot of memories – A case study in the analysis of digital video production by young learners. *Education, Communication and Information,* 5 (1)

Reid, M., Burn, A. and Parker, D. (2002) *Evaluation report of the Becta digital video pilot project*. Becta/BFI

Schuck, S. and Kearney, M. (2004) *Students in the director's seat: teaching and learning across the school curriculum with student-generated video*. Sydney: Faculty of Education, University of Technology, Sydney

12
Digital cameras

Chapter objectives

Digital cameras are providing opportunities to children – and their teachers – to work using photography with a freedom and economy that is unprecedented. The potential readily to use visual images in addition to text in order to record information and communicate ideas has important implications for what we understand by literacy. In this chapter we shall introduce some basic technical considerations that are important for the successful use of digital cameras in the classroom, and then identify some straightforward applications of digital photography, both in activities designed for children and to meet teachers' own professional needs and demands.

What are digital cameras?
Digital cameras share a common purpose with film-based cameras: they both record images. The technical means by which this end is achieved differs, though. The traditional camera uses film. The film is sensitive to light, and changes on exposure. The film is then processed, outside of the camera, resulting in paper- or transparency-based pictures. In a digital camera the image is taken, or 'captured', but then it is also processed and stored as a file within the camera itself (Ang, 2002).

In a digital camera, processed images are held on a memory card. From this medium the images may be transferred to a computer, usually by a USB cable or on recent computers by inserting the memory card into a drive on the computer, for further manipulation or incorporation in other files. Alternatively, many recent printers can accept the memory card directly and print from it, so by-passing the computer altogether.

What do the programmes of study for Key Stage 1 and 2 include?

The use of digital cameras is not specifically identified in the programmes of study. However, they might be utilised in various contexts. At Key Stage 1 children should be taught to gather information (1a), enter and store it (1b) and retrieve it (1c). They should be taught to use text, tables, images and sounds to develop their ideas (2a). They should also be taught to share their ideas by presenting information in a variety of forms (3a) and to present their work effectively (3b).

At Key Stage 2, children should be taught to talk about the information they need (1a), how to prepare information (1b), how to organise and reorganise it (2a), how to share and exchange it (3a), as well as consider its suitability for its audience and its quality (3b).

At all stages children should be taught to review, modify and evaluate their work as it progresses (4a, 4b and 4c).

What does the ICT scheme of work include?

The ICT scheme of work does not refer directly to the use of digital cameras, but they might usefully be involved in 2B (Creating pictures), 3A (Combining text and graphics), 4B (Developing images using repeating patterns) and Unit 5A (Graphical modelling). More importantly, perhaps, a digital camera can be employed in a range of cross-curricular contexts, some of which are suggested later in this chapter.

What do teachers need to know before using digital cameras in the classroom?

The proliferation of interest in digital photography has resulted in a wide range of digital cameras being available. These vary considerably in functionality. More expensive digital cameras offer the sophistication of single lens reflex (SLR) viewing and manual control over shutter speed and aperture. However, these features may not be of much use in the primary classroom and could create unhelpful layers of complexity. A simple camera will be cheaper and appropriate for most purposes.

Unfortunately, the ease with which images can be recorded, transferred and stored by digital cameras has led to their misuse by unscrupulous individuals. Both trainees and serving teachers need to be aware and respectful of parental concerns about images of their children being taken. Schools will have their own policies in respect of photography, frequently guided by their local authority. A regular strategy is for the school to obtain written parental permission for their child to be involved in photography at the beginning of each school year, or when the child enters the school. The understanding will be that the images are used only in the course of educational activity. Before using a digital camera in school, it is vital to ensure that you will be complying with your school's policy on photography.

From the perspective of the teacher's own professional needs, a digital camera can be a helpful ally. For example, a picture of the outcome of a design technology project, or a photograph of PE or a dance or drama production will serve as a helpful record for assessment purposes. It is certainly quicker to create than a written account, and is likely to convey what was happening much more clearly.

For a teacher's own continuing professional development, photographic documentation can bring to life his or her work in the classroom and his or her contribution to the wider life of the school. It is also first-hand testimony, evidence in a form that is much more convincing than a written claim can be.

What do teachers need to know about digital cameras?

For a teacher, the way in which a digital camera works has a number of advantages. The most important of these is speed. Images are available for children to use almost instantaneously. There is no delay while a film is sent away for processing. This immediacy means that the momentum of a project is maintained and the children are able to use the images that they have taken to continue their work. The facility through which unwanted images can be deleted without any waste, and the possibility of taking a large number of pictures at a time are other benefits of digital photography. Finally there is the cost benefit. The price of digital cameras has dropped rapidly in the last few years to the extent that they are now regularly bundled as part of a package of computer products. Furthermore, once purchased, there are few running costs. Film and processing are no longer recurring expenses. Digital cameras consume batteries quickly, but this potential cost can be minimised by buying a camera with a rechargeable battery.

Many 'still' digital cameras, even quite cheap ones, are able to record moving images in mpeg format. Not surprisingly this functionality is not as developed as that found on a dedicated digital video camera, and the length of clip that it is possible to create will be constrained by the capacity of the camera's memory card. Nevertheless, the possibilities for creating short videos on a digital camera should be kept in mind.

What are the key features of digital cameras?

There are two significant technical parameters that are typically used by manufacturers to describe digital cameras: resolution and zoom. The resolution of which the camera is capable is measured in pixels – or more usually megapixels (one million pixels). As we have seen in Chapter 8 on graphics software, a pixel is a rectangular dot in a single colour. Putting lots of pixels together in an image provides the illusion of continuous gradations of colour. The smaller the pixel, the better defined the image will appear. If the same size of picture is rendered in 1024 × 768 pixels it will look better, and, dependent in its size, is less likely to appear 'blocky' than if it is shown in 640 × 480 pixels. However, in this example the image file at higher resolution will be two and a half times larger than the same image at lower resolution, so taking up proportionately more space on the memory card. As we have considered in Chapter 8, if the children are using the images they create for desktop publishing, incorporation into web pages or to send by e-mail, then small images at relatively low resolutions will be sufficient and more economical in every respect, not least ink.

It is worth noting that, conventionally, images are recorded with dimensions in a ratio of 4:3, consistent with the usual proportions for computer monitors. Some cameras have the capability for other settings such as 3:2.

A digital camera usually incorporates a zoom lens, typically allowing the image to be enlarged up to three times, and so enabling the user to change the field of view between wide angle and telephoto. The camera may also offer a digital zoom function, which takes over when the limit of the optical zoom is reached. However, because of the way it functions, the digital zoom tends to deteriorate the picture quality.

Most digital cameras are provided with an LCD screen. This is helpful in enabling the user to review immediately the images that have been taken, providing the opportunity to ensure that appropriate images are captured before returning to the classroom and to delete those that are not needed, so freeing up space on the memory card. This facility enables the adoption of a totally different approach to photography in contrast to film technology, where mistakes are costly in terms of developing unwanted pictures. Digital photography allows a much more spontaneous, experimental attitude to be embraced.

Other important features that are usually found on a digital camera include a flash that can be utilised to assist recording images in poor light or at night. As with a conventional film camera, there are limits to the capability of the flash in an open space, but the technology now enables good-quality close-up shots to be achieved in the dark. The camera is also likely to have various controls such as a timer, options for close-up and distance work and adjustment of the white balance.

Progression of knowledge, skills and understanding

It is likely that a digital camera will be used inside or outside the classroom primarily for recording objects or events, rather than for artistic purposes. As such, a point-and-click operation may be all that is needed. However, older children should be encouraged to think more about the composition of the photographs they can take, and may want to explore the effects and settings that are provided.

Although there is a large number of different brands and models of digital camera available, there has fortunately been convergence in their design, and many features will be recognisable from one camera to another. This means that for children, and their teachers, understanding gained of how one camera works will have substantial transferability if they are faced with a new model.

What are the capabilities and limitations of digital cameras?

Digital cameras provide a fast and effective way of creating a photographic record and have a wide range of possibilities in the classroom. However, they are costly and fairly fragile items of equipment that need to be treated with care. For classroom purposes it may well be that buying a simple camera with limited functionality is a practical and less expensive option.

It is probable that a school will have sufficient cameras for only a handful of children to be using them at any one time, so their management during a lesson, and planning for their integration into projects and activities, need to recognise this resource limitation.

Digital cameras and the core subjects

Digital cameras and science

Digital cameras are essentially recording devices, so their potential in science, to assist the children in providing an account of what they have done and observed, is obvious. Their utility is particularly apparent in fieldwork. On returning to the classroom the children will have the visual reminders of the investigations that they have carried out, and will be able to incorporate these images into their reports.

Digital cameras and mathematics

Digital cameras are very effective in helping children make links between abstract ideas that they learn in the classroom and the world around them. Children can be encouraged to take photographs of their environment and identify the shapes and nets that they have recorded.

Children may walk around the school and take images which show examples of regular shapes, e.g. door as rectangle, sand tray as circle. The children may view the images on a screen with their teacher and talk through their selections. It may not be necessary to keep the images in the long term. Alternatively, children may undertake a similar activity looking for examples of acute, right and obtuse angles. The children may download selected images and import them into a word processing document to sit alongside their notes.

Digital cameras and English

Children's books are usually enhanced by their illustrations and logically their own writing will be made more attractive and perhaps clearer through the incorporation of digital images that they have composed. It is important that the pictures the children use do genuinely complement and enrich the text, and are not just a technological version of the borders with which teachers encouraged children to decorate their work if they finished their writing quicker than anticipated. Talk to the children about how the words and pictures interplay to give meaning.

Images can be imported into painting software – children may paint themselves into a Viking village scene, with appropriate clothing and props, for instance, and from there create a story of their life as a Viking.

PRACTICAL TASK PRACTICAL TASK PRACTICAL TASK PRACTICAL TASK

Create a resource bank of photographic images that might be used in the classroom, but which it may be impractical for the children to take themselves. For example, photographs of your town – the station, the market place, the park, key buildings such as the fire station and hospital – will be invaluable for a local study in geography. You will be able to use the photographs for whole-class work, perhaps on an interactive whiteboard, while the children will be able to include them in their reports or presentations.

REFLECTIVE TASK

To provide you with greater insights into the power of visual images, experiment with adults' image manipulation software (such as Paint Shop Pro and Adobe's Photoshop). Even relatively simple operations such as cropping photographs to unconventional proportions can affect significantly the impression they give. Try creating a collage, combining elements of two or more images – as is sometimes done somewhat unscrupulously by the press to create fake pictures to support a scandalous story.

A SUMMARY OF **KEY POINTS**

> **Successful use of digital cameras.**

> **Applications of digital photography.**

> **Activities to meet teachers' needs.**

Moving on

A useful way to familiarise yourself with the possibilities for digital photography is to use a camera to create your own e-portfolio. Take pictures of the children working, of displays that you have created, and if practical ask a colleague (or the children) to take pictures of you leading the class. Your images can later be assembled as a presentation, or incorporated into the pages of a personal website or blog.

REFERENCES AND FURTHER READING REFERENCES AND FURTHER READING

Ang, T. (2002) *Digital photographer's handbook*. London: Dorling Kindersley

Becta (2007) *Creativity in digital media awards* **http://www.becta.org.uk/corporate/display.cfm? section=21&id=2663** Accessed 17 January 2007

Becta (2007) *How to use a digital camera in drama* **http://schools.becta.org.uk/index.php? section=tl&rid=518** Accessed 17 January 2007

Becta (2007) *Ten ways to use a digital camera in religious education* **http://schools.becta.org.uk/ index.php?section=tl&rid=8108** Accessed 17 January 2007

Becta (2007) *Using photography, audio and video recording equipment to gather data* **http:// partners.becta.org.uk/index.php?section=rh&rid=11118** Accessed 17 January 2007

Futurelab (2006) *Creat-A-Scape* **www.createascape.org.uk/** Accessed 17 January 2007

13
Virtual learning environments (VLEs)

Chapter objectives

In this chapter some of the theory and practice surrounding the implementation of VLEs will be introduced. It is intended to give trainees a sound basis from which to begin to consider how to usefully incorporate such technologies in their own pedagogical practice.

The theory

VLEs have been identified as a key tool within the agenda for anytime, anywhere learning. Furthermore, the DfES (2005) sees such tools as being central to its personalised learning agenda, wanting to 'encourage all organisations to support a personal online learning space for learners' (p.10). However, whilst there is obviously educational potential through online collaboration and personalised spaces, it is fair to say that there is much academic debate about both the nature and design of online environments and the pedagogical strategies which can be developed to maximise their potential for learning. So what are VLEs?

There are two main elements to VLEs currently. Firstly, a VLE can be seen simply as a dynamic web space in the sense that content can be easily updated or uploaded without the need for any knowledge of html code. This means that information and files (including multimedia) can easily be made available to children beyond the limitations of the school timetable and building. Secondly, many VLEs offer a range of online tools such as discussion forums, blogs and wikis. Such tools offer yet further opportunities for children to extend their learning beyond the classroom environment, for example by continuing a debate about the differences between children's lives in Victorian times compared with today. Similarly, children might be given a

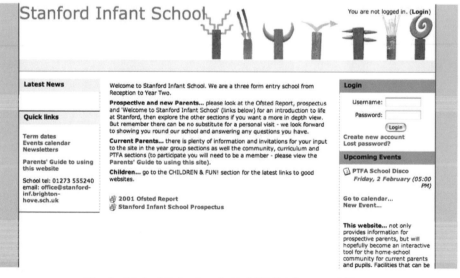

Stanford Infant School website/VLE Brighton and Hove

Virtual learning environments (VLEs)

homework task over the course of a week to work online in small groups to create a poem using a wiki. This way, children can collaborate online to generate and edit text, keeping a history of contributions at each stage. The key attraction of accessing such social software through the portal of a VLE is that, to a certain extent, important issues of safety online can be addressed, as it is possible to regulate access and membership. However, important issues remain regarding online conduct which will be dealt with later in this section.

So as it can be seen, a VLE is a much more dynamic web space than a website, facilitating wider ownership within the school community and reciprocal interaction, in comparison with a more static website which is usually updated by a web designer or creator. Many schools are now seeing the potential that such technologies offer to establish a virtual community around the actual school community incorporating children, teachers, parents, prospective parents, governors and the wider community as the home page of this school website illustrates well.

Setting up a VLE

There is a range of commercial and open-source software available for establishing a VLE. Blackboard is a commercially available application which many trainee teachers will have had experience of whilst undertaking their training. However, the VLE-cum-website referred to above has been set up with open-source software called Moodle, which can be down-loaded freely (**http://moodle.org/**). The software can be run on most servers or a spare client machine that is set up as a server. Whilst the installation of Moodle is not beyond an enthusiastic amateur, it is probably best left to a technician rather than a busy teacher with other commitments. Setting up the VLE to ensure its sustainability and effective use is a far more challenging task.

Whilst essentially a VLE offers some solution to the issues of Internet safety it is vital that teachers establish an agreement with children about what is acceptable conduct within the VLE. For example, the need for sensitivity when responding to or sending messages should be explored with children. Similarly, the facility to upload images or multimedia content by all users means that children will need to be encouraged to self-regulate and question the appropriateness of their content. Any agreement should also clearly indicate what sanctions will be put into effect should any of the users break the code of conduct. All of this needs to be established at the outset and referred to regularly to remind users of their responsibilities. Whilst such measures, and the risk of children sending inappropriate messages to each other, can seem daunting, it can also be seen as an important process for children to engage with. Children and young people are increasingly engaging in online communication (Livingstone and Bober, 2004; Owen *et al.*, 2006; Turvey, 2006).

PRACTICAL TASK PRACTICAL TASK **PRACTICAL TASK** PRACTICAL TASK

Devise your own online code of conduct. What expectations would you have concerning children's online conduct and the way they relate to each other online? What would be appropriate sanctions for children who break the code of conduct? This will enable you to effectively negotiate an online code of conduct in practice.

Embedding a VLE within effective practice

When planning to use a VLE alongside face-to-face teaching it should be remembered that not all children have access to the internet at home. Measures should be taken to minimise the impact of equal opportunities issues that are likely to arise. For example, children could be given access to the school computers outside of school hours if appropriate supervision is available. A VLE can be a relatively safe environment in which they can learn how to use online tools appropriately and effectively to support their learning across the curriculum as the following example illustrates.

CLASSROOM STORY

A class of 30 Year 5 children have been working with a group of trainee teachers both face-to-face and online. The theme of the project was bullying, based upon the work the children were doing in PSHE. Initially, the children and trainee teachers needed to get to know each other so each child planned and acted a 15-second mime about themselves which was captured on a digital still camera with a video facility. These movie clips were then uploaded into a discussion forum called 'Guess Who' by the children. Over the course of the week at school and out of school, children and trainee teachers tried to work out as much about each other as they could from their mimes and then left messages for each other. After further face-to-face tasks an online discussion was held on strategies to beat bullying. Further tasks included using a wiki to generate an anti-bullying rap, which was then put to music and uploaded as an mp3 file. A final online discussion was held to evaluate the children's raps. Throughout this project, the VLE was an important catalyst enabling children's creative work to be viewed by a wider audience and also extending the opportunities to reflect upon activities beyond the classroom environment.

REFLECTIVE TASK

Talk with some children about their use of online communication tools. To what extent do they use e-mail, instant messaging, blogs? What kinds of access do they have to these technologies in the home?

A SUMMARY OF **KEY POINTS**

> VLEs can offer new ways of learning to supplement face-to-face practices

> It is important to establish expectations and rules regarding online conduct and safety

> Care needs to be taken to ensure that those without access to the internet at home are not discriminated against.

Moving on

Consider the extent to which the VLE that you have had access to throughout your teacher training has played a role in your own learning and professional development. Think about the ways in which you have used VLE as a learner and how you might now incorporate this technology in your own practice as a teacher.

REFERENCES REFERENCES **REFERENCES** REFERENCES **REFERENCES** REFERENCES

DfES (2005) *Harnessing technology: transforming learning and children's services.* **www.dfes. gov.uk/publications/e-strategy/** Accessed 30 January 2007

MOODLE development site (2007) **http://moodle.org/** Accessed 30 January 2007

Livingstone, S. and Bober, M. (2004) UK children go online: surveying the experiences of young people and their parents **http://personal.lse.ac.uk/BOBER/UKCGOsurveyreport.pdf** Accessed 30 January 2007

Owen, M., Grant, L., Sayers, S. and Facer, K. (2006) *Social software and learning*, **www.futurelab.org.uk/research/opening_education.htm**> Accessed 30 January 2007

Turvey, K (2006) Towards deeper learning through creativity within online communities in primary education. *Computers and Education*, 46 (3), 309–21.

FURTHER READING FURTHER READING **FURTHER READING** FURTHER READING

Becta (2003) *Virtual learning environments* **http://partners.becta.org.uk/index.php?section=rh&catcode=_re_rp_ap_03&rid=11252** Accessed 30 January 2007

DFES (2003) *Towards a unified e-learning strategy* **www.dfes.gov.uk/consultations/conResults.cfm?consultationId=774** Accessed 30 January 2007

Gillespie, H., Boulton, H., Hramiak, A. and Williamson, R. (2007) *Learning and Teaching with Virtual Learning Environments*. Exeter: Learning Matters.

14
Mobile technologies

Chapter objectives

One of the exciting aspects of ICT is that the technology itself is evolving quickly and providing opportunities for innovation and experiment. In this chapter we will summarise the different kinds of mobile technology that are already available, conscious that the picture is constantly changing. We will go on to review some of the ways in which mobile devices might be utilised in primary schools. What we will encounter is considerable variety in the contexts in which mobile technology can be applied, which leads to consideration of the implications for primary teachers and ICT co-ordinators in taking strategic decisions about the equipment that is important and relevant for them.

What are mobile technologies?

Mobile technologies have emerged as a corollary of the miniaturisation of electronic components. Early examples would include the transistor radio and, in the late 1970s, the evolution of the 'Walkman' from mini-cassette players and reel-to-reel tapes. However, in the last few years there has been an explosion in the range and diversity of ICT equipment that is small enough to be carried around conveniently, and it is to these more recent innovations that the term 'mobile technologies' is more usually applied. They include PDAs, mobile phones and MP3 players such as Apple's iPod. We will also refer to laptops, or 'notebook' computers, and tablet PCs, although strictly these are 'portable' rather than 'mobile', due in part to their physical size (Anderson and Blackwood, 2004).

The development of smaller components has also enabled the convergence of technologies into single units of equipment. For example smartphones, such as O2's XDA and T-mobile's MDA, combine a PDA with other components that provide the functionality of a mobile phone.

What do the programmes of study for Key Stage 1 and 2 include?

It is fair to say that the current programmes of study did not anticipate the widespread adoption of mobile technologies in the classroom. However, mobile technology has become commonplace in our lives. Accordingly, including its use in curriculum activities is only a reflection of what is happening in the world beyond the school gates. In particular, teachers might devise opportunities for Key Stage 1 children to use mobile technologies to gather information (1a), to enter and store it (1b) and to retrieve it (1c). Children should also be taught to select from and add to information (2b) and to try things out and explore what happens in real and imaginary situations (2d).

The breadth of study requirements are particularly relevant in this context. For these younger children there should be chance to work with a range of information to investigate the different ways it can be presented (5a) and to talk about the uses of ICT inside and outside school (5b).

At Key Stage 2 children should be taught to talk about the information they need (1a), how to prepare it (1b) and to interpret it and check its relevance (1c). They should be taught to organise and reorganise information (2a), to evaluate the effect of changing values and to identify patterns and relationships (2c). Particularly relevant in considering mobile technologies, they should be taught how to share and exchange information (3a), as well as consider its suitability for its audience and its quality (3b).

Under breadth of study, Key Stage 2 children should work with a range of information to consider its characteristics and purposes (5a), and work with others to explore a variety of information sources and ICT tools (5b). Similarly to Key Stage 1, they should investigate and compare uses of ICT inside and outside school.

At all stages children should be taught to review, modify and evaluate their work as it progresses (4a, 4b and 4c).

What does the ICT scheme of work include?

Although mobile technologies are not identified specifically in the programmes of study they might be incorporated in a range of activities linked to the scheme of work. For instance, at Key Stage 1 the tape-recording task suggested in Unit 1C (The information around us) could reasonably be updated to involve the use of a PDA to make sound files. Unit 3E (E-mail) could usefully be extended to include text messaging on mobile phones, enabling the children to compare and contrast the conventions and implications of communicating by the two media.

What do teachers need to know before using mobile technologies in the classroom?

In considering the use of mobile technologies inside – and outside – the classroom, teachers will need to establish what is practical in terms of funding. This is likely to be a team decision involving all staff. Some schools have made the choice to buy a class set of laptops, PDAs or even iPods, but they are a minority (especially in the UK; the evidence from the world wide web is that PDAs have greater currency in American classrooms). It is unlikely that PDAs will replace the school's need for desktop or laptop computers, so if a set of PDAs is bought, will staff in the school as whole have the commitment to use them? If not, then it is questionable whether the PDAs will be more than an expensive novelty.

Apart from cost considerations, the increasing diversity of affordable ICT suggests that teachers in future will need to choose what is most appropriate for their classroom.

What do teachers need to know about mobile technologies?

The range of mobile technology available is substantial and it may be useful to summarise the features of the main types of mobile equipment that are currently marketed.

A laptop computer in principle has all the functionality of a desktop computer but with the additional benefit of being powered by a rechargeable battery and so transportable. With mobility in mind, the size and weight of laptops are minimised and so they usually have a smaller screen and keyboard. The reduction in size of the components makes laptops more expensive than a desktop computer of comparable specification. Laptops can also be more difficult to use. The keyboard is not raked, which makes typing physically harder, and some users have difficulty using the touch pad to control the pointer. These concerns can be overcome by attaching a standard keyboard and mouse, or by using a docking station and mouse. Laptops are more expensive than the equivalent desktop models, but have the advantage of being easy to transfer from one location to another. In a school this potentially enables more effective use of a valuable resource as the laptop is moved from one class-room to another according to need. Some schools have bought class sets of laptops which are stored on a specially designed trolley with recharging facilities, so constituting a portable computer suite. Manufacturers have recently tended to refer to laptops as 'notebooks'.

Tablet PCs are characterised by having a pen-shaped stylus as an input device. With appro-priate handwriting-recognition software provided, the stylus enables the user to enter text using their usual handwriting rather than the keyboard. The stylus is also easier to user than a mouse or touch pad for drawing. There are two main types of tablet PC. The 'slate' comprises the screen as a flat top to the main unit, accompanied by a detachable keyboard. The more expensive alternative employs a screen that rotates to enable it either to fold down on top of the keyboard, so that the PC is used as a slate, or to be angled above the keyboard so that the PC can be used in notebook fashion. In tablet PC mode, the screen can be oriented vertically, making it even more flexible to use than a standard laptop. For example, it can be passed around a classroom and, using a data projector and wireless connection, children can take their turns to make a contribution which will be shared instantly by the whole class.

Personal digital assistants (PDA) were initially conceived as personal organisers, but their functionality was quickly extended so that now they are typically supplied with simple versions of office software, Internet connectivity and sound recording facilities. The expecta-tion now is that PDAs will allow connection and synchronisation with a desktop computer. Some PDAs have mobile phone ('smartphone') capability, including photography. Input is usually by a stylus, like the tablet PC using either handwriting recognition software or a virtual keyboard on screen. In the last few years PDAs such as the BlackBerry and Palm Treo have been provided with small physical keyboards.

The use of mobile phones has been considered in relation to teaching and learning. Many schools ban children from bringing their phones into the classrooms, concerned about the possible distraction and also the risk of theft (BBC, 2005). However there is an argument that children's enthusiasm for these devices can be harnessed to support the development of their literacy and oracy skills (Attewell, 2005) and, more generally, for communication (Cole, 2003).

MP3 players store and play audio files, usually music. MP3 is a reference to the file format which at one time was dominant for music, but the devices are perhaps better referred to as digital audio players (DAPs) as other formats such as Windows Media Audio (WMA) and Advanced Audio Coding (AAC), used on Apple's iPod, are now also popular. The hardware itself falls into three main categories. Portable CD players originally could play only purchased (or copied) CDs, but can now usually manage downloaded MP3s or other formats burned onto a CD-R. The problem with portable CD players has always been the suscept-ibility of the technology to jolts. More robust alternatives usually preferred now are flash-based players, which have no moving parts. These store the music files on memory cards.

They are often provided with removable disk drive support, which means that they can be used for storage in the same way as a memory stick. For a few pounds more there are other options such as built-in microphones to enable speech recording. The third type of DAP is based on hard drive technology. These players are not quite as strong as flash-based equipment, but currently they have the advantage of higher capacity. This might not be critical if their use were restricted to music files, but it has meant that some products, such as the (fifth generation) iPod are now effectively personal media players, capable of playback of video and still images as well as audio files.

What are the key features of mobile technologies?

While the transportability of mobile devices is their obvious shared feature, it is also worth considering how they will be integrated with other equipment. It would probably be a mistake to think of a PDA as a replacement for a fully functioning desktop (or laptop) computer. Rather, its portability can be exploited, but through synchronisation with the full-size computer; data collected 'on the move' can be processed further in the classroom. For example, if a Calendar entry – a time and date for an appointment – is made in a PDA during a staff meeting it can later be synchronised with Calendar on the teacher's home computer (it was this kind of facility, rather than any educational application, that originally drove forward the development of PDAs). This procedure effectively backs up the information and also makes it accessible on a large screen.

There are two main ways in which data transfer between devices may be set up: either cables can be used or a wireless connection can be established. Peer-to-peer wired connections, which do not require a server, between laptops or tablet PCs and a desktop computer can be established. However, in the longer term it is probably easier and more useful to provide the laptop or tablet PC with a link onto the network through a network point. Smaller mobile devices such as PDAs and digital audio players are conventionally linked to a single desktop (or laptop, or tablet PC) computer through a USB cable. The computer holds software which enables the user to control the mobile device.

However, laptops, tablet PCs, PDAs and some mobile phones nowadays are generally fitted with some form of wireless communication capability which allows them to send and receive data from other devices. One or both of two technologies may be available. Bluetooth is relatively simple to establish and should work satisfactorily as long as the distance between devices is not great, nor is the requirement for bandwidth substantial. Alternatively, WiFi may be offered. This entails the device having a wireless card (strictly a wireless network interface controller, WNIC) and the potential to connect to a network through an access point. In this way the set-up of WiFi has parallels to conventional wired Ethernet networking. Its advantage is that it is more powerful than Bluetooth and enables secure networks to be established in public places such as railway stations and coffee shops. Using a PDA or laptop to access the Internet with such flexibility is a strong recommendation for mobile technology.

What do mobile technologies have to contribute to teaching and learning?

Investigations into the opportunities for mobile technologies to support teaching and learning have been ongoing for some time now (see Passey, 1999, for an early, influential report).

It is arguable, though, that evidence to support the benefits of mobile technologies for teaching and learning is so far scanty (see Naismith *et al.*, 2005 for an objective overview) and may have depended on resources and time that, though possible in an experimental situation, would not be scaleable. We have noted, for example, that some educationalists see potential for the use of mobile phones for school use. Yet this possibility has not been widely adopted. Technical, financial and practical constraints can all be readily identified. Ironically it may also be that children and young people see the mobile phone as representative of their independence from adults. In this case they may anyhow be reluctant to see their phones hijacked for the school's purposes.

Nevertheless, if all these reservations can gradually be overcome it would seem that mobile technologies offer exciting prospects by extending the classroom both spatially, or geographically, and temporally, so that learning does not have to take place within any fixed parameters of location or time. This shift to what has been dubbed 'anytime, anywhere' learning is consistent with other social trends such as '24/7' availability of services and flexible working patterns for adults.

CASE STUDY CASE STUDY CASE STUDY CASE STUDY CASE STUDY CASE STUDY

As an example of 'anytime, anywhere' learning, the music software Gigajam teamed up with Leicester City Local Authority and the East Midlands Broadband Consortium to offer music lessons which pupils can access at home or elsewhere outside of school hours. The pupils receive practical and theoretical guidance, which include video and audio files. Access is through Leicester's Community Gateway. Initially a pilot was undertaken involving just four schools but the success of the project was such that now all Leicester City schools have access to at least the first five lessons of each of the four courses offered by Gigajam: guitar, bass, keyboards and drums (Gigajam, 2006).

Podcasts, which might be either sound or video files that are transferred automatically onto mobile devices (or other computers), are a relatively recent phenomenon which could be exploited profitably by education. Files are offered through a feed by the information provider (which would be the school, or individual teacher) to a 'subscriber' (the learner; the idea of a subscription in this instance does not necessarily imply that a payment is made). On the Internet, feed readers, or 'aggregators', most popularly in RSS (Really Simple Syndication) format, are used to keep subscribers in touch with any changes made to pages. This is particularly helpful for fast-changing news websites. However, the principle could also be applied to release lessons in the form of talks or demonstrations to pupils which they would download and play back at a time to suit themselves.

RESEARCH SUMMARY RESEARCH SUMMARY RESEARCH SUMMARY

Mudlarking in Deptford was a project devised by Goldsmiths College and Futurelab to explore 'how associative histories, stories and visions of Deptford Creek can be woven into a guided tour of the area – one in which the participant actually produces the tour'. The aim was explicitly to subvert the traditional 'guided tour' concept so that it was placed in the hands of the learners rather than the guide (or teacher). Using PDAs with GPS (Global Positioning System) and camera facilities, the children were able to collect and store images and their ideas (Futurelab, 2006).

Wolverhampton Local Authority has explored the use of PDAs in the primary classroom. A major outcome of the project has been that the personal 'ownership' of the PDA by the children, made possible by the relative low unit cost of the equipment, has proved extremely motivating. Specific gains in certain areas have also been reported, notably reading through the use of e-books (Perry, 2005).

The value of a PDA for a teacher's professional use should not be underestimated. Apart from providing a portable electronic diary, the PDA offers a range of possibilities for maintaining records. For example, the spreadsheet (e.g. Pocket Excel) can be set up so that children's achievement during a lesson can be recorded as it happens rather than retrospectively. A discreet entry into the PDA, taken as the lesson progresses, is much less obtrusive than making a note into a desktop or laptop computer, and can be made as the teacher moves around the class. The PDA's compactness and easy mobility may also be used to carry notes around during a lesson, either of the plan itself or relating to individual children.

PRACTICAL TASK PRACTICAL TASK PRACTICAL TASK PRACTICAL TASK

The only practical approach to starting to think about the ways in which mobile technologies might be applied in teaching and learning is to explore them thoroughly so that you become familiar with their characteristics and limitations. Once you have done this at a personal level you will be better placed to determine a role for mobile technologies in the classroom, and to persuade others (including those in the school who manage budgets) that what you are proposing is worthwhile. Accordingly, choose one of the mobile technologies that appeals to you, and which, somehow, you can finance, and use it regularly over several weeks to discover its capabilities.

REFLECTIVE TASK

Talk with children about mobile technologies. With which technologies are they familiar through personal use? Do you foresee any difficulties in teaching children the technical aspects of mobile technology use?

A SUMMARY OF **KEY POINTS**

> **Mobile technologies available to schools.**

> **Use of mobile devices in primary schools.**

> **Applications and implications.**

Moving on

As indicated earlier, whether a school opts to explore the use of a particular mobile technology will be influenced by a number of factors such as cost and staff expertise. Talk with colleagues to establish with which technologies they are personally familiar, and whether these might have application in the classroom or in out-of-school contexts.

REFERENCES REFERENCES **REFERENCES** REFERENCES REFERENCES

Anderson, P. and Blackwood, A. (2004) *Mobile and PDA technologies and their future use in education.* JISC Technology and Standards Watch: **www.jisc.ac.uk/uploaded_documents/ACF11B0.pdf** Accessed 9 August 2006

Attewell, J. (2005) *Mobile learning inspires the hard-to-reach.* London: Learning and Skills Development Agency. Accessed 4 January 2007 **www.lsda.org.uk/files/pdf/press/26apr2005.pdf**

Attewell, J. (2005) *Mobile technologies and learning* **www.m-learning.org/docs/The%20m-learning%20project%20%20technology%20update%20and%20project%20summary.pdf** London: Learning and Skills Development Agency. Accessed 5 January 2007

BBC (2005) *Schools support mobile phone ban* **http://news.bbc.co.uk/1/hi/england/merseyside/4551556.stm** Accessed 5 January 2007

Becta (2004) *What the research says about portable ICT devices in teaching and learning*. Coventry: Becta, available online at **www.becta.org.uk/page_documents/research/wtrs_porticts.pdf** Accessed 5 January 2007

Cole, G. (2003) *Ring tone revolution*. **http://education.guardian.co.uk/elearning/story/0,,869659,00.html** Accessed 4 January 2007

Futurelab (2006) *Mudlarking in Deptford* **www.futurelab.org.uk/showcase/mudlarking/index.htm** Accessed 5 January 2007

Gigajam (2006) *Anytime, anywhere music lessons for Leicester City pupils* **www.gigajam.com/news-77-Anytime,+anywhere+music+lessons+for+Leicester+City+pupils.html** Accessed 5 January 2007

Heppell, S. *et al*. (2004) *Building learning futures... a research project at Ultralab within the CABE / RIBA 'Building Futures' programme* (p9). **http://rubble.heppell.net/places/media/final_report.pdf** Accessed 5 January 2007

Naismith, L., Lonsdale, P., Vavoula, G. and Sharples, M. (2005) *Literature review in mobile technologies and learning*. Futurelab series report 11. **www.futurelab.org.uk/research/reviews/reviews_11_and12/11_01.htm** Accessed 5 January 2007

Passey, D. (1999) *Anytime, anywhere learning project evaluation focus*. Lancaster: Lancaster University/AAL

Perry, D. (2005) *I was pants at IT* – Wolverhampton LEA 'Learning2Go' mobile learning – PDAs in schools project, Evaluation Phase 1, End of First Year Report August 2005 **http://wgfl.wolverhampton. gov.uk/PDASite/content/docs/dpa%20Report%2011.pdf** Accessed 9 January 2007

Wikipedia (2007) *Bluetooth*, *wireless*, *RSS*, and many other topics provide clear, helpful further information on mobile technologies

15
Interactive whiteboards

What are interactive whiteboards?

Interactive whiteboards (IWBs) are touch-sensitive boards which allow teachers and children to engage directly with material projected on a screen from a computer via a data projector. They have their conceptual origins in commercial contexts where they were introduced to enliven presentations and dialogue in the boardroom and elsewhere. In large part due to government policy they have now been widely adopted in schools in the United Kingdom. In the last few years the success of the technology has been recognised to the extent that interactive whiteboards may now be found in American classrooms, in some countries in Europe and even in the developing world. Promethean, one of the major suppliers in the UK, has been involved in a project in Botswana that uses solar-powered boards to bring video-conferencing and the Internet to remote villages.

Since their introduction into schools a substantial body of anecdotal evidence and small-scale studies has been published to suggest that there are real and significant gains to be made by the use of interactive whiteboards in the classroom. These opportunities have been summarised by the National Whiteboard Network, the arm of the *Primary National Strategy* charged with supporting the introduction of IWBs into schools, as the potential to:

- *Improve the quality of interactions*
- *Improve teacher assessment through the promotion of effective questioning*
- *Enhance modelling*
- *Redress the balance of making resources and planning for teaching*
- *Increase the pace of learning*

National Whiteboard Network (2006)

What do the programmes of study for Key Stage 1 and 2 include?

Interactive whiteboards have been introduced into schools subsequent to the formulation of the current programmes of study and so ostensibly the requirements can be fulfilled without their use. Furthermore, the interactive whiteboard is, akin to the traditional blackboard or whiteboard, genuinely a cross-curricular tool and it is probably not useful to think of its implementation as grounded in the ICT subject content. That said, it is nevertheless arguable that good classroom use of the IWB will contribute to the children's capability at Key Stage 1 to select from and add to information (2b) and to try things out and explore what happens in real and imaginary situations (2d). It will also contribute to the children's awareness of the different ways in which information may be presented (5b). At Key Stage 2, use of the IWB will be one way in which children can be taught about how to prepare information (1b), how to develop and refine ideas (2a) and how to share and exchange information (3a). Under breadth of study, the IWB represents one of the ICT tools that Key Stage 2 children might explore (5b).

As with all applications of ICT, children at all stages should be taught to review, modify and evaluate their work as it progresses (4a, 4b and 4c).

What does the ICT scheme of work include?

As with the programmes of study, the ICT scheme of work pre-dates the widespread adoption of interactive whiteboards as a tool for teaching and learning and so they are not referred to in the rubric. Additionally, the relevance of the IWB is not so much something that should be learned about *by* children, as learned *with* them. In this sense we are dealing with equipment whose role complements that of the computer itself, rather than a topic – such as word processing or database – for which the development of knowledge, skills and understanding is necessary.

What do teachers need to know before using an interactive whiteboard in the classroom?

Technically, interactive whiteboards work by enabling the teacher and children to control the computer by touching the board, either with a special pen or with their finger. The touch is understood by the computer in the same way as it recognises mouse movement and clicks.

There are two main technologies that have been implemented in the design of IWBs used in the classroom which can broadly be characterised as 'hard' or 'soft' boards. Hard boards have a grid of copper wire behind the solid surface. These boards need special pens which are tracked by the grid using electromagnetism. Soft boards use 'resistive' technology. The board has a polyester surface membrane which is flexible, though strong, and separated from a rigid second layer by a small air gap. As the finger or pen is used to depress the surface, the contact is registered by the board and transmitted to the computer.

The 'feel' of the two different boards is quite distinctive, and teachers usually decide that they have a preference for one type of board rather than the other. Sometimes this partiality may simply be the result of familiarity. It can also be influenced by the software that is provided with the board. The software is not interchangeable, although there has been considerable convergence in functionality as the different manufacturers have recognised the utility of particular tools.

The different programs associated with the respective boards furthermore imply that resources prepared using one software are not automatically transferable to another. Conversion can be achieved, but currently it is not always straightforward. It is noticeable that resources offered by the government and other national organisations are provided separately for the two main brands of IWB on the market, Promethean and SMART. Teachers need to consider that if they build up a bank of resources for one type of board it will not easily be converted to the other. For this reason alone schools have tended to adopt a whole-school approach to the purchase of IWBs, and have decided on one brand rather than the other. This decision may well have been prompted by the policy of some local authorities to support one type of board to the effective exclusion of others.

What do teachers need to know about interactive whiteboards?

In order to use an interactive whiteboard three items of equipment are necessary: the whiteboard itself, a computer and a data projector. The computer is connected to both the projector and to the interactive whiteboard. The physical organisation of this equipment is important. In particular, decisions must be taken as to whether the equipment is fixed or mobile, with the IWB held on a trolley and the data projector and computer moved around with it. On first consideration a mobile IWB is attractive as it means that this expensive equipment can be deployed in several classrooms. However, there are disadvantages to this arrangement. Each time that the equipment is moved it will have to be recalibrated. Additionally, even on a good trolley the IWB is an awkward shape to manoeuvre. Data projectors, too, are not robust and are vulnerable if not handled carefully. Schools are now tending to arrange for their IWBs to be permanently installed on a wall. If at all possible, ceiling mounting the data projector is preferable, too. Health and safety concerns would support this option. Trailing leads should always be avoided in the classroom, and trunking used for cables where at all possible. This is going to be less practical if the mobile alternative is chosen.

An additional benefit to a fixed installation is that encasing the projector in a ceiling-mounted unit provides security for what is otherwise an attractive, portable target for thieves.

The computer used to control the IWB can be a standard desktop computer. Its positioning will to a certain extent depend on the geography of the classroom; there is no need for it to be close to the whiteboard. Many schools use laptops for this purpose, which have the benefit of enabling teachers to prepare resources away from the classroom.

The positioning of the board in the classroom needs careful consideration. There must be sufficient space on either side of the board for the teacher or children to stand and avoid being in the path of the projector. The projected light will be affected by other light sources such as windows and overhead lights. Blinds or curtains may be necessary. The height of the board is also a factor. At the very least the teacher must be able to reach the top of the board, both to calibrate it and to access menu items in program windows, and as far as is practical the children should be able to use as much of the board as possible. However, the board also needs to be visible to the class. In many classrooms benches or small platforms have been set up so that shorter users can write on the whole board. There is an obvious safety consideration here; balancing on a stool is not an acceptable alternative.

The size of the board is important. Generally speaking, the larger the board, the easier it will be for the class to use. Detail will be difficult to make out on a small board from the back of the room. While this may not be problematical when using resources designed specifically with the whiteboard in mind, the size of text will be a concern when, for example, demonstrating menu items in a program window. Promethean boards are now being marketed with a diagonal dimension of 95 inches, which should be large enough for most classrooms, but may still not be enough for some school rooms such as the hall and, possibly, a larger computer room. The largest SMART board currently offered has a 77-inch diagonal, and a similar sized RM Classboard is available. Needless to say there is a cost implication involved in opting for a larger board.

Increasingly schools are recognising that the full potential of an interactive whiteboard is realised only if good-quality audio equipment has been integrated. Many programs and web pages that might be used on the interactive whiteboard depend to a greater or lesser extent on audio facilities, sometimes to give feedback on choices that the user has made. It is important that the sound can be heard by the whole class, and ideally the source should be close to the board itself, rather than the computer, so that there is close identification of sound and projected image.

The IWB should not be used with conventional whiteboard pens. Although the IWB can be wiped, marks will inevitably be left and will be picked out by the light from the projector. Wherever space has allowed, teachers have tended to retain their old whiteboard, or alternatively use a whiteboard (or paper flipchart) mounted on an easel, in addition to the IWB.

RESEARCH SUMMARY RESEARCH SUMMARY **RESEARCH SUMMARY**

A helpful summary of research into interactive whiteboards was published by Becta in 2003. Among the general benefits that are concluded are motivation, which is widely reported (e.g. Levy, 2002), the efficiency with which teachers are able to present web-based and other resources (Walker 2003) and the opportunities for interaction and discussion in the classroom (Gerard, et al., 1999). The summary also lists factors that support effective use. These include, significantly, the importance of teachers becoming familiar with the technology (Levy, 2002; Glover and Miller, 2001) and also practical considerations such as the position of the boards to avoid sunlight and any obstructions (Smith, 2001).

What are the key ways of using an interactive whiteboard?

There are two main ways in which a teacher may use an interactive whiteboard. It can be used very effectively with the pen or finger simply replacing the mouse. For example, a PowerPoint presentation can be managed at the board, clicking for each new slide, rather than the teacher needing to go to the computer in order to move on. This becomes particularly useful for the children if the presentation has been designed to include choices activated by hyperlinks, so that the children are able to decide or at least to see what option has been taken. Similarly, for the teacher to work at the board to show the children how to use software has more impact, and maintains better pace, than the teacher demonstrating remotely, hoping that the children can follow the pointer, even if she has gone to the board first to show the children what will happen.

Alternatively, the teacher can use the native software of the whiteboard. At its most straightforward, the software provides a selection of tools that enable annotation and other manipulation such as gradually revealing parts of the desktop. These tools can be used in 'real time', and combined with the strong visual impact of what is on screen, perhaps from a web page, can make for lively lessons that engage the children well. However the software can also be used to prepare resources in advance of the lesson to create files that will be used interactively with the children. In SMART these files are known as notebooks, while in Promethean they are flipcharts. RM offer an alternative software called Easiteach. Creating notebooks, flipcharts or Easiteach files with interactive features is not difficult, but time spent becoming familiar and adept with the software will be repaid.

As a first step to developing your own library of IWB resources try replicating an example that you have downloaded from the world wide web. This will enable you to gain confidence with the software, putting you in a position to bring your own creativity and imagination to designing your own notebooks or flipcharts.

What do interactive whiteboards have to contribute to teaching and learning?

It is worth briefly considering the claims noted on p193 from the National Whiteboard Network in relation to the potential of interactive whiteboards. Four of them refer to gains that may be made over 'traditional' teaching approaches. The judgement that an ICT solution offers an improvement over teaching by alternative means is always a good litmus test; if ICT does not bring an enhancement, then why bother with it?

Perhaps the most important of the five gains is the increased pace of lessons that IWBs allow. This benefit has been widely reported by teachers. If the lesson is well prepared the teacher will be able to use resources quickly and smoothly to move from one point to another. File organisation on the computer is important for quick access, and it will usually be helpful to organise desktop shortcuts in advance of the lesson. The teacher also needs to know how to use the resource itself. This is not as straightforward as it may seem. Some resources such as the interactive teaching programs offered by the DfES at **www.stan dards.dfes.gov.uk/primary/publications/mathematics/itps/** have been created with a lot of thought but are not necessarily intuitive to use. Planning, and specifically consultation of the supporting guides, will help to ensure that the lesson itself maintains good pace.

If the teacher has sufficient digital resources to hand, and knows how he or she intends to use them, then the good pace to the lesson that follows will give space for two other of the benefits identified by the National Whiteboard Network, improving the quality of interactions and improving teacher assessment through the promotion of effective questioning. The quality of interactions should also be helped by the richness of the resources that the class is sharing.

Modelling is well suited to work on the interactive whiteboard. For young children, to see and manipulate representational images and icons has a strong impact and will often make the teaching point much more clearly than verbal or textual explanations.

The final claim of the National Whiteboard Network, that IWBs have the potential to redress the balance of making resources and planning for teaching, is perhaps more contentious. Resources are available for downloading from the world wide web, and many of these are of high quality, such as the interactive teaching programs (ITPs, mentioned above) and materials that the National Whiteboard Network has itself commissioned. Some local authorities have been active in developing resources (and have been generous enough to offer them on open access). There are also some proprietary software titles, designed with IWB use particularly in mind, which may be purchased. However, searching for the right resource takes time and in some circumstances it may be quicker, and provide a tailor-made outcome, to create the resource from scratch. Once the teacher has a file for use on the interactive whiteboard, though, it is re-cyclable, and the initial effort made to secure exactly the right material will be repaid in subsequent years. Within a school teachers may also share resources and develop online libraries, using filing systems provided by the IWB software.

What are the capabilities and limitations of interactive whiteboards?

The full impact of interactive whiteboards may need more time to assess, as the technology is only now emerging from its adoption phase. Some of the perceived benefits such as motivation (Smith, 2000) could arguably be related to novelty. At the same time the IWB does affect teaching style. The technology self-evidently lends itself to whole-class teaching more than to group work. Even if a teacher decided to work with one group at the IWB while the rest of the class was occupied in other activities, there would be the likelihood of children being distracted, especially if sound and video were involved. As with any whole-class work, the teacher needs to ensure that all of the children are engaged. Planned and targeted questioning will be a key technique to this end. Ironically, the children's interactivity with the board may not be as fundamental. In the early days of the introduction of IWBs it was reckoned that giving the children direct access to the board would be central to the success of the technology. However, it became apparent that bringing young children, especially, frequently to the front of the class incurred a time overhead and impaired the pace of the lesson – the very benefit that the IWB is supposed to bring. Accordingly some teachers tend to restrict the interactivity to their demonstrations on the board, rather than always bring a child to the front of the class to work on a resource. Obviously there is a balance to be struck.

Another surprising consideration is whether the interactive whiteboard is genuinely being used interactively. If the data projector is essentially only beaming what is on the computer desktop, or if the interactivity is low level, such as moving on slides sequentially in a PowerPoint presentation, then it is questionable whether the IWB is necessary. Unfortunately this criticism even applies to some of the resources posted on the National Whiteboard Network website. At a more sophisticated level, some schools are exploring the potential of wireless devices such as remote keyboards, tablet PCs or slates, and gyro mouses. The intention here is for the input equipment to be passed around the class, without the children coming to the board. This provides an interesting alternative approach, but in the primary classroom, at least, there will be a concomitant loss of physical connection directly between the teacher or children and the board which might represent a pedagogical disadvantage. The hand causing something to move or change directly on the board, in full view of the whole class, is very powerful.

REFLECTIVE TASK

Break down the elements of a lesson you have observed (or given) in which extensive use was made of the interactive whiteboard. Identify which parts of the lesson were necessarily interactive, and which were more a matter of projecting images or text, or making use passively of other multimedia resources.

Interactive whiteboards and the core subjects

On the face of it, interactive whiteboards are cross-curricular and it is possible to conceive of resources being prepared for any subject. However, it is noticeable that the focus of the National Whiteboard Network has been on literacy and mathematics. Most of the resources on the NWN website (**www.nwnet.org.uk**/) are for one or other of these two subjects. The interactive teaching programs (**www.nwnet.org.uk**/), initiated by the DfES earlier than the instigation of the National Whiteboard Network, focus on mathematics alone. This tendency is perhaps not so surprising. The visual representation and manipulation of numbers (by counters) and shapes are highly appropriate content for work on the IWB.

Provision of free resources for science from government sites is not as well developed. Partly this may be for reasons of cost. Interesting and accurate representations of scientific phenomena and experiments take time to produce. However, there is good proprietary software available from companies such as Sherston, 2Simple, CATS, 4Learning, Kar2ouche, ClicSoft, Boardworks, The Big Bus and Inclusive Technology. Their science CD-ROMs all come with bold, clear text and images and have probably been designed with whole-class teaching using the interactive whiteboard in mind.

A SUMMARY OF **KEY POINTS**

> **Interactive whiteboard basics.**

> **Key ways to use interactive whiteboards.**

> **Interactive whiteboards and their contribution to teaching and learning.**

Moving on

Teachers often liken their 'performance' in the classroom to a stage role in which the success of a lesson is in part gauged by how well they have engaged their audience of children. If teachers include an interactive whiteboard as one of their props then it is important that it is used effectively and efficiently. This does not mean that the whole lesson is scripted. Indeed one of the exciting aspects about the use of, say, web resources and an interactive white-board is that the opportunity is there to respond quickly and easily to the questions or suggestions of the audience, following hyperlinks and creating searches. What is necessary, though, for a professional lesson is that teachers are confident with the technology and regard it as their ally. This needs time for preparation and practice.

REFERENCES AND FURTHER READING REFERENCES AND FURTHER READING

Becta (2006) *Enhancing teaching and learning with interactive whiteboards* **http://schools.becta. org.uk/index.php?section=il&catcode=nwslttr_index&icttypeid= 1&icteditionid=5&ictsectionid=&ictsubsectionid=&ictitemid=118** Accessed 3 January 2007

Becta (2006) *The benefits of an interactive whiteboard* **http://schools.becta.org.uk/index.php? section=tl&catcode=ss_tl_use_02&rid=86** Accessed 3 January 2007

Becta (2003) *What the research says about interactive whiteboards* **www.becta.org.uk/page_ documents/research/wtrs_whiteboards.pdf** Accessed 31 December 2006

DfES (2004) *Interactive teaching programs* **www.standards.dfes.gov.uk/primary/publications/ mathematics/itps/** Accessed 3 January 2007

Gerard, F. *et al*. (1999) cited in Becta (2003) *Using SMART Board in foreign language classrooms*. Paper presented at SITE 99: Society for Information Technology and Teacher Education International Conference, San Antonio, Texas, 28 February–4 March

Glover, D. and Miller, D. (2001) cited in Becta (2003) Running with technology: the pedagogic impact of the large-scale introduction of interactive whiteboards in one secondary school. *Journal of Information Technology for Teacher Education*, 10 (3), 257–276

Levy, P. (2002) cited in Becta (2003) *Interactive Whiteboards in learning and teaching in two Sheffield schools: a developmental study*. Sheffield: Department of Information Studies, University of Sheffield

Smith, A. (2000) *Interactive Whiteboard Evaluation* **www.mirandanet.ac.uk/cgi-bin/journals/search_ ej.pl?runtype=casedisplay;cid=124;ejtype=all;origin=mnet** Accessed 3 January 2007

Smith, H. (2001) cited in Becta (2003) *SmartBoard evaluation: final report*. Kent NGfL. **www.kented. org.uk/ngfl/ict/IWB/whiteboards/report.html** Accessed 31 December 2006

Walker, D. (2003) cited in Becta (2003) Quality at the dockside. *TES Online*. 3 January, pp. 66–67

16
The Internet

Chapter objectives

This chapter aims to introduce the reader to ways in which the Internet is used to support and enhance learning. It will include accounts of the major online tools and environments for educational use. In recent years larger numbers of teachers and children have been working in spaces which are not open to the wider Internet, secure password-protected online areas known as virtual learning environments (VLEs) (see Chapter 13). There are also exciting developments which exploit the potential of the Internet for collaboration, publication and communication using the tools of 'Social software'. A further objective of this chapter is to introduce these tools to the reader and discuss ways in which they may be used.

The Internet and education – an introduction

It is a given that the Internet is now a feature of life within and outside formal settings of education. Its influence is all-pervasive in daily activities from shopping, to downloading music and video and banking. There are increasing numbers of viewers online for the various video-sharing sites such as YouTube which are drawing people away from the traditional broadcast media. The latest computers from both Mac and PC vendors place the Internet and media-sharing at the heart of their respective operating systems in such a way as to make it seem obvious and inevitable that a user would be part of the online world from the moment the computer is switched on. This is a radically different approach from the early days of personal computers.

Whilst we cannot assume that all learners have access to these all-pervasive facilities and services at home, there are very many ways to be connected and use the Internet even without personal ownership of a computer. For school children this is sometimes the computer in the classroom or network room at school, perhaps even after school in community use of the facilities in an extended day or in a local library. Many mobile phones provide some level of access online and the terminals of local Internet cafes are rarely less than full. Of course some forms of the external use refer to older children who are using the computer outside of school time.

It was in 1997 that the incoming government first decided to set in motion the means by which schools and learners could become connected to the wider Internet and to each other. The programme proposed:

- **connecting all schools to the Internet;**
- **increasing the speed of school Internet connections;**
- **developing quality, interactive digital teaching and learning resources.**

The metaphor for this construction was the creation of the National Grid for Learning. Although this term is no longer used nationally, there are still local areas joining together in regional 'grids for learning'. A grid for learning is a helpful analogy with the electricity grid even if the comparison is not completely accurate. However, it does still chime with a range of other initiatives championed by the government in the recent e-learning strategy which envisages a world of 'anytime, anywhere' and 'personalised' learning.

At this point it would be useful to survey some of the tools and facilities which are available to Internet users. Many of these you may already be familiar with. Feel free to scan down past e-mail and conferencing if that is the case and rejoin the text in discussion of items about which you may be less knowledgeable, such as social software or VLEs.

What is the world wide web?

In everyday communication people refer to the Internet and/or the world wide web (WWW) interchangeably. Technically the WWW is in fact only one part of the Internet, being made up of hypertext pages containing text, images, sounds and animations interconnected via hyperlinks. These pages provide information, opinion, archive material, music, video and up-to-the moment news and images. Some provide software and games to download, while others act as portals or gateways, existing merely to provide links to a range of other pages. Anyone can publish pages on the WWW. All web pages are written in coding languages such as the original hypertext mark up language (HTML). Your browser interprets the files and makes them readable and presentable onscreen.

Where do e-mail, discussion groups and conferencing come in?

The Internet is a communications tool and much of the communication it facilitates takes place via the world wide web. However, it also supports two other main categories of communication: e-mail and discussion or conferencing.

E-mail (electronic mail) allows a user to send electronic messages to other users. There are many parallels with letter writing, although a range of e-mail-specific conventions, often referred to as 'netiquette', have grown up, such as a lack of formality, tolerance of spelling errors and a prohibition on spam (unsolicited or junk email). Messages often arrive in a basic text format, although formatted text documents, graphics or other files can be sent as attachments and increasingly as part of the e-mail message itself. E-mail can facilitate rapid and sometimes low-cost communication across the world or next door.

REFLECTIVE TASK

The term 'netiquette' refers to the conventions associated with the use of e-mail. Consult a range of sources – for example, Becta, your e-mail software help, a search tool home page, a school e-mail policy – and research this. How might you introduce and develop this idea with children?

E-mail and discussion boards

Electronic discussion or conferencing takes a variety of forms and formats. There are electronic bulletin boards or newsgroups where information or queries can be posted related to a specific subject or interest. These often lead to detailed exchanges of information and opinion between a range of contributors. Some individuals find it useful to watch the discussion without necessarily contributing themselves and they are referred to as lurkers. Access to such asynchronous discussions can be restricted, for instance, to members of a professional association, or they can be open.

A similar function can be provided through e-mail. In this instance it is called a 'listserv' and is essentially an e-mail distribution list with all participants automatically being circulated with each contribution. A newsgroup or listserv may be mediated by an individual who checks each contribution for relevance before it is posted.

E-mail and the electronic discussion possibilities described above are known as 'asynchronous'. Users can read others' contributions and respond at a time convenient to them. Communication is not dependent on the contributors being available at the same time.

Access to synchronous discussion, where the participants are online at the same time, is also available through a range of tools from instant messaging through to video chat (in, for example, Skype or iChat AV). Electronic conferences can be established where specified participants meet online and contribute to a real-time discussion. Conferencing can utilise text, audio or video (video conferencing). Generally, specific software is used for each of these.

What do the programmes of study for Key Stages 1 and 2 include?

The relevant parts of the curriculum for ICT for these areas includes the following. At Key Stage 1 children should be taught to gather information from a variety of sources (1a), retrieve stored information (1e) and to use text, tables, images and sounds to develop their ideas (2a). They should also be taught to share their ideas by presenting information in a variety of forms (3a) and to present their work effectively (3b).

At Key Stage 2, children should be taught to talk about the information they need, how they can find and use it (1a), to prepare information (1b) and to interpret information and check its relevancy (1e). They should also be taught how to share and exchange information (3a) as well as consider its suitability for its audience and its quality (3b).

Accessing the world wide web

The web browser on your computer is the piece of software that enables the user to view and navigate web pages. Internet Explorer (IE) is the browser bundled in with your Windows PC and Safari is the browser used on the Mac (although you can have a Mac version of IE). Other browsers are available and a popular choice is the freeware package Firefox, downloadable from the Mozilla website (Mozilla.org, 2007).

Navigating the world wide web

As you may already know from your own use of the Internet, navigation is via pointing and clicking on hypertext links. These links (often text coloured blue, although they can be buttons or images) take the user from one hypertext document to another. The cursor will become a hand symbol when it is moved over a hypertext link. For habitual users of the Internet this is something that is done without thinking. You will find that there are children who use these interfaces instinctively but there will be others who will need some specific input into simple navigational tasks.

Although any website may have any number of pages linked together, each of these pages is essentially a separate document and has its own individual uniform resource locator or URL. This is the web page address and it is this unique URL which enables navigation through the almost limitless range of web pages. URLs may at first appear confusing, although familiarity quickly enables the user to decode and even predict some URLs. Briefly, using as an example the URL **http://www.wkac.ac.uk/education/**

- **http stands for hypertext transport protocol and means the document is being accessed through hypertext;**
- **www.stands for world wide web;**
- **wkac is the name of the server being accessed, in this case King Alfred's College, Winchester, and this is the server on which the web page being accessed is stored;**
- **.ac stands for academic – all academic institutions in the UK have this as part of their URL; http:// www.ex.ac.uk/ is Exeter University;**
- **.uk means that the site is based in the United Kingdom; similarly .es is Spain; an address without a country designation is usually based in the US;**
- **/education is the directory or pathway on the server in which the specific page is located, i.e. where the document is stored.**

When you find something, remember that you can do one of two things. Firstly, you can add the site to your list of 'Bookmarks' or 'Favourites' so that you do not have to search for it again. However, if you are on another person's computer this will simply add the link to their personal list of sites they need. In order to see the link from any computer you will need to set up some online bookmarks with a resource such as del.icio.us (see social software section).

Searching the world wide web

Locating useful resources on the open world wide web is time consuming and can be difficult. Search engines such as Google produce hundreds of possible pages as results from plain text searches, only some of which will be relevant and useful. Many teachers search for useful information as part of the planning process and gather together some useful links or pages as a list in advance of a lesson. Unless you are specifically teaching and learning about searching (which is something that is essential to do at some point) it will be a waste of the children's time to use up part of the time for basic resource location.

The reason for their variability is that search engines are huge simply huge databases which users can search with keywords or phrases, e.g. AltaVista **www.altavista.com/**. Search engines automatically trawl the web looking for sites and index them by keyword. This can mean that every word in a website is indexed regardless of context or relative importance, resulting in huge numbers of hits for any word or phrase searched, many of which will not be useful. Results are usually ranked in order of relevance, which can be helpful, although the criteria used to decide relevance may not match with the user's own ideas. Searching with combinations of words or phrases can result in fewer, more appropriate hits. Many search engines support a range of strategies and tools for refining searches. Practice may also improve the user's effectiveness in using a search engine.

Directories are the second common type of search engine and they allow users to progressively narrow down their search area by choosing categories and sub-categories. e.g. Yahoo! **www.yahoo.com**/. There are some similarities to branching tree databases. Some form of human mediation is usually involved in organising these directories and productive searching may as a result be faster. The number of websites included in a directory is likely to be smaller than that covered by a search engine. Most search directories also support keyword or phrase searching.

Children's Internet access at school is often filtered by the local authority or regional broadband supplier, meaning that open text searches on the Internet are usually (though not always) safer. It is unwise to use the more popular adult search engines in a school setting where the access is not controlled. The most popular, Google, is almost certain to produce at least some results in an open text search which you would not wish to have to discuss with your pupils (see also the section below on Internet safety policies). If you are looking for resources with children, and you want them to use a search engine facility themselves, it is a good idea to use the safer junior version of the search engine, such as 'Yahooligans', a cut-down version of 'Yahoo' (**www.yahooligans.com**)

REFLECTIVE TASK

Use a range of common search tools to search for:

- **a website you know of;**
- **information related to a specific part of the National Curriculum programmes of study, for instance, the Earth and beyond;**
- **a newsgroup relevant to your subject specialism.**

What do you notice? Do you find one of the tools or types of tools more suited to your needs and interests than another? Why do you think this might be? How can you increase the efficiency of your own searching? What useful knowledge, understanding and techniques have you discovered which you could utilise within the classroom?

Advanced searching

Most search tools now support both keyword and categorised searching. For many users, especially when starting out, search tools can be frustratingly unproductive. Perseverance and the use of some advanced or Boolean searching strategies will usually turn up something useful.

Boolean searching involves the use of operators such as AND, OR and NOT. These can be used to refine searches by combining or excluding words or phrases:
AND narrows a search, such that only sites that contain both keywords will be displayed, e.g. information AND technology;
OR widens a search, to include sites containing one or other, or both, of the keywords used, e.g. information OR technology;
NOT narrows a search, by excluding sites containing the keyword, which follows it, e.g. information NOT technology.

Often the Boolean operators must be in upper case, although it is important to check in the search tool being used. Some tools use the plus and minus sign to provide similar functions. Other useful strategies supported by a number of search tools include:

- the use of quotation marks around phrases, such as "information technology" – this will ensure that only sites in which the words appear in this order are found;
- wild cards – symbols which can be entered at the beginning or end of keywords or phrases, such as 'tech', and the search engine will then look for matches which contain words beginning with tech, but with a range of endings, such as technology, technologies, techniques and technical. The symbol used varies between search tools.

Search tools vary enormously. They also develop and change. It is worthwhile exploring the guidance given by the tools themselves – there is usually a wealth of information pointing towards more efficient and effective use. You could also use the website **www.searcheng inewatch.com** which is a comprehensive listing of search engines together with tutorials and rankings of the various services.

Focused searching

There are many sites designed for teachers, providing access to resources, teaching ideas and discussion opportunities. Many of these are free, though there are some commercial services for which a subscription is payable. Searching in sites like these is likely to provide results more quickly than using general search tools. Additionally, the material provided may also be more closely matched to teachers' needs. One example is the BBC site **www.bbc.co.uk/schools/** which provides access to a huge range of curriculum resources.

A search tool with a UK focus can be helpful. This will reduce the range of sites searched, but results may be more closely matched to the user's requirements; using the UK version of Google is one example (**www.google.co.uk**). Similarly, some other search engines and directories will allow the user to search for UK sites only if required.

Internet safety and Internet acceptable use policies

Some of the dangers inherent in the use of the Internet are widely known and acknowledged. Whether it is access to unacceptable content or inappropriate contact with strangers online, these factors give rise to grave concerns by parents and carers. Less immediately harmful perhaps but equally pervasive on the world wide web is the plethora of wholly inaccurate and pernicious information, versions of history which serve extreme political views and are presented as fact (Holocaust deniers, for example).

Responsibility for children's safety resides with the management of the school and the LA and parents have a right to expect safe and secure Internet access at their children's school. At the same time, panic and denial of access merely hands the control of the medium to those who would wish to use the Internet for profit, exploitation and criminal activity.

Clearly, the potential for access to sources previously unavailable to support the curriculum, and tools to support communication is something that should be exploited for the benefit of all learners, notwithstanding the very justifiable concerns which are felt. For this reason Internet safety policies exist to guarantee as far as possible safe access and responsible use of the Internet for learners. All schools making use of the Internet should have an appropriate policy, often called an Acceptable Use Policy, which clearly outlines the potential benefits and risks and how these are managed within the school. Policies are usually written and reviewed in consultation with parents and there are model versions available from government websites for education and parents' information sites (see resources list at the end of the chapter). If in doubt about how this policy operates in your school, you should seek the advice of the senior management and/or ICT co-ordinator.

Since most access in schools is now fast, broadband and supplied under contract by Regional Broadband Consortia (RBCs), the filtering of inappropriate content is often carried out remotely by the LA or RBC itself. Teachers can report sites which they feel are harmful and these are added to the list for blocked access. Encouraging a culture where children feel able to report things they see which make them feel uncomfortable fosters a responsible attitude and begins to educate learners about how they would deal with these issues in the wider world beyond the classroom.

What are the key features of the Internet and world wide web?

Communication

The power of the Internet lies in the communication facilities it supports. The range of facilities caters for diverse needs, interests and preferences. Cluster schools doing the same topic might set up a shared area on an LA intranet to share resources and ideas. Children can pose questions direct to war veterans or zookeepers or Year 7 children in the local secondary school via e-mail. Video conferencing can be a vehicle for developing questioning (and answering) skills.

CLASSROOM STORY
Artists in non-residence

A class of Year 4 children and their teacher undertook a research project involving video conferencing with a practising artist. The artist, an abstract expressionist, first discussed and planned a sequence of activities during a video conferencing meeting with the teacher. Over a term groups of children with their teacher met weekly with the artist online. The children showed and discussed their work. The artist was able to share resources, such as images of his own work and that of others on photoCD, to support the discussions. The class asked questions ranging from queries about the artist's influences and inspiration to the price of finished paintings. Together, the teacher, artist and class planned an exhibition to display the children's abstract work. The artist was able to advise the children on issues such as the impact of framing pictures.

The project was an opportunity for professional development for the class teacher as well as an exciting learning experience for the children.

Information and resources

This is the information age. The world wide web contains unimaginable amounts of information. Some of it is incorrect, some of it is out of date, some of it is not relevant, but some of it is of a high quality and generously shared by its originator with the worldwide online community. Access to such a wealth of information is revolutionising many aspects of day-to-day life.

The Internet – some example resources

There is an unprecedented range of resources available via the Internet, mostly freely available, including:

- **channels for discussion and exchanges with peers with similar interests;**
- **activities developed by others and shared;**
- **free software downloads ;**
- **lesson plans and ideas;**
- **video clips;**
- **audio clips;**
- **examples of children's work.**

The ideas and activities introduced here are intended only to give a brief introductory feel for the range of ways in which the Internet can be utilised to support and enhance teaching and learning in mathematics, science and English. They are not intended to be comprehensive, merely to go some way towards illustrating the breadth of possibilities and to provide starting points for the customisation of ideas and the generation of others. Examples introduced under mathematics, for instance, may be just as applicable to one or more of the other areas. Other useful sources include professional journals (*Primary Science Review*, *Reading*, *Interactive*, *Child Education*, *Junior Education*, etc.), websites (National Grid for Learning, Becta, etc.) and schemes of work (science, ICT, etc.).

In English there are very many websites which support a range of literacy-related activities. For example, Kent National Grid for Learning has developed a range of big books online at Infant Explorer featuring Sebastian the (**www.naturegrid.org.uk/ infant**/). These can be read online and are supported by a range of worked lesson plans and activity ideas and resources. Children are encouraged to e-mail Sebastian with their work, which may be displayed on the pin board. Sebastian also publishes a blog.

**'Sebastian the Swan' home page –
direct access at** *www.sebastianswan.org.uk*

Another example is the Children's Story site at **www.childrenstory.com** which enables the user to select a fairy story and hear it being read. Activities such as these can be followed up in a range of ways away from the computer.

For science, there may well be areas of the subject that are difficult to resource or provide few opportunities for practical activities. These are well catered for with child-centred web resources. The NASAKIDS site **www.nasa.gov/audience/forkids/home/index.html** is visually engaging, often modelling through video and animation concepts which are counterintuitive and otherwise difficult to communicate.

For mathematics there is a wide range of activities available online which can reinforce the acquisition of basic skills at the BBC's school portal at **www.bbc.co.uk/schools**.

Children and their teachers can access websites to look for mathematics investigations which may then be carried out away from the computer. Such opportunities maximise use of limited computer resources as well as providing access to well-thought-out activities. There is an increasing range of activities to support young children's mathematical activities, which may also be used to develop hand–eye co-ordination as well as reinforce early mathematics.

Many of the websites have teachers' areas with worksheets, activity ideas and lesson plans. For an example see the mathematics area of Teaching Ideas at **www.teachingideas.co.uk** or **www.educate.org.uk**, which contain activity ideas and resources which may help teachers in managing the setting and marking of homework.

REFLECTIVE TASK

Download a lesson idea, worksheet or other resource from a suitable website. Draw up a lesson plan for a stated age group and subject focus, detailing how you would make use of the resource to enhance or extend children's learning. (See Chapter 2 on planning for primary ICT for ideas on how to do this.)

Irrelevance of geographical location

Anyone connected to the Internet can communicate with anyone else similarly connected, irrespective of the distance between them. They can also access any of the world's web pages regardless of the location of the server on which they are stored. Schools in geographically isolated locations can access resources such as online galleries when journeys to traditional galleries would be difficult or impossible. Similarly, virtual field trips allow children to explore a variety of close and distant locations. E-mail communications between children from schools a mile to a continent apart provide a range of learning opportunities.

PRACTICAL TASK PRACTICAL TASK **PRACTICAL TASK** PRACTICAL TASK

Access the Cyber Geography Research website, **www.cybergeography.org**, and explore the Atlas of Cyberspaces. What do you notice about the network?

What does the Internet have to contribute to teaching and learning?

Finding things out

The opportunities for finding things out via the Internet are almost limitless. Teachers can research subject knowledge, teaching ideas and resources. Accessing such information efficiently and effectively is vital to ensure that they and their classes can benefit from the professional information at their disposal.

Well-organised and well-managed research activities on the world wide web can be visually and intellectually engaging as well as developing children's understanding of electronic texts and the use of a range of media to communicate information effectively. The development and practical application of higher-order reading skills, such as keyword searching, skimming and scanning, are key, as are strategies for effective use of search tools. Caution must, however, be exercised as noted above because not all the information accessed may be current, appropriate or even accurate.

E-mail and video conferencing provide opportunities for asking direct and purposeful questions, as well as making comparisons and collecting data. Similarly, there is a range of 'ask an expert' websites, through which children can seek information directly from historians or authors.

The world wide web also provides children with opportunities to find things out from other children via web pages. This can be valuable in all sorts of ways, such as providing models at levels children can aspire to – children's poems, for instance, as most poems children read are written by adults. Children's science, geography or RE work may be sources of information expressed in language accessible to primary children.

Developing ideas and making things happen

Collaboration is facilitated by communication and the Internet provides a variety of channels for this. Children can contribute stories, poems and reviews to a range of websites. They can also respond to others' contributions. Such sites also model authors' story-starts and provide plentiful opportunities for reading online. See the sections on VLEs and social software for further ideas and information on this.

Children may post part-completed or drafted work on school web pages and invite e-mail responses to help them develop their work. This might be a D&T design, a poem or a piece of music. Responding to others' work can help children articulate and apply their own knowledge, skills and understanding.

Exchanging and sharing information

Many of the points considered above also have relevance for the exchange and sharing of information. Person-to-person exchanges, such as through electronic pen pals, are facilitated by the Internet. This can add an element of speed to the communication, maintaining interest and relevance for the correspondents.

The global online community works because people are prepared to share information and resources with others, usually without charge. There are a number of sites where schools can access environmental data on weather from around the country and the world. Schools can post their own data, either as a *quid pro quo* for utilising information from other schools, or merely for the satisfaction of adding to the wealth of available resources. This is particularly easy to achieve where the school has an automatic weather station. Similarly, publishing children's project work on the web enables them to share it with people they know, parents and other relatives, as well as people they don't, such as children in an elementary school in the USA. Posting lists of links to useful online resources can save other teachers time and effort.

Issues in using the Internet

Staying focused

The Internet and especially the world wide web can be enthralling – the temptation for random exploration can be hard to resist. Teachers will need to manage children's tasks in order to ensure both their safety and the productivity of the activity. Use of bookmarked sites only, tightly focused tasks and time limiting can be appropriate strategies.

Reading level and language issues

The vast majority of web pages are aimed at an adult audience and may thus be difficult for primary children to comprehend. There are a number of strategies teachers can deploy in order to provide access to material which is accessible, including:

- **the use of the search tool Ask Jeeves for Kids!, which has a reading level option and is designed to select sites which answer the query posed at an appropriate reading level;**
- **utilising web pages specifically written for children;**
- **utilising web pages recommended by other teachers;**
- **utilising children's work on school web pages.**

Teachers may also be concerned about American web pages which display not only differences in vocabulary but also in the spellings of words. Children are exposed to US (and Australian) vocabulary through television, as are adults, and appear to have little difficulty with comprehension. Alternative spellings may provide more of a challenge, although they can also provide a teaching and learning opportunity. Teachers can make explicit the differences and discuss these with children – for instance, searching for information on the theme of 'colour' in a US-based search tool may be unproductive, although a parallel search using the US spelling could also be attempted.

Copyright and the web

Material placed on the world wide web remains the intellectual property of the author and is subject to copyright whether or not this is specifically stated. Copyright extends beyond text to images, animation and sound. However, it is generally accepted that material placed on the web is there for other people to use. Sometimes it will not be possible to copy and paste an image from a web page, because the author has arranged the programming to prevent this. Similarly, it may be possible to listen to a sound file, but not to download it. It is good practice to acknowledge the source of any material from the web and to encourage children to do the same. Further information is available from the Copyright Licensing Agency, **www.cla.co.uk** and the Copyright Web Site at **www.benedict.com/**.

Currency and authenticity

There is a lot of concern about the currency and authenticity of materials available on the world wide web. The potential to access up-to-the moment satellite weather photographs, breaking world news stories, images from space as they are received from missions or real-time video of bird eggs hatching is exhilarating. However, there are lots of websites which are not regularly maintained and in which the information displayed may be outdated. This can be frustrating and schools must also do their bit to ensure that their own web pages are current. Many web pages include information giving the date on which they were last updated. This can be a useful guide.

Authenticity is often harder to assess. Anyone can upload information to the world wide web or circulate it via e-mail, newsgroups or listservs. There is no editing process, as there is with any published book, newspaper or magazine, and thus material, particularly from unfamiliar sources, must be viewed critically. It may be partial, misleading or inaccurate. Comparing information from the Internet with that from other sources for substantiation and corroboration can be a teaching and learning objective in itself. Some high-quality websites are subject to an editing process, such as the BBC, **www.bbc.co.uk** and newspapers, e.g. **www.guardian.co.uk**.

Vocabulary and jargon

A vast new vocabulary is emerging related to ICT, a lot of it related to the Internet and some of it found in this chapter. In common with children's language development in maths or science, it is important that they develop a vocabulary which enables them to articulate their ideas, understanding, intentions and problems. Deciding when and how much vocabulary to introduce is an important professional consideration for teachers.

Printing from websites

Web pages can be printed using the icon on the browser, or selecting Print via a menu. This will print the whole of the current web page, which may be rather more than is expected. There is nothing to limit the length of web pages to the amount visible on screen at any one time, or even to A4. The web page author can make the page any length at all. Printing out long pages can be time-consuming and also expensive. It is useful to get into the habit of copying and pasting text and images to be printed into a word processing package and to encourage this strategy with children. This ensures that only the text and for images actually required are printed, and the document length can be assessed before a decision on printing is made.

Digital division

There is increasing concern that the Internet is leading to a digital division in society in the UK, with information (and skill) haves and have-nots. Concern focuses on the potential for children (and adults) who do not have access to online resources to be seriously disadvantaged as a result. This issue is increasingly relevant for primary schools as home computer ownership continues to expand. Many children live in families for whom computer ownership is never likely to be a reality. Schools are beginning to consider the implications for entitlement and equality of opportunities. Free Internet access is now available via many public libraries and the availability of such community facilities is increasing. Some schools are beginning to make computer facilities available before and after school.

School websites and publishing on the Internet

Many schools have websites which provide a medium of communication and publication for the school community. Over the last few years many of these school websites have been absorbed into VLEs and other social software environments (see below for further information).

Publishing on the Internet is available at a number of different levels. If you become interested in publishing for yourself and others you could consider using one of the social software tools for blogging (see below) or you could learn use a web-publishing package which generates the necessary coding in the web page authoring language HTML. Popular versions of this include Microsoft FrontPage and Dreamweaver. Both are available at educational discounts but the costs remain high in terms of the learning curve and training is essential to make the most of the facilities they have. As you will see from the sections below on VLEs and social software there are other possibilities for publishing which involve creating content from templates and other authoring tools provided freely.

Social software – tools for communicating, collaborating and publishing

Changes in the way the Internet is used more widely in recent years have the potential to affect the way in which it is used in formal settings in education. These have sometimes been characterised as being a whole new 'version' of the Internet, known as 'web 2.0'. This is misleading in some ways in that, to an end user, the main structures and navigational interfaces are the same. What is substantially new, however, is the increase in the use of 'social software' sites which depend on communication, shared understandings of ways of sorting ideas, resources and finally, of self-publication/broadcast.

For primary ICT use the exploration of some of these sites is problematic in that many of them are open-ended, open-source and open-use (and abuse). However, the tools which have emerged that make these sorts of sites possible have, on occasion, been adopted and adapted into safe environments for education. Such tools as 'blogs' or 'wikis', can and do form parts of VLEs (see Chapter 13) enabling children to produce and edit their own online versions of themselves and their work which, in turn, invites communication from peers in the form of comments, questions, criticisms, etc. Co-authoring and collaboration before the advent of this 'social software' has been a feature of primary school life for many years, even if it is problematic in an individualised assessment programme such as the one currently still in place. What 'social software' allows is increasingly rich and vibrant forms of writing and media production.

Children of primary school age may encounter some of the older tools of 'social software' outside of school. Sites such as MySpace are places where users publish their likes, dislikes, blogs, biographies, pictures, etc., and invite friends to join them in associated messaging services. Examples which younger people may use more than MySpace include Bebo, which, at the time of writing, is aiming to be a younger person's version of the former.

Templates enable the creation of sophisticated-looking pages online. It should be stressed at the outset that all of these sites are places where the content is sometimes inappropriate. The onward links from people's pages, however innocent they appear at first, cannot all be vetted and verified. For this reason there is a tendency for such sites to be blocked for users in schools. However, the principle of one's own desktop and publishing space with the associated freedom to publish, comment and collaborate in a safe way is enshrined in many local and regional VLEs. In one case, that of think.com, the idea is writ large in the form of a global environment for educational publication from school-age users. Provided your school is registered and the users are verified and agree to the rules, the collaborative tools are freely available (think.com, 2007).

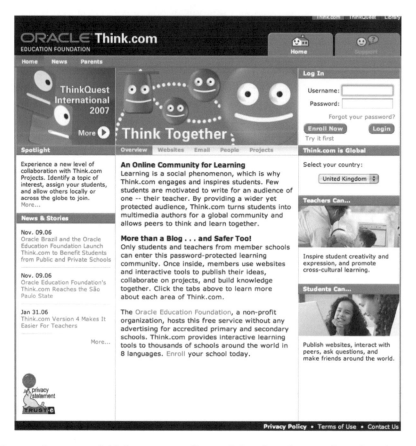

The opening page of think.com, an online social and work space for education users

You will have noted that the tagline for think.com is 'Think together' – this is what people are doing when they are sharing their resources, such as digital images, online. Websites such as Flickr are a rich source of digital photographs, uploaded by users and given tags to make them searchable by others, including those uploading and using the same tags. Thus, pictures of, for example, a trip to the Science Museum in London to view a gaming exhibition, 'Game on' could be uploaded to Flickr or similar and given label categories, known as 'tags' of 'London' 'Museum' 'Computer game' 'Science' 'Exhibition'. People viewing Flickr may search for the pictures which you have taken and uploaded by the tag you have used. Furthermore, you and your class may search for pictures taken of the same place – sometimes at the same time – for the purposes of onward communication, shared commentaries on public spaces etc.

Furthermore, Flickr and similar sites are a way to share images between home and school with the caveat that you still require a shared Internet policy to enable publishing of pictures featuring children who may be recognised. The same sort of sharing and tagging applies to video images in sites such as YouTube which are becoming popular exhibition spaces for digital video projects (see Chapter 11).

The idea of co-authoring is extended into factual writing by the creation of online reference texts in wikis – collaborative writing tools. Thus, Wikipedia has grown exponentially into an enormous reference resource, edited (and policed) by its creators to allow contributions from a wide range of co-authors all of whom are writing from personal knowledge and experience. Although generally considered to be one of the safer sites for social software authors to visit, there is by no means universal understanding or approval of the site in formal educational circles. The tools which allow collaborative writing have, however, sometimes been adapted into wikis in shared areas in VLEs (see Chapter 13 for additional commentary on this).

A further social software tool which you should consider for your own personal use is one of the many sites which allow the tagging and categorisation of particular bookmarked websites. You can create an online collection of websites which you use regularly by tagging them with labels that enable you to locate them more frequently. The advantage over traditional bookmarking is that the list is available on any computer you are working on which is connected to the Internet. If you move location frequently, or use more than one computer in a day, these sites enable you to keep track of the useful resources you discover. There is also the possibility of enabling sharing of seeing what other people are finding through their use of a particular tag. One example of these sites is del.icio.us. As usual, one of the caveats here is a thorough exploration of the safety policy of the school and the site yourself to ensure that children are not at risk in the site and that they will report to you anything that makes them uncomfortable. The other caveat is to remember that sites move re-purpose themselves. It is always worth checking resource recommendations and functionality for yourself. One suggested purpose of del.icio.us is to create group lists of resources in an online account administered at the school, perhaps one per class. Again, here, the point will be the safety angle and the lack of wishing to duplicate on functions which may have been adapted into your local VLE already (see del.icio.us, 2007).

A SUMMARY OF **KEY POINTS**

> **The Internet is a global network of computers supporting communication through the world wide web, e-mail and conferencing and there are special features which make it useful in supporting teaching and learning.**

> **Schools are increasingly active in the online community, searching, retrieving, analysing and synthesising information as well as developing, trialling and publishing their own.**

> **Critical evaluation of web-based resources is vital to ensure suitability, accuracy and safety.**

> **Through its many facets the Internet has the potential to support teachers in their day-to-day work in the classroom as well as their continuing professional development.**

Opening page of del.icio.us social bookmarking site

Moving on

Consider the wide range of opportunities you have seen for the use of the Internet in teaching and learning. In your induction year, and into the future, consider the likely impact of the use of blogging and social software, possibly within a VLE, on your role in the classroom. Think about how this might be a way to join subjects together in cross-curricular projects and look for ways to develop this in your professional life.

FURTHER READING FURTHER READING FURTHER READING FURTHER READING

BBC schools website (2007) **http://www.bbc.co.uk/schools/** Accessed 30 January 2007

Becta (2003) Virtual learning environments, **http://partners.becta.org.uk/index.php?section=rh&cat code=_re_rp_ap_03&rid=11252>** Accessed 30 January 2007

Cybergeography web research site (2007) **www.cybergeography.org** Accessed January 30 2007

DfES (2003) Towards a unified e-learning strategy, **www.dfes.gov.uk/consultations/conResults.cfm? consultationId=774** Accessed 30 January 2007

DfES (2005) Harnessing technology: transforming learning and children's services, **www.dfes.gov.uk/ publications/e-strategy/** Accessed 30 January 2007

Delicious social bookmarking site (2007) **http://del.icio.us** Accessed 30 January 2007

QCA/DfES (1999) *Curriculum Guidance for the Foundation Stage*. QCA/DfES

QCA/DfES (1999) *The National Curriculum*. QCA/DfES

Higgins, S. *et al*. (1999) *500 ICT tips for primary teachers*. Kogan Page. (1999)

Monteith, M. (ed.) *IT for learning enhancement*. Intellect Books

Livingstone, S. and Bober, M. (2004), UK children go online: Surveying the experiences of young people and their parents **http://personal.lse.ac.uk/BOBER/UKCGOsurveyreport.pdf** Accessed 30 January 2007

MOODLE development site (2007) **http://moodle.org/** Accessed 30 January 2007

Owen, M., Grant, L., Sayers, S. and Facer, K. (2006) Social software and learning **www.future lab.org.uk/research/opening_education.htm>** Accessed 30 January 2007

QCA/DfES (1998, rev. 2000, 2003) *Information and communications technology: A scheme of work for Key Stages 1 and 2*. QCA DfES

Smith, H. (1999) *Opportunities for ICT in the primary school*. Trentham Books

Somekh, D. and Davis, N. (eds) (1997) *Using Information Technology Effectively in Teaching and Learning*. London: Routledge

Think.com (2007) **http://www.think.com** Accessed 30 January 2007

Turvey, K. (2006) Towards deeper learning through creativity within online communities in primary education. *Computers and Education*, 46 (3), 309–321

17
Music and sound

Chapter objectives

The intention of this chapter is to introduce a range of ways in which ICT can be utilised creatively within music education. However throughout the chapter we emphasise the caveat that technology should not replace traditional ways of learning about and making music in the primary school but offer new opportunities to engage with the subject.

Audio revolution

The importance of music and sound in people's lives is often underestimated. Indeed creating, performing and listening to music are fundamental activities that can play a significant part in the emotional, social and intellectual development of the individual. The music industry has undergone radical change in the last five years due to the digitisation of music and the ease with which music can be created, accessed and shared in compressed file formats such as MP3s. Powerful music composition programs connected to an electronic keyboard, to a certain extent, enable children to engage immediately with the elements and language of music without necessarily understanding formal music notation. Similarly, the significance of audio seems to be enjoying a resurgence as new forms of expression and communication emerge such as the podcast. The ease with which quality digital audio recording can be created through a desktop or laptop computer puts these new forms of communication and expression well within the grasp of primary school children. This chapter will introduce a range of applications, and examine how these can be utilised to support children's learning in music specifically but also how audio in general can be utilised creatively across the curriculum.

The programmes of study for ICT

In using musical composition software children in both Key Stage 1 and 2 will to varying degrees be required to review, modify and evaluate their work as it progresses, listening to their outcomes and making changes to their compositions as appropriate (4abc). Children in Key Stage 1 will be developing ideas and making things happen as they begin to manipulate sound to develop their ideas (2a). They will share their ideas in a variety of forms including audio (3a). In using online musical games and simulations, children will be learning about the elements of music in real and imaginary situations (2d).

At Key Stage 2, again, children may use simulated musical games to identify patterns and relationships (2c), perhaps between graphical representations of sound and their outputs, changing variables such as pitch, tempo and rhythm. Increasingly, in their use of multimedia they will develop and refine their ideas, bringing together audio with moving or still image (2a). In thinking about the mood and atmosphere of their musical compositions, they will have to be increasingly sensitive to the needs of their audience (3b).

In their breadth of study children at Key Stage 1 will work with a range of information (5a) and may have the opportunity to explore a variety of tools (5b) such as keyboards, composition software, MP3 players, CD players. At Key Stage 2, children will work with others to investigate a range of tools and information (5ab)

Composing and performing music

GarageBand is a piece of software that comes with Apple Mac computers and is particularly suited to music composition activities. The software contains pre-recorded musical loops which can be previewed and then dragged onto the score, building up tracks and layers of music which can then be mixed using the dynamic and balance controls. However, the real creative potential of this software is in the way that live instruments including the voice can be recorded. This opens up a number of possibilities such as creating and recording a rap, a song or creating a soundscape to accompany a poem written by a child or group of children. It is also possible to connect a midi keyboard to the computer so children can create, record and then orchestrate their own melodies.

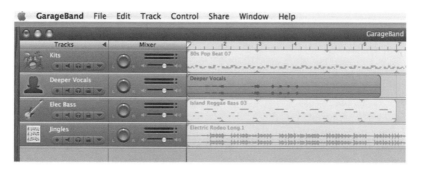

GarageBand Apple Mac – user interface

There are a number of applications like GarageBand that work in a similar way, for example, with children dragging pre-recorded samples and loops into their own compositions then adapting these by applying effects and editing them. These include Dance Ejay, Music Maker, RM Music Explorer and 2Simple Music Toolkit. However, it is important that teachers recognise both the limitations and potential of such software and it is useful to ask some key questions:

- **How far can any pre-recorded samples be adapted and changed?**
- **Is there any facility for recording and combining live instruments?**
- **To what extent can children generate their own melodies and rhythms?**
- **Does the software support any links between different types of media (sound, still/moving image)?**

Another piece of software that is particularly flexible is Audacity. Although there are no sample sounds for children to use, they can record their own sounds into the computer then edit these by cutting and splicing them as well as applying effects. Multiple layers of sound can also be built up to create complex textures of sound. This software particularly lends itself to spoken word and music projects such as creating a soundscape to accompany and add mood to a poem. The software is open source and can be downloaded at **http:// audacity.sourceforge.net/**.

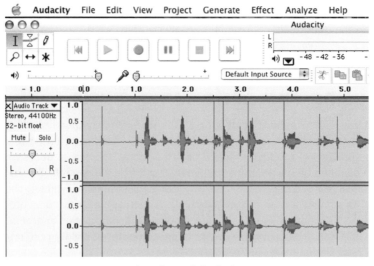

Interface of Audacity

CLASSROOM STORY

A class of Year 5 children have been working with a trainee teacher, creating the words for a class rap on an anti-bullying theme. Over the course of a week groups of the children use music composition software to set the words to music. The trainee teacher asks the children to think how they are going to accompany their rap. What kinds of instruments will they use? How will they make sure that as they build up the different layers of music, the all-important words and message they are trying to convey is not lost? What form will their rap take? Will they have a refrain that is repeated at intervals throughout or some other structure? How will the piece end: all instruments fading out together or phasing out the instruments one by one? As the children begin recording their rap, they make mistakes, which become evident as they listen to and evaluate their work as it progresses. At different stages they decide to rehearse and practise coming in at the correct time before actually recording.

REFLECTIVE TASK

Consider this classroom story in relation to the programmes of study for music and ICT available from National Curriculum Online at the following address: **www.nc.uk.net/webdav/harmonise?Page/@id=6016**

What aspects of the programmes of study for both subjects could be addressed through the activity described in the classroom story?

Combining audio and visual

Once children become familiar with using musical composition software to compose and record music digitally, this opens up a number of possibilities for exciting projects combining audio with still and moving image. There are some specific software packages that have been developed to facilitate this. One such package is Sound2Picture, a multimedia resource to help children learn about film music. It contains copyright-free digital video and audio materials, which children can combine and mix to create the required mood and atmosphere. However, new software is often not necessary to initiate such projects. PowerPoint supports audio and this facility can be utilised in many ways. One idea might be to create an online gallery of children's artwork for a whole-school assembly by getting them to scan their work or photograph it. They could then create or choose an appropriate short piece of music to accompany their slide and artwork. Windows Movie Maker is also standard on most new PCs these days. Children could create their own short pieces of music to accompany a short movie clip they have shot. The key to success with such projects initially is to try this out yourself first and to keep the pieces of music created to a manageable length. The impact of combining music and image is often rewarding and children enjoy experimenting with different types of music to create different moods.

Podcasts and podcasting

What is podcasting? This is a method of publishing files to the Internet, allowing users to subscribe to a feed and receive new files automatically by subscription, usually at no cost, whenever they log onto the internet. The latest update is automatically downloaded to the subscribers' preferred device, whether this is an MP3 player, PDA or mobile phone. Again, there is a great deal of educational potential with this technology. Teachers might consider creating their own educational podcasts or children themselves could create a podcast to accompany a historical or geographical field trip to their local area. Podium by Textease is a very intuitive piece of software that enables children to create and broadcast their own podcasts. Together with the software and computer, all that is needed is a microphone and web space to publish the podcast to.

PRACTICAL TASK PRACTICAL TASK **PRACTICAL TASK** PRACTICAL TASK

Experiment with images and music. Using PowerPoint create three slides and insert the same image on to all three slides (this might be a photograph you have or an image downloaded from a website). Now go to a copyright-free music download site such as **http://freeplaymusic.com/** and download three contrasting clips of music to your desktop. In PowerPoint go to Insert > Movies and Sound > Sounds from file to locate the audio files you have downloaded. When you are prompted to decide how to play the clips, select Play automatically with slide. View your three slides and consider how the music impacts upon your viewing of the pictures.

Listening to and appraising music

Many primary school classrooms are equipped with interactive whiteboards, which again offer a wealth of opportunities for sharing and discussing ideas about music as they usually have good-quality audio integrated within the system. However, together with rich audio resources to enhance children's experience, there is also the capacity to use a range of media to explore musical ideas. For example, the interactive whiteboard could be used to create a graphic score which the class interpret using percussion instruments. Alternatively a class might be asked to appraise a particular Cézanne landscape. How does it make them feel? What is the mood? Is there a clue in the colours used? They could then go on to appraise different pieces of music and decide which is suitable for the painting. Indeed, the opportunity to bring together a rich array of digital media in one place can be a powerful tool in developing children's aesthetic appreciation of music through listening and appraising as this next classroom story illustrates.

CLASSROOM STORY

A music advisory teacher is giving a demonstration lesson with a Year 2 class. They are looking at how the elements of music can be used to depict a real event. They begin by performing a poem projected on the interactive whiteboard about a steam train. The teacher draws the children's attention to the sounds created in the poem. Next they watch and listen to a short video clip of a steam train as it blows its whistle and releases steam, finally coupling with its carriages and accelerating gradually out of the station. They talk about the different sounds they have heard in the sequence. In the main part of the lesson they create their own soundscape to accompany the video, using percussion instruments and body sounds, also discussing how to depict the gradual acceleration of the train through tempo. Finally, the teacher introduces the children to a new piece of music – 'The little train of the Caipira' by Villa Lobos, which depicts exactly what they have been creating, using different instruments of the orchestra to represent the different sounds and manipulating tempo to illustrate the train gradually getting up to speed. The children listen carefully, identifying and appreciating the different elements to this piece of music, which they can now understand, having explored this event themselves through text, moving image and audio.

(Peter Walker,
Advisory Teacher for Music,
Brighton and Hove)

There can be no doubt that the range of ICT tools now available to the primary teacher offers new ways of enabling children to find out about a range of music as illustrated in this classroom story. However, to make the most of these new opportunities a secure subject knowledge of music is essential in order to develop children's understanding further and use the technology effectively.

Some practical issues

There are some important factors concerning file types and saving work when using digital audio. Most software supports MP3 and WAV files. However, MP3 files compress the data more to give smaller file sizes which is an important factor to consider if children's work needs to be transferred between machines or indeed uploaded to the school website or virtual learning environment. Audacity can be used to convert between file types. Another important factor when working with digital audio is to understand how to save work success-fully to save disappointment. If creating a PowerPoint presentation that has inserted audio or movie clips, the sound clips themselves are not in fact inserted into the document but merely linked to it. This is the same when compiling rich multimedia using programs such as Windows Movie Maker or iMovie. The implications of this are that if the project is saved and then opened on another machine, the audio or movie clips will not work because the program will be looking for the linked files in the location they were saved on the original machine. Thus if children have created a PowerPoint presentation with audio and this is going to be played to the whole school on a different machine in the hall, it is necessary to go to File and then select Package for CD. It is possible to navigate to your memory stick and save your work on this. However, by packaging for CD you are ensuring that all of the digital assets (audio/movie files) you have linked to in your work are kept together in one folder, enabling this work to be played on any machine.

A SUMMARY OF **KEY POINTS**

> There is a wealth of software and hardware that can be utilised to enrich children's experiences and learning in music.

> It is vital for teachers to develop their own capabilities with audio and music applications before implementing them in the classroom.

> A sound knowledge and understanding of the music curriculum should underpin any use of technology to support children's learning in music.

> ICT should not be used as a substitute for traditional ways of making music.

Moving on

There is an array of software and hardware to support children's development of knowledge and understanding in music and the main focus of this chapter has been on those resources, which lend themselves towards more creative uses of technology in music. For teachers to make effective use of ICT in music they must have a critical view of the technology and an understanding of the opportunities it affords both the teacher and the learner in relation to the development of their subject knowledge. It may be, for example, that it is far better for children to beat a real drum to a piece of music or song than create a rhythmic pattern in a computer program if we want to develop their ability to hold a steady beat. Similarly, to develop children's control of pitch they need plenty of opportunities to find their own voice through singing and performing live music together. With this in mind, investigate critically the links at the end of this chapter to familiarise yourself with the range of ICT-based resources to support children's development in music. You will need to ensure that you have the appropriate plugins such as Macromedia Shockwave and QuickTime Player in order to operate some of the web-based resources. If planning to use such software to support your teaching of music, make sure that the relevant plugins are installed.

FURTHER READING FURTHER READING **FURTHER READING** FURTHER READING

www.hitchams.suffolk.sch.uk/ictmusic/index.htm Accessed 19 January 2007

Becta (2007) Using web-based resources in primary music **http://schools.becta.org.uk/index.php? section=cu&catcode=ss_cu_ac_mus_03&rid=3689** Accessed 19 January 2007

Creating Music (1999) **www.creatingmusic.com/** Accessed 19 January 2007

BBC (2007) Making Tracks **www.bbc.co.uk/radio3/makingtracks/sequenza.shtml** Accessed 19 January 2007

Becta (2006) *How to use ICT in music* **http://schools.becta.org.uk/index.php?section=cu&cat code=ss_cu_ac_mus_03&rid=456** Accessed 19 January 2007

Kent NGfL (2004), Music **www.kented.org.uk/ngfl/subjects/music/index.htm** Accessed 19 January 2007

REFERENCES REFERENCES **REFERENCES** REFERENCES REFERENCES REFERENCES

http://freeplaymusic.com/ Accessed 19 January 2007

www.nc.uk.net/webdav/harmonise?Page/@id=6016 Accessed 19 January 2007

http://audacity.sourceforge.net/ Accessed 19 January 2007

Walker, P. (2006) *Infant Multimedia Music Scheme.* Brighton and Hove Music and Performing Arts www.bhmpa.org.uk/school_zone/music_curriculum_support/ Accessed 19 January 2007

Section C
ICT and the professional teacher

The rapid development of ICT brings in its wake a series of challenges to which teachers must respond. In this third section we provide an overview of three aspects of teachers' involvement with ICT which are not directly curriculum–related but which are nevertheless critical for effective and positive use of ICT in the classroom. These are:

- **professional use of ICT;**
- **computers in your classroom;**
- **ethical and legal issues.**

Q17 of the Standards for QTS identifies the need for teachers to 'Know how to use skills in . . . ICT to support their teaching and wider professional activities' (TDA/DfES, 2007). ICT should be a teacher's helpful ally administratively, for example providing ready means for maintaining pupils' records of progress as well as offering diverse opportunities for the preparation of resources. In Chapter 18 on the professional use of ICT we offer some ideas as starting points for both improved personal capability and continuing professional development.

Teachers have a clear duty of care for the children in their classroom, highlighted in the five outcomes of *Every child matters* covered by the Children Act 2004. Being electrically powered, computers, and associated peripherals, bring a particular burden of responsibility for safe operation. Primary age children may have little or no previous experience as users of electrical equipment, while typically computers in schools are being sited in locations that were not originally designed for this purpose. It would be impractical to provide an exhaustive list of 'dos' and 'don'ts' in respect of health and safety, but Chapter 19 in this section includes guidelines on how to make your classroom as free from risk as possible, as well as referring the reader to appropriate interpretations of the relevant legislation.

The new ways of communication that ICT offers have raised a range of ethical and legal issues with which we, as a society, are grappling to come to terms. Many of these are not completely new problems; for example, there have always been opportunities for plagiarism, or for the dissemination of undesirable material. However, the need to take a moral stand and deal with potential threats has been markedly accentuated by the speed and ease with which information can now be transmitted. The earlier chapter on the Internet has discussed some of the questions involved. Chapter 20 on ethical and legal issues turns our attention to two other significant areas for ICT in education, copyright and data protection, contributing to the promotion of positive values and attitudes (covered by paragraph Q2 of the Standards), but also in a pragmatic way aiming to avoid unnecessary pitfalls.

18
Professional use of ICT

Chapter objectives

It is a requirement of the Standards that teachers, 'Know how to use skills in...ICT to support their teaching and wider professional activities' (DfES 2007). In this chapter we shall consider the demand from two angles: personal capability and the use of ICT to source relevant information.

Personal capability

The requirement to use ICT to improve efficiency sounds obvious, but in reality a teacher might question the need to adopt ICT as a tool for their professional practice when manual alternatives appear to be quicker. The short answer to this objection is that selective use of ICT will repay the investment of time made to gain proficiency with the keyboard, other hardware and appropriate software. Facility with the keyboard is particularly helpful. Acquisition of keyboard skills is in some ways analogous to learning to drive – and takes about the same amount of time. For those who want to develop typing skills, an electronic tutor such as Mavis Beacon or Accu-Type is invaluable. The course need not necessarily be followed to its conclusion but to a point when you are using most of your fingers and moving around the keyboard with some fluency. This will only improve with further practice.

In a similar way, cumulative benefit is derived from learning software. Modern word processors, desktop publishing packages and spreadsheets have wide-ranging functionality. To a novice they may seem daunting, treacherous and unwieldy, but in time it will prove quicker to use them than relying on 'traditional' pen-and-paper approaches. Time saving possibilities include:

- using a template in your word processor so that a lesson plan can be called up repeatedly;
- using a spreadsheet to keep pupils' records (for example, marks) that can readily be sorted into order and converted into graphical representations to demonstrate progress;
- using desktop publishing to produce professional-looking worksheets; although clip art should be used judiciously it is nevertheless a tremendous time saver;
- using digital photography (both still and video) to record children's work;
- using the Internet for classroom resources and to supplement subject knowledge.

Further ideas are available on a number of websites, including Terry Freedman's useful IT in Educational Administration web page.

Professional development using ICT

In their work in the classroom, teachers will be supporting children in the use of ICT to source information. This is a key skill; the capability to access information is now critical. While reference is often made to a 'knowledge-based' society, there is a strong argument that it is not holding knowledge personally that is now important, so much as knowing how to reach it when it is needed. Does it matter whether you retain the fact that the Battle of Bosworth was in 1485 if you can find it out in a few mouse clicks?

Teachers can help themselves professionally to keep up to date by using ICT in a variety of ways, the most important of which is accessing information via the Internet. There is a number of key sites with which all teachers should be familiar. A useful starting point is provided by the Department for Education and Skills site (**www.dfes.gov.uk**), not just for its own content – which includes news and discussion of current issues in education – but for links it offers (**www.dfes.gov.uk/links.shtml**) to other key national bodies.

Teachernet (**www.teachernet.gov.uk/**) is a less formal site which nevertheless provides a wealth of information for teachers, ranging from details on pay and conditions to downloadable resources. The site claims over 2,000 lesson plans. An area of professional development using ICT that is receiving increased attention is the creation of e-portfolios. The DfES has developed e-portfolio resources on Teachernet that support teachers in tracking their career and professional development.

Teachers' TV (**www.teachers.tv/**) is a digital television channel for education professionals (heads, teachers, support staff and governors). Programmes cover a range of topics, ranging from curriculum foci to more general themes such as tackling challenging behaviour. The effectiveness of the medium is that it is visual. Watching teaching and learning take place, supported by an informed commentary, provides insights that would be difficult to achieve through the written word alone.

Teachers' TV can be accessed through Freeview (digital terrestrial), satellite, cable or, currently in limited areas of the country, DSL (via the telephone line). Scheduling is over 24 hours; programmes tend to be short, usually 15 minutes or half an hour, and are generally repeated during a week. However, remembering to watch, or set the video recorder, may escape many busy teachers. Fortunately many of the programmes are archived on the Teachers' TV website, **www.teachers.tv/searchArchive.do**

The British Educational Communications and Technology agency (Becta) which has its site at **www.becta.org.uk** , offers a substantial range of materials, specifically on the use of ICT, to support teachers. Information and advice sheets are constructed logically, with non-specialist teachers in mind, and make clear both technical and pedagogical aspects of their themes.

An online resource that offers an immediate impact on efficiency is the National Curriculum site, **www.nc.uk.net**, from where all the current National Curriculum documents may be downloaded. They are offered in alternative forms, as Acrobat (.pdf) files or as text files (.rtf). The Acrobat files (for which you will need Acrobat Reader, which can be downloaded from the Internet free of charge) are presented in the same style as the print edition. Perhaps more useful, however, are the text versions which can be edited in a word processor and so incorporated in planning documents and for other aspects of administration. Similarly, schemes of work can be obtained from the QCA at **www.qca.org.uk**, in either Acrobat or Word (.doc) format.

The related National Curriculum in Action site, **www.ncaction.org.uk/**, is a very supportive resource, particularly for beginning teachers. It provides examples of children's work with commentaries and assessments of the National Curriculum level that is represented.

The Standards site (**www.standards.dfes.gov.uk/**) is the online home of a range of national initiatives, including the *Primary National Strategy*. The site carries a lot of background information that provides insights into the development of the ideas that make such an impact on the way that teachers teach and children learn. Case studies of the initiatives in action are also provided.

It is important that teachers should have access to inspection evidence, and foremost among sources for this is the Ofsted site at **www.ofsted.gov.uk**. The site provides access to all of the inspection reports carried out on schools (and other educational institutions such as local authorities and teacher training providers). This is a huge repository of information. It would be difficult to conceive how it might be made so readily available and kept so up to date other than by the Internet. It is also worth remembering that Ofsted produces, and posts on the Internet, reports on subject and curriculum issues aggregated from its findings in individual schools. This is authoritative research that complements material that teachers might glean from other sources.

There are many other governmental and quasi-governmental sites that hold helpful information for teachers. The General Teaching Council of England (**www.gtce.org.uk**) and the Training and Development Agency for Schools (**www.tda.gov.uk/**) are two further locations that repay a visit. Most of these are very effective technically; they have been designed carefully and offer an interface that is attractive and intuitive. Not surprisingly, privately produced sites, which tend to offer curriculum resources rather than statutory information and administrative support, are of less consistently high quality, in terms of both content and presentation. They reflect forcefully the somewhat anarchic nature of the Internet, and it is worth being circumspect about material when the provenance is uncertain. One option here is to route your search for resources through an organisation that has already vetted them, such as Becta.

Commercial organisations such as Living Library (**livlib.eduweb.co.uk**) provide a substantial service, but on subscription.

Sites referred to in the text were current in September 2006.

REFERENCES AND FURTHER READING REFERENCES AND FURTHER READING

Freedman, T. (1998) IT and ICT in Educational Administration Home Page at **http://easyweb.easy net.co.uk/~etfreedman/indexa.htm** Last modified 15 May 2003. Accessed 1 September 2006

DfES (2007) Cutting burdens **www.teachernet.gov.uk/wholeschool/remodelling/cuttingburdens/** Accessed 1 September 2006

19
Health and safety

Chapter objectives

In this chapter we shall review the health and safety considerations that apply to the use of computers and other aspects of ICT in schools. As a starting point, we shall point to the current legal requirements. However, the extent to which legislation deals with specific aspects of the use of ICT in schools is limited and so we will also cover some practical considerations which contribute to the sense of responsibility for health and safety that every good teacher will have in her classroom.

Legal requirements

Under the Health and Safety at Work etc. Act 1974 and the Management of Health and Safety at Work Regulations 1999, employees – which includes classroom teachers – 'must:

- *take reasonable care of their own and others' health and safety;*
- *co-operate with their employers;*
- *carry out activities in accordance with training and instructions;*
- *inform the employer of any serious risks.'*

(Teachernet 2007)

While the current health and safety legislation resides primarily in documents issued by the Health and Safety Executive (see Further reading), and while ultimate responsibility lies with management, teachers need to think beyond the strictly legal to consider what constitutes good practice.

Room layout

Very few primary schools were designed from the outset to accommodate computers, and so in many cases the siting of equipment is at best a compromise with the overall physical arrangements of the classroom. The convention in the primary school originally was for computers to be dispersed around the school, usually one, two or possibly three to each classroom. Where they are positioned amongst the desks, tables, chairs, bookshelves and cupboards will to some extent be dictated by circumstances, but even so there are guidelines worth following. None of these is more than common sense, but they bear summarising.

It is important that the computer is positioned so that the monitor is not subject to reflection, either from artificial light or from sunshine. Not only is glare distracting, but it may also cause headaches and strain if users are subjected to it for long.

The computer should be as close to a power supply as possible. This will minimise confusion if anything goes wrong. More prosaically, but just as important, keeping the length of electrical flex to a minimum reduces proportionately the risk of someone tripping over it. If the cable supplied is too long, and an alternative of more appropriate length is unavailable, it is preferable to loop and tape or tie the surplus together (to minimise the build-up of a magnetic field the loop should not be too tight).

For convenience many schools have bought trolleys so that computers can be moved easily from room to room. These are fine, as long as they are designed well, with the work surface at an appropriate height for the children – which won't be the same throughout a primary school – and with sufficient area for the 'footprint' of your equipment. The dimensions merit checking as trolleys may not have convenient workspace for overflow, especially if the expectation is for more than one child to be using the computer at any time. Again, attention must be paid to ensure that cable is not flapping loosely around the system.

The question of space often becomes even more acute in those schools that have decided to dedicate a room to an ICT suite. The challenge is to accommodate children and computers in a room that was in all likelihood designed with only children in mind. Rows of computers are arranged around the wall, with little space for writing or source materials – or a co-worker. Additionally, turning to face the teacher is hard for the children.

Possibly associated with a lack of space may be problems caused by excessive heat and humidity. Computers give off a significant amount of heat and fumes; especially if grouped together, consideration of improved ventilation may become important. Schools may need to give consideration to the installation of air-conditioning units.

Setting up the computer

Linking the components that make up a single computer system, one that is either new or has been dismantled for a move, is not difficult and there is no reason for a teacher to be disconcerted by this task. However, as with all electrical equipment, there is a potential hazard if care is not taken, and the obvious precaution is to ensure that the equipment is disconnected at the mains before making any adjustments to the cables that make up the system.

Computers in operation are not drawing much power from the mains, which means that a single computer, monitor and peripherals can share just one socket without problem. However a gang, rather than a splitter (which is more likely to become dislodged if leads are accidentally bumped), should provide this access. Also, one gang per socket is the rule, and gangs should not be daisy-chained. In a room in which several stations are planned professional advice should be sought. Both tidiness and safety will dictate that mains leads, and any data cables for networking, should be concealed in trunking, with as little flex as possible lying on the work surface.

The mains lead to the computer usually provides a kettle-type connection. This is generally effective and safe, as long as the lead has been pushed firmly home onto the projecting pins. Some monitors are provided with a lead with similar connections so that they can draw power from the computer. However, it is preferable for the monitor to have its own, sepa-rate, earthed plug into the gang or wall socket.

Data from the computer to the monitor are run through an RGB cable, RGB representing red, green and blue – the colours used to make up the picture on the screen. RGB cables should come equipped with two retaining screws on each connector, which provide a secure link between the computer and monitor. Usually the cable has 15 pin D-shaped connectors at either end, with the direction of the cable made obvious by the configuration of the pins.

The same is true for the connection of other peripherals. Computer manufacturers over the last few years have gone out of their way to make clear which device goes into which socket, often using colour coding to assist. The keyboard and mouse, which are standard input devices, often have reserved sockets. However, they may alternatively be supplied to connect through USB (universal serial bus) ports. These are a more efficient alternative to the older nine-pin serial port (which you will still find on some computers). Most peripherals – printers, cameras, memory sticks, scanners – are now manufactured with USB connections. They are usually efficient and require no manual installation of supporting software.

All of the above makes the assumption that the equipment is sound and in good working order. Old or frayed leads must be replaced, and the teacher must be vigilant in watching for any accidental damage, such as cuts to plastic insulation or wear to plugs, that may have been sustained. If repairs, rather than connecting and setting up ICT equipment, are involved, then professional help should be sought.

Danger, children at work

Teachers must be clear that, while ultimate legal duty for health and safety in the classroom lies with employers, in practice they are responsible for the safe operation of computers in their classrooms. A cable that has not been correctly attached is a potential hazard and on a daily basis only the teacher is in a position to check this. For the same reason, none of the setting up discussed in the previous section should be delegated to primary age children. Apart from electrical safety, computer equipment is often heavy and should be moved only by an adult.

Yet children are going to be the main computer users in your classroom, and so they too need to know how to work efficiently and safely at the computer. For older Key Stage 2 children this may extend to switching the computer on themselves, and perhaps even to switching on at the mains too. However, the teacher must be on hand to supervise either of these tasks.

Monitors have improved considerably in quality over recent years but it is still not advisable for children (or adults) to sit in front of a screen for extended periods. There is no substantive evidence that eyesight is adversely affected by spending a long time in front of a VDU (visual display unit), nor is the level of radiation emitted close to breaching safe levels set out in international recommendations. However, reading a screen for long periods without a break can cause a headache.

Teachers need also to be aware of rare, but serious, effects that can arise. A few people suffer from photo-sensitive epilepsy which is triggered by flickering light. However, they can often still work successfully with a monitor, especially given that the quality of this equipment has improved so substantially over the last decade. Similarly, some people experience skin irritations as the result of working with monitors. The cause of this response may be a range of factors, possibly attributable to the computers drying out the atmosphere, in which case air flow and humidity into the room should be improved.

Another reason to discourage extended time in front of the computer is to make it practical for the user to maintain good posture. Slouching, while generally unattractive and unhealthy, will also be detrimental to the relationship of the user's wrists with the keyboard. The lower arms should be held off the desk and be about horizontal. Children in the classroom are unlikely to be using a computer continuously long enough to be susceptible to repetitive strain injury, but if they can be encouraged to sit properly at the computer from early on it will stand them in good stead for the future. For similar reasons, an ergonomic chair with adjustable height and backrest is recommended. This will enable children – who vary tremendously in height – to sit with their feet on the floor (or on a rest) and with their thighs parallel to the ground.

Working with VDUs, published by the Health and Safety Executive (updated 2006), is a very practical guide, as well as offering an outline of the legislation current in this area.

REFERENCES AND FURTHER READING

Becta (2000) Health and Safety with ICT Information Sheet **www.becta.org.uk/technology/ infosheets/general.html** (downloadable in html or pdf format) Accessed 31 July 2000

Health and Safety Executive (2006) *Working with VDUs* Revision 3 downloadable leaflet from the Health and Safety Executive website **www.hse.gov.uk** Accessed 3January 2007

Health and Safety Executive (1992) *Display screen equipment work – Health and safety (display screen equipment) regulations 1992*. HSE Books, PO Box 1999, Sudbury, Suffolk CO10 6FS

Health and Safety Executive (2004) *Getting to grips with manual handling*. Downloadable leaflet from the Health and Safety Executive website **www.hse.gov.uk** Accessed 3 January 2007

Teachernet (2007) Responsibility for health and safety in schools **www.teachernet.gov.uk/whole school/healthandsafety/visits/responsibilities/visitsresponsibilitiessection1/** Accessed 3 January 2007

20
Ethical and legal issues

Chapter objectives

The rapid development of ICT over the last few years has presented a range of new social and legal challenges. Some of the ethical questions that are raised have already been considered in the chapter on the Internet. However, the innovatory opportunities for learning, working and leisure presented by ICT have further consequences for the legal framework in which they operate, and the rapid pace of change has added an additional layer of complexity to these tangled arrangements.

This chapter intends to provide an awareness of some of the issues involved. However it is not intended to be a comprehensive guide, and if the reader has a concern over a particular circumstance in which the legitimacy of an action might be debatable, it is sensible to seek further advice.

Copyright

Even before the advent of computers the question of copyright was a vexed one for schools. The current legislation in the United Kingdom is, though, unequivocal and thorough. It applies to anything published (including text and artistic production, which might itself be literary, musical, graphic or dramatic in nature). It extends, too, to other technological media apart from computers, such as films, audio and televised programmes. In short, the likelihood is that anything you might want to copy is covered by the legislation.

Some of the confusion over copyright for schools may originate in the concept of 'fair dealing' which is embodied in the Copyright, Designs and Patents Act, 1988 (this Act still forms the basis of legislation in this country, though its impact has been modified by EU harmonisation). Becta's helpful guidance (Becta 2000) summarised this idea succinctly:

> 'Fair dealing' is really a permitted form of defence if accused of infringement, limited to particular purposes of which the best known is 'research or private study', but case law has established that producing multiple copies for classes is certainly not 'private study'.

The inference is clear. Educational institutions are not in any way exempt from copyright legislation. However, many schools and colleges have paid a fee to the Copyright Licensing Agency (CLA). This provides limited rights to make copies of some copyright material. Copying is restricted to works published by organisations that have joined the scheme, but this in fact covers most British publishers (a major exception, however, is printed music). More restrictive, though, is the scope of the CLA scheme in applying only to printed material. The exact allowance for copying (usually photocopying) differs between institutions and has been varied in recent years; it would be sensible to check your school's current agreement to ascertain precisely what is permitted.

If we switch our focus more particularly to ICT, the same principles apply. In practice, a computer program should be regarded as a literary work, with its authors and distributors enjoying the same rights and privileges as if they had produced a book. Software publishers are usually very careful to stipulate what the purchaser has bought. In general, 'buying software' only gains title to a licence to install and use the software, not to the software itself. The text of the licence will give details about how many copies of the software may be made. The starting point is that only one will be allowed, in order that data may be transferred to a computer's hard disk. However, it is often possible to buy at economic rates licences to cover a whole site, or multiple stations within a purchasing institution.

Teachers have an obligation to ensure that software-licensing conditions are not breached in their school. In some circles the conditions under which software has been purchased are broken with the excuse that additional, illegal copies are not hurting anyone because the transmission is electronic; no physical material is appropriated. However, the disk and packaging are negligible elements of the software bundle. What is at stake is the author's intellectual property, and an unauthorised copy represents its theft. Apart from the ethical argument against software theft, there is also the highly pragmatic consideration that, especially amongst smaller educational publishers, loss of revenue will jeopardise future development of material.

Several organisations are involved in monitoring the use of software to ensure that breaches of copyright are avoided. Foremost of these in the United Kingdom is the Federation Against Software Theft (FAST), which has its website at **www.fast.org.uk**. FAST does not simply act to police software use, however; it is a valuable source of advice and support to computer users.

The Internet poses considerable challenges to the enforcement of copyright law, not least in the difficulty of monitoring all the material that is held and is available for download. Nevertheless, copyright laws do apply. Even if copyright ownership is not declared, it should be reckoned as applicable, unless its rightful owner has explicitly placed the material in the public domain.

Teachers will need to determine how best to introduce children to the concept of copyright. While this is a more urgent question in secondary schools, the increase in computer use, particularly at home, by primary age children means that breach of copyright as well as plagiarism from the Internet or CD-ROM may well arise in your classroom. While it may not be appropriate to introduce a formal system of referencing to young children, spending time to explain why sources should be acknowledged will only be to their long-term benefit.

Data protection

Teachers and schools need to know of their obligations regarding data confidentiality. These duties are enshrined in data protection legislation. In essence this dates back to the Data Protection Act of 1984, which was introduced in response to growing concern about the impact of advancing computer technology on personal privacy. Considering its vintage, it was far-sighted, providing both rights for individuals and a demand on organisations (or individuals) who held and used personal information to adopt responsible practices, even for data such as names and addresses, which might not be considered to be particularly sensitive.

Ironically the original Act was limited to information held on computer, which exempted data records held by 'traditional' methods on hard copy. Another difficulty with the 1984 Act, which perhaps could not be foreseen, was that the growing internationalisation of computer use through the Internet would facilitate unscrupulous transfer of data to locations outside of UK jurisdiction. Partly to improve the regulations in these areas, but also partly in response to an EU directive issued in September 1990 aimed at harmonising legislation across the member states, the 1984 Act was replaced by a revision, formulated in 1998 and taking effect in March 2000.

Like the original Act, the current legislation is based on eight principles. The detail of these has been rearranged from the earlier requirements, primarily to accommodate the new eighth principle. The list has been summarised by the Information Commissioner as follows:

> *... anyone who processes personal information must comply with eight principles, which make sure that personal information is:*
> - *fairly and lawfully processed;*
> - *processed for limited purposes;*
> - *adequate, relevant and not excessive;*
> - *accurate;*
> - *not kept longer than necessary;*
> - *processed in accordance with the data subject's rights;*
> - *secure;*
> - *not transferred to countries without adequate protection.*
>
> (ICO, 2007)

There remain exemptions to the Act. These include personal data held in connection with domestic or recreational matters and personal data that the law requires the user to make public, such as the electoral register. On the other hand, the principles provide for individuals to be able to access data held about themselves, and to insist on the data being corrected if they are erroneous.

Schools are subject to the Data Protection Act, and it is difficult to envisage a school not being registered. Staff who keep records on pupils on a home computer, and, indeed, under the 1998 Act, paper records, come under the scope of the legislation, and their schools should be aware of this.

FURTHER READING FURTHER READING **FURTHER READING** FURTHER READING

Becta (2000) Copyright and ICT Information Sheet **www.becta.org.uk/technology/infosheets/general.html** Accessed 31 July 2000 (no longer available)

Becta (2006) *Intellectual property, copyright and school internet use* **schools.becta.org.uk/index.php?section=is&rid=9983&pagenum=2&NextStart=1&pagenum=1&NextStart=1** Accessed 3 January 2007

ICO (Information Commissioner's Office) (2007)

Data Protection Commissioner (2000) *Data protection* **www.ico.gov.uk/what_we_cover/data_protection.aspx** Accessed 3 January 2007. Summaries and the full text of the Data Protection Act can be downloaded from this site.

Index

Achieving QTS

The Achieving QTS series continues to grow with nearly 50 titles in 8 separate strands. Our titles address issues of teaching and learning across both primary and secondary phases in a highly practical and accessible manner, making each title an invaluable resource for trainee teachers.

We've updated and improved 13 of our bestselling titles in line with the new Standards for QTS (September 2007). These titles are highlighted with a * in the list below.

Assessment for Learning and Teaching in Primary Schools
Mary Briggs, Angela Woodfield, Cynthia Martin and Peter Swatton
£15   176 pages   ISBN: 978 1 903300 74 9

Assessment for Learning and Teaching in Secondary Schools
Martin Fautley and Jonathan Savage
£16   160 pages   ISBN: 978 1 84445 107 4

*Learning and Teaching in Secondary Schools (third edition)
Viv Ellis
£16   192 pages   ISBN: 978 1 84445 096 1

Learning and Teaching Using ICT in Secondary Schools
John Woollard
£17.50   192 pages   ISBN: 978 1 84445 078 7

Passing the ICT Skills Test (second edition)
Clive Ferrigan
£8   80 pages   ISBN: 978 1 84445 028 2

Passing the Literacy Skills Test
Jim Johnson
£8   80 pages   ISBN: 978 1 903300 12 1

Passing the Numeracy Skills Test (third edition)
Mark Patmore,
£8   64 pages   ISBN: 978 1 903300 94 7

*Primary English: Audit and Test (third edition)
Doreen Challen
£9   64 pages   ISBN: 978 1 84445 110 4

*Primary English: Knowledge and Understanding (third edition)
Jane Medwell, George Moore, David Wray and Vivienne Griffiths
£16   240 pages   ISBN: 978 1 84445 093 0

*Primary English: Teaching Theory and Practice (third edition)
Jane Medwell, David Wray, Hilary Minns, Vivienne Griffiths and Liz Coates
£16   208 pages   ISBN: 978 1 84445 092 3

*Primary ICT: Knowledge, Understanding and Practice (third edition)
Jonathan Allen, John Potter, Jane Sharp and Keith Turvey
£16   256 pages   ISBN: 978 1 84445 094 7

*Primary Mathematics: Audit and Test (third edition)
Claire Mooney and Mike Fletcher
£9   52 pages   ISBN: 978 1 84445 111 1

*Primary Mathematics: Knowledge and Understanding (third edition)
Claire Mooney, Lindsey Ferrie, Sue Fox, Alice Hansen and Reg Wrathmell
£16   176 pages   ISBN: 978 1 84445 053 4

*Primary Mathematics: Teaching Theory and Practice (third edition)
Claire Mooney, Mary Briggs, Mike Fletcher, Alice Hansen and Judith McCullouch
£16   192 pages   ISBN: 978 1 84445 099 2

*Primary Science: Audit and Test (third edition)
John Sharp and Jenny Byrne
£9   80 pages   ISBN: 978 1 84445 109 8

*Primary Science: Knowledge and Understanding (third edition)
Graham Peacock, John Sharp, Rob Johnsey and Debbie Wright
£16   240 pages   ISBN: 978 1 84445 098 5

*Primary Science: Teaching Theory and Practice (third edition)
Rob Johnsey, John Sharp, Graham Peacock, Shirley Simon and Robin Smith
£16   144 pages   ISBN: 978 1 84445 097 8

*Professional Studies: Primary and Early Years (third edition)
Kate Jacques and Rob Hyland
£16   256 pages   ISBN: 978 1 84445 095 4

Teaching Arts in Primary Schools
Raywen Ford, Stephanie Penny, Lawry Price and Susan Young
£15   192 pages   ISBN: 978 1 903300 35 0

Teaching Design and Technology at Key Stages 1 and 2
Gill Hope
£17   224 pages   ISBN: 978 1 84445 056 5

Teaching Foundation Stage
Iris Keating
£15   200 pages   ISBN: 978 1 903300 33 6

Teaching Humanities in Primary Schools
Editor: Pat Hoodless
£15   192 pages   ISBN: 978 1 903300 36 7

Teaching Religious Education: Primary and Early Years
Elaine McCreery, Sandra Palmer and Veronica Voiels
£16   176 pages   ISBN: 978 1 84445 108 1

Achieving QTS Cross-Curricular Strand

Children's Spiritual, Moral, Social and Cultural Development
Tony Eaude
£14   128 pages   ISBN: 978 1 84445 048 0

Creativity in Primary Education
Anthony Wilson
£15   224 pages   ISBN: 978 1 84445 013 8

Creativity in Secondary Education
Jonathan Savage, Martin Fautley
£16   144 pages   ISBN: 978 1 84445 073 2

Teaching Citizenship in Primary Schools
Editor: Hilary Claire
£15   192 pages   ISBN: 978 1 84445 010 7

Teaching Literacy Across the Primary Curriculum
David Wray
£14   144 pages   ISBN: 978 1 84445 008 4

Achieving QTS Extending Knowledge in Practice

Primary English: Extending Knowledge in Practice
Jane Medwell and David Wray
£16   160 pages   ISBN: 978 1 84445 104 3

Primary ICT: Extending Knowledge in Practice
John Duffty
£16   176 pages   ISBN: 978 1 84445 055 8

Primary Mathematics: Extending Knowledge in Practice
Alice Hansen
£16   176 pages   ISBN: 978 1 84445 054 1

Primary Science: Extending Knowledge in Practice
Judith Roden, Hellen Ward and Hugh Ritchie
£16   160 pages   ISBN: 978 1 84445 106 7

Achieving QTS Practical Handbooks

Learning and Teaching with Interactive Whiteboards: Primary and Early Years
David Barber, Linda Cooper, Graham Meeson
£14   128 pages   ISBN: 978 1 84445 081 7

Learning and Teaching with Virtual Learning Environments
Helena Gillespie, Helen Boulton, Alison Hramiak and Richard Williamson
£14   144 pages   ISBN: 978 1 84445 076 3

*Successful Teaching Placement: Primary and Early Years (second edition)
Jane Medwell
£12   160 pages   ISBN: 978 1 84445 091 6

Using Resources to Support Mathematical Thinking: Primary and Early Years
Doreen Drews and Alice Hansen
£15   160 pages   ISBN: 978 1 84445 057 2

Achieving QTS Reflective Readers

Primary English Reflective Reader
Andrew Lambirth
£14   128 pages   ISBN: 978 1 84445 035 0

Primary Mathematics Reflective Reader
Louise O'Sullivan, Andrew Harris, Gina Donaldson, Gill Bottle, Margaret Sangster and Jon Wild
£14   120 pages   ISBN: 978 1 84445 036 7

Primary Professional Studies Reflective Reader
Sue Kendall-Seater
£15   192 pages   ISBN: 978 1 84445 033 6

Primary Science Reflective Reader
Judith Roden
£14   128 pages   ISBN: 978 1 84445 037 4

Primary Special Educational Needs Reflective Reader
Sue Soan
£14   136 pages   ISBN: 978 1 84445 038 1

Secondary Professional Studies Reflective Reader
Simon Hoult
£14   192 pages   ISBN: 978 1 84445 034 3

Secondary Science Reflective Reader
Gren Ireson and John Twidle
£16   128 pages   ISBN: 978 1 84445 065 7

To order please phone our order line 0845 230 9000 or send an official order or cheque to **BEBC, Albion Close, Parkstone, Poole, BH12 3LL**
Order online at www.learningmatters.co.uk